DATE DUE

GAYLORD

PRINTED IN U.S.A

A DAY AT THE RACES

THE MGM LIBRARY OF FILM SCRIPTS

Ninotchka

North by Northwest

Adam's Rib

Singin' in the Rain

A Day at the Races

A Night at the Opera

A Day at the Races

Screenplay by Robert Pirosh, George Seaton,
and George Oppenheimer
Original story by Robert Pirosh and George Seaton

A VIKING FILM BOOK

NEW YORK / The Viking Press

Published in 1972 in a hardbound and paperbound edition by
The Viking Press, Inc.
625 Madison Avenue, New York, N.Y. 10022
Published simultaneously in Canada by
The Macmillan Company of Canada Limited
SBN 670-25887-3 (hardbound)
      670-01947-x (paperbound)
Library of Congress catalog card number: 79-178819
Printed in U.S.A.

ACKNOWLEDGMENT
Robbins Music Corporation: From "A Message from the Man in the Moon." Lyrics: G. Kahn, Music: B. Kaper and W. Jurmann. Copyright 1937, Renewed 1965, Robbins Music Corporation. "Blue Venetian Waters," Words: G. Kahn, Music: B. Kaper and W. Jurmann. Copyright 1937, Renewed 1964, Robbins Music Corporation. "Tomorrow Is Another Day," Words: G. Kahn, Music: B. Kaper and W. Jurmann. Copyright 1937, Renewed 1964, Robbins Music Corporation. "Barn Sequence," words and music by Roger Edens. Copyright 1937, Renewed 1964, Metro-Goldwyn-Mayer. Rights throughout the world controlled by Robbins Music Corporation. "All God's Chillun Got Rhythm," Lyrics: G. Kahn, Music: B. Kaper and W. Jurmann. Copyright 1937, Renewed 1964, Robbins Music Corporation.

Production	Metro-Goldwyn-Mayer
Produced and directed by	Sam Wood
Screenplay by	Robert Pirosh, George Seaton, and George Oppenheimer
Original story by	Robert Pirosh and George Seaton
Music by	Bronislau Kaper and Walter Jurmann
Musical Director	Franz Waxman
Lyrics by	Gus Kahn
Musical arrangements	Roger Edens
Choral and orchestral arrangements	Leo Arnaud
Orchestration	George Bassman and Paul Marquardt
Musical numbers staged by	Dave Gould
Director of Photography	Joseph Ruttenberg, A.S.C.
Art Director	Cedric Gibbons
Associates	Stan Rogers and Edwin B. Willis
Musical presentation	Merrill Pye
Film Editor	Frank E. Hull
Recording Director	Douglas Shearer
Wardrobe	Dolly Tree
Associate Producer	Max Siegel
Length	8,202 ft.
Time	111 minutes
Released	1937

DR. HUGO Z. HACKENBUSH — Groucho Marx
TONY — Chico Marx
STUFFY — Harpo Marx
GIL STEWART — Allan Jones
JUDY STANDISH — Maureen O'Sullivan
EMILY UPJOHN — Margaret Dumont
WHITMORE — Leonard Ceeley
MORGAN — Douglass Dumbrille
FLO MARLOWE — Esther Muir
DR. LEOPOLD X. STEINBERG — Sig Rumann
SHERIFF — Robert Middlemass
SOLO DANCER — Vivien Fay
DR. WILMERDING — Charles Trowbridge
DOCTORS — Frank Dawson, Max Lucke
MORGAN'S JOCKEY — Frankie Darro
DETECTIVE — Pat Flaherty
MESSENGER — Si Jenks
RACE JUDGE — Hooper Atchley
JUDGES — John Hyams, Wilbur Mack
NURSE — Mary MacLaren
DOCTOR — Edward LeSaint
DRUNK — Jack Norton
EXTRA — Carole Landis
SINGERS — Ivie Anderson and the Crinoline Choir

NOTE: Because the final film differs so much from the script, this volume includes both the original script and the dialogue and action in the film itself.

THE ORIGINAL SCRIPT

Fade in:
Overhead Shot—Standish Sanitarium
Grounds—Night—Newcombe

Dissolve to:
Trucking Shot
> *The gate of the Standish Sanitarium.* We TRUCK PAST *a sign near the gate on which is written:*

> "THE STANDISH SANITARIUM
> ESTABLISHED 1878
> QUIET PLEASE"

> *As we pass the sign the* VOICE *of* GIL *is heard over the* SOUND TRACK, SINGING *"Lady Fair," etc., etc.* CAMERA TAKES IN *the front view of the sanitarium, and* PANS UP. *Lights go on in several windows.*

Cut to:
Judy, in Bed
> *The* SONG *rises in volume. She stirs in her sleep, half awakens. Then suddenly, on a high note, she becomes completely awakened, sits up in bed, and listens a moment. Her attitude changes to one of annoyance as she glances at the clock beside the bed which reads: 2:30. She shakes her head and* SIGHS *audibly.*

Cut to:
Exterior, Sanitarium
> *There is a large oak tree, but no sign whatsoever of the singer— the* SONG *continues. Suddenly, a window opens and the angry face of the* HEAD NURSE *peers out. She looks around bewilderedly, trying to locate the singer.*

3

HEAD NURSE: Stop that racket!
The SONG *trails off a bit.*

Cut to:
Judy's Room
She has gotten out of bed and, with an expression of grim purpose on her face, is putting on a wrap. She looks very charming and feminine, but definitely angry. She comes to the window and looks at an oak tree with a grim expression.

Cut to:
The Oak Tree, *in close proximity to* JUDY'S *window.*
Perched on a high branch, half hidden by foliage, with a small portable phonograph to which he is SINGING *softly, is* GIL STEWART. GIL *grins broadly and continues to* SING. *His lyrics at this moment are, "Upon the Midnight Solitude."*

Cut to:
Shot of Judy in the Window and Gil in Tree
JUDY *(sarcastically)*: This is a fine time for a concert!
GIL *(singing)*:

If I forget the time and season, there is a reason.

Cut to:
Close Shot—Gil Singing
GIL *(singing)*:

I've got a message from the man in the moon for you, just you.

Cut to:
Close Shot—Judy
JUDY: Sh! Sh!

Cut to:
Close Shot—Gil

4

GIL *(still singing)*:

He said to tell you there's a bench in the park for two, just two.

Cut to:
Close Shot—Judy
JUDY: Gil, please.

Cut to:
Close Shot—Gil Singing
GIL *(lowering his voice)*: I know you should be sleeping, and I'm keeping you awake, but I'm just delivering a message he told me to take.

Cut to:
Close Shot—Judy
JUDY *(indicating the windows above)*: Quiet—the patients!

Cut to:
Two Shot—Gil in Tree and Judy in Window
GIL *(singing)*:

I've got the message saying, love will be 'round to call and then.

JUDY: Go away.
GIL *(singing)*:

If we don't meet him, he may never be 'round to call again.

JUDY: Perfect.

Cut to:
Close Shot—Gil (Continuing Singing)
GIL:

The evening found me lonely, and I thought you might be lonely too, so I brought a message from the man in the moon for you.

Cut to:
Close Shot—Judy

JUDY: And I have a message for you, I don't ever want to see you again. For weeks you've annoyed me with your silly antics—but this is the limit. *(She turns and walks away from the window)*

Cut to:
Shot—Gil in Tree and Open Window
GIL *(starts to sing again)*:

> Lady Fair.

Judy comes back.
JUDY: Look here, Gil Stewart, this may be funny to you—
GIL *(indignantly)*: *Funny?* I came here to *propose*—to offer my hand in holy wedlock!
JUDY *(laughing)*: That's *really* funny.
GIL: Well, what's the matter with me?
JUDY: What isn't the matter with you? You're selfish—You're shiftless—You're jobless—You're—
GIL: Wait a minute! Didn't I hold down a job for almost a year—? Didn't I save up my money—?
JUDY *(with contempt)*: Yes—To study voice and instead you bought a race horse and gave up your job. *(She glares at him)* Good night! *(She turns and walks back into her room)*
GIL *(again starts singing)*:

> Lady Fair, marry me.

JUDY *(coming back)*: If you don't go away—
GIL: Not until you say yes.
JUDY: Never! Now will you go?
GIL: *Not till you say yes.*

> CAMERA TAKES IN *half a dozen windows from which lean infuriated* PATIENTS, *in assorted night attire, who* BAWL *and* HISS: "Yes!" *Simultaneously,* GIL *is deluged with pitchers of water . . . shoes . . . wastebaskets, etc. One of these hits the phonograph, still* PLAYING. *There is a loud grating* SOUND *as the needle scratches and the phonograph* BANGS *to the ground.*

Fade out

Fade in:

Exterior, Just Outside of Conference Room—Day

Pick up JUDY *hurrying toward the conference room;* CAMERA PANS WITH HER *and carries her into the conference room, where, on the long table, company books are piled. Three serious-faced doctors are standing.* WHITMORE, *the sanitarium manager, is nervously pacing.* MORGAN, *the race-track owner, back to the* CAMERA, *is standing staring out of the window.* JUDY *enters, she doesn't notice* MORGAN.

JUDY *(brightly)*: Good morning! *(Then seeing the serious faces)* Oh—I'm sorry about last night—all that noise and—

WHITMORE *(interrupting as he moves toward her)*: Judy, it's something more serious.

MORGAN *turns from the window (he is holding three promissory notes in his hand).* MORGAN *moves toward* JUDY.

WHITMORE: Mr. Morgan wants those notes paid when they come due next month.

JUDY *(to* MORGAN—*smiling)*: Why, of course. We always pay them—*(To* WHITMORE*)*—Don't we?

WHITMORE *(quickly to* JUDY, *explaining)*: You mean the interest. Mr. Morgan means the principal—fifty-five thousand dollars—

JUDY *(to* MORGAN*)*: I understood those notes were held by the bank.

MORGAN: I've taken the notes over from the bank.

JUDY *(to* WHITMORE, *bewilderedly)*: But—I—I can't understand. . . . You're my business manager—why didn't you tell me about this?

WHITMORE *(solicitously)*: I didn't want to worry you, Miss Judy— I hoped to get an extension on the notes. *(He turns to* MORGAN, *feigning sincerity)* Mr. Morgan, can't you give us more time?

JUDY: Yes, why can't you carry us along the way the bank did?

MORGAN *(definitely)*: This place has been losing money for months.

JUDY: But there must be something we can do. Surely, the memory of my father, his worth to the community, must count for something.

MORGAN *shrugs.*

FIRST DOCTOR (*angrily—to* MORGAN): But, Mr. Morgan—this institution is a landmark.

SECOND DOCTOR: All your lucrative interests—the casino, the race track, have been built around it.

MORGAN: I wish I could afford to be sentimental, Miss Standish, but— (*He shrugs*).

WHITMORE: I'm sorry, Judy.

JUDY: But if we had the right man as chief of staff, we'd be all right. And Mrs. Upjohn highly recommends a doctor she met in Florida.

> MORGAN *and* WHITMORE *exchange looks of apprehension.*

WHITMORE: Are you going to take the advice of a hysterical patient?

MORGAN: The time is so short—what could he accomplish?

JUDY (*determinedly*): He can try—it's our only chance.

> WHITMORE *looks worriedly at* MORGAN, *as though to give him a cue.* MORGAN *steps in.*

MORGAN: Look here, Miss Standish—I don't want you to think I'm being hard—I can take over this place next month without paying you a cent . . . as it is, I'll give you a check for five thousand dollars now, in return for immediate possession.

JUDY: But I don't want the money, I want the sanitarium.

WHITMORE: I think it's a very generous offer, Miss Judy.

> JUDY, *dazed, looks at the* DOCTORS *appealingly, but gets no encouragement.* MORGAN *takes a legal-looking document from his pocket and hands it to* WHITMORE. WHITMORE *takes up a pen and tenders it to* JUDY.

WHITMORE: As your father's friend, I strongly advise it.

> JUDY *looks around for some sign of encouragement and gets stony silence. She looks at the document, picks up the pen, and slowly prepares to sign.* WHITMORE *and* MORGAN *scarcely conceal their satisfaction. Suddenly we hear* MRS. UPJOHN's *excited* VOICE.

MRS. UPJOHN'S VOICE: Judy! Judy!—

> *The door bursts open to admit* MRS. UPJOHN, *who is bubbling over.*

MRS. UPJOHN: I have the most exciting news for you—Judy, he's here! He's here!

JUDY *(startled, looks at her)*: Who?

MRS. UPJOHN: The doctor I met in Florida last year. He's come to take charge.

WHITMORE *(curtly)*: I'm afraid, Mrs. Upjohn, you're a trifle late—Miss Standish is turning her sanitarium over to Mr. Morgan. *(to* JUDY, *indicating paper)* Here, Miss Judy—

MRS. UPJOHN *(taking the pen)*: I tell you, he's a second Pasteur!

JUDY *(sadly—with a smile)*: I'm afraid we need a second Houdini. *(She turns to* MORGAN, *who is furious at this intrusion).*

MRS. UPJOHN *(waving the idea aside)*: Hugo—ah—I mean, Dr. Hackenbush, he'll do miracles. *(tearfully)* Why, I didn't know there was a thing the matter with me until I met him.

MORGAN *(to* JUDY, *impatiently shoving the document toward her)*: You'd better sign, Miss Standish—I'm due at the race track!

MRS. UPJOHN *(pushing the paper back to him)*: She'll sign nothing. *(Glaring at* MORGAN, *who glares back)* And if you're late for the races—run along—run along! We mustn't keep the doctor waiting.

She gives him a shoo-shoo.

WHITMORE *(to Judy)*: You're making a great mistake.

MORGAN: She certainly is.

JUDY *looks wonderingly at them.*

MRS. UPJOHN *(assuring* JUDY*)*: Don't let them bully you. With Dr. Hackenbush in charge, I'm sure that my trustees will let me help you. *(With a wave of dismissal to* MORGAN*)* Good-by, Mr. Morgan.

MORGAN: Miss Standish, it's up to you.

JUDY *(looks bewildered)*: I have a month at least—I can try this new doctor.

MORGAN *starts for the door, sore as hell, then turns.*

MORGAN *(barking to* JUDY*)*: You'll wish you'd taken this check.

WHITMORE *(going after him)*: But, Mr. Morgan—Mr. Morgan—

MORGAN *goes out, followed by* WHITMORE. JUDY *looks after them wonderingly.*

Cut to:

Corridor, *as the two men halt a moment for intimate conversation.* MORGAN *turns on* WHITMORE.

MORGAN *(angrily)*: Well, you certainly fixed things right!

WHITMORE *(nervously)*: Don't worry—*I'll* take care of this doctor.

Cut back to:

Conference Room

MRS. UPJOHN: Oh, I'm so excited! My metabolism—I'm sure this will cause a relapse. *(She hurries to the door)* Oh, Doctor!—Doctor Hackenbush!

> MRS. UPJOHN *then hurries out of the door of conference room, the one* MORGAN *and* WHITMORE *exited through.* CAMERA MOVES WITH HER *to corridor, which is long and spacious. At the end, in the background, we see a very nice sun porch. There are two rooms in the foreground—one on each side—the left one is marked* "DOCTORS' RECREATION ROOM" *and the one on the opposite side is marked* "NURSES' RECREATION ROOM." MRS. UPJOHN *crosses to door of the* "Doctors' Recreation Room"—*enters* CALLING—

MRS. UPJOHN: Dr. Hackenbush—Hugo!

> *As she disappears into the room, the door marked* "Nurses' Recreation Room" *opens—a female* GIGGLE *is heard and* GROUCHO *appears in doorway. (He is carrying his medicine kit and handbag.) As he looks back he says—*

GROUCHO *(speaking back into room)*: That will make you head nurse—

> *We hear* MRS. UPJOHN'S VOICE—

MRS. UPJOHN'S VOICE: Oh, Hugo—

> GROUCHO *reacts and quickly closes nurses' door and starts pacing impatiently as* MRS. UPJOHN *reappears in doorway opposite—sees* GROUCHO *and with a—*

MRS. UPJOHN'S VOICE: Oh, there you are—*(She crosses saying—)* Come, they're waiting.

> *She turns to her right, starting for conference room. He turns*

10

left—realizes his mistake, turns and hurries after her. CAMERA
MOVES WITH THEM *into conference room, where* JUDY, WHIT-
MORE, *and* THREE DOCTORS *are curiously looking* GROUCHO
over. GROUCHO *quickly crosses to them, hands his bags to*
WHITMORE.

GROUCHO: Here, boy—take these bags, and run up to my room,
and here's a dime for yourself.

WHITMORE *automatically takes bags.*

MRS. UPJOHN: No, no, Doctor. Mr. Whitmore is our business
manager.

GROUCHO: Oh, I'm terribly sorry! Here's a quarter.

WHITMORE *drops bags in disgust.*

MRS. UPJOHN: You must not take the doctor too seriously. He's
probably tired after his long trip.

GROUCHO: Why shouldn't I be tired? Did you ever ride four on
a motorcycle? And me top man!

MRS. UPJOHN *(to* THREE DOCTORS*)*: This is Dr. Hugo Z. Hackenbush—your new chief of staff. Oh—oh—oh, Doctor! What shall
I do? *(Bowing business)*

GROUCHO: Just a minute until I calm these paralytics.

GROUCHO *bows a couple more times to* DOCTORS.

MRS. UPJOHN: And now, Doctor, I'd like you to meet Miss Standish, owner of the sanitarium.

GROUCHO *(more bows to* DOCTORS*)*: Just keep on going until I
get back. *(To* JUDY*)* How do you do, Miss Standish, you're the
prettiest owner of a sanitarium I've ever seen.

JUDY: Thank you!

GROUCHO: You've a charming place here. *(Looking at picture on
wall)* Ah, I knew your mother very well. *(Pointing at picture)* I'll
let you in on a little secret. Many, many years ago I proposed to
your mother.

JUDY: But that's my father!

GROUCHO: No *wonder* he turned me down!

MRS. UPJOHN: Now, Doctor, I'd like you to meet your new
associates.

11

ASSOCIATES: Johnson, Bellevue Hospital, Nineteen-eighteen. *(Bows low)* Franco, Johns Hopkins, Twenty-two. *(Bows low)* Wilmerding, Mayo Brothers, Twenty-four. *(Bows low)*

GROUCHO: Dodge Brothers, late Twenty-nine. *(He bows low)*

JUDY: Doctor, I'm happy to welcome you as our new chief of staff. I hope you'll be able to pull the sanitarium out of its difficulties.

MRS. UPJOHN: The sanitarium is having a little financial trouble.

GROUCHO *(grabbing his bag, slaps his hat on backward and runs out.* MRS. UPJOHN *grabs him by the coattails)*: I get it! I'm not going to get paid. Good-by, boys!

MRS. UPJOHN: Please don't go! I'll take care of your salary!

GROUCHO: Oh, yeah! The last job I had, I had to take it out in trade and this is no butcher shop. Not yet anyhow!

MR. WHITMORE: Judy, it seems to me if I may say so, we're making a rather hasty decision.

MRS. UPJOHN: Surely you don't question the Doctor's ability?

MR. WHITMORE: No, not exactly, but running a sanitarium calls for a man with peculiar talents.

GROUCHO: You don't have to look any further. I've got the most peculiar talents of any doctor you've ever met.

MR. WHITMORE: I suggest looking further into his record.

GROUCHO: My record is unblemished. If you don't believe it, I'll show you my parole papers. *(He shows parole papers)*

JUDY: I'm satisfied with Mrs. Upjohn's recommendations. And now, I'll advise the rest of the staff. *(She exits)*

MR. WHITMORE: Tell me, Doctor, just what was your medical background?

GROUCHO *(hesitatingly)*: You mean, medically?

MR. WHITMORE: Yes.

GROUCHO: Well, at the age of fifteen I got a job in a drugstore, filling prescriptions.

MR. WHITMORE: Don't you have to be twenty-one to fill prescriptions?

GROUCHO: That's for grown-ups! I just filled them for children.

MR. WHITMORE: No, no, Doctor! Where did you get your training as a physician?

GROUCHO: Well, to begin with, I took four years at Vassar.

MRS. UPJOHN: Vassar! That's a girls' college!

GROUCHO: I found that out the third year. I'd a-been there yet but I tried to make the swimming team.

MR. WHITMORE: The doctor seems reluctant to discuss his medical experiences.

GROUCHO: Well, medically, my experiences have been most unexciting except during the flu epidemic.

MR. WHITMORE: Ah! And what happened?

GROUCHO: I got the flu.

MRS. UPJOHN: Now, Doctor, I think it's time for my pill.

GROUCHO: Take it some other time.

MRS. UPJOHN: But Doctor, you told me to make them regularly.

GROUCHO *hands pill to* MRS. UPJOHN.

MR. WHITMORE: Just a moment, Mrs. Upjohn! That certainly looks like a horse pill to me!

He pushes GROUCHO *aside, grabs the pill from* MRS. UPJOHN *and examines it sneeringly.*

GROUCHO: Oh, you've taken them before, huh?

MRS. UPJOHN: Doctor, you sure you haven't made a mistake?

GROUCHO: You have nothing to worry about. The *last* patient I gave one of those to won the Kentucky Derby.

MR. WHITMORE: May I examine this please? Isn't that awfully large for a pill?

GROUCHO: Well, it was too small for a basketball so I didn't know what to do with it. Say, you're awfully large for a pill, yourself!

MR. WHITMORE *(to* ONE OF THE DOCTORS*)*: Doctor Wilmerding, what is your opinion?

ASSOCIATE: It must take a lot of water to swallow that!

GROUCHO: Nonsense! You can swallow that with five gallons.

MR. WHITMORE: Isn't that a lot of water for a patient to take?

GROUCHO: Not if she has a bridge in her mouth. You see, the

13

water flows under the bridge, and the patient walks over the bridge and meets the pill on the other side. (BUGLE *call*) So it's war! *(He starts to leave)*

MRS. UPJOHN: No, Doctor, that's from the race track.

GROUCHO: Race track? Then what am I doing here? *(He steps out of the French window)*

Fade out

Fade in:
Establishing Shots of Race Track

Dissolve to:
Angle—Raking Exterior, Mounting Stables

A HOT-DOG VENDER *is just coming out of the stable.* MORGAN *suddenly appears on the scene, sees the* HOT-DOG VENDER, *and his face is contorted with anger. The* VENDER *ducks and* MORGAN SHOUTS *angrily (as he hurries toward entrance stall that* VENDER *came out of).*

MORGAN: That little——

Cut to:
Interior, Mounting Stall—Camera Shooting Toward Entrance—Angle Takes in Full Stall

HARPO, *dressed as jockey, standing next to his* HORSE. *He is looking around furtively and is just about to eat a hot-dog sandwich—it is up to his mouth, when, suddenly, he hears and recognizes* MORGAN'S VOICE. HARPO'S *face falls with fear and he quickly looks around for a hiding place for the hot dog. His eyes fall on the back of the* HORSE *in the stall next door and he slips the hot dog underneath the saddle between the* HORSE'S *back and the curve in the rear of the saddle (unnoticed by the* PEOPLE *in that stall), then quickly covers his actions as* MORGAN *comes in.* MORGAN *looks at* HARPO.

MORGAN *(furiously)*: You've been eating?

HARPO *pantomimes innocence.*

14

MORGAN *roughly grabs* HARPO—*yanks his mouth open and looks—then roughly searches him—then shakes him roughly.* MORGAN *still grips him tightly—threateningly.*

MORGAN—While you're my jockey you keep your weight down! You understand? *(*HARPO *nods)* And you'd better win this race— or else . . .

Just then BEEF *sidles into the stall and* TALKS *to* MORGAN *in very low tones. While this conversation is going on,* HARPO *is looking into the next stall longingly at his sandwich and trying to retrieve it, but the* JOCKEY *in the next stall is in the way, adjusting the saddle on his* HORSE.

BEEF *(in a whisper)*: Hey, Boss—someone bet a lot of money on your horse. They've knocked the odds down one to two.

MORGAN: What? *(Then to* HARPO, *who is practically climbing over the stall in his effort to get at the sandwich.* MORGAN *pulls him back)* Come back here!—I'm switching my bet! *(He leans over to* HARPO, WHISPERS *to him)* Forget what I told you about winning—you're going to pull that horse. Understand? *(*HARPO *shakes his head)* What? *(Grabs* HARPO *to him)* I said—*you're going to lose!* *(*HARPO *nods)* That's better. Now get out there!

There is the sound of a BUGLE. JOCKEYS *all start to mount.* HARPO *gets up on his* HORSE *too, and looks over longingly at his sandwich on the* HORSE *next door. The* HORSES *file out,* CAMERA FOLLOWING. HARPO *tries to jockey into a position behind the* HORSE *with the sandwich. He finally succeeds and is just about to reach over and get it when he sees* MORGAN. *He quickly pulls back his hand, and pretends that he has been stroking the* HORSE *instead.* MORGAN *looks at him angrily.*

(NOTE: *If you want an additional gag here, the* MAN *who leads the* HORSES *around might put* HARPO *back in line angrily, when he starts to edge up on the* HORSE *ahead to get the sandwich—simply* YELLING: "Get back in line!"*)*

Dissolve to:
The Track—with Horses Thundering Along
HARPO'S HORSE *is the last one, directly behind the* HORSE *with*

the sandwich. HARPO *is keeping in back of him, trying to reach his sandwich.*

Cut to:

Morgan and Whitmore, *watching the race. They exchange nods of satisfaction.*

Cut to:

Racetrack—the Stretch

Suddenly, the HORSE *with the sandwich starts pulling ahead,* HARPO *right on its tail, still trying to get the sandwich. The* SANDWICH HORSE *forges ahead into the lead,* HARPO *coming up to second. Just as the* TWO HORSES *get close to the finish,* HARPO *reaches over and grabs the sandwich. As he passes abreast of the* JOCKEY *on the* SANDWICH HORSE, *the* JOCKEY *is whipping his* HORSE *with his crop and hits* HARPO'S *hand, the sandwich dropping to the ground. Simultaneously,* HARPO *drops the reins, his* HORSE *spurts forward and comes in first.*

Morgan and Whitmore, *angrily looking on.*
WHITMORE: Is that what you call losing?
MORGAN *(furiously)*: That little worm double-crossed me! Well, that makes it a perfect day! First we miss out on the sanitarium—and now this!

Cut to:

Harpo, *cantering up to the* JUDGES' *stand. The* JUDGES *put a huge laurel wreath on him. He salutes the* JUDGES, *throws his whip, swings one leg over the* HORSE, *and rests the other on the stirrup. The stirrup (a trick elastic affair), stretches to the ground and* HARPO *descends to the ground as if on an elevator. He acknowledges the* APPLAUSE, *and takes hold of each end of the floral wreath and starts jumping rope through the crowd.* WE FOLLOW HIM *as he skips rope to where* MORGAN *and* WHITMORE *await him angrily.* HARPO *swings the floral horseshoe over* MORGAN'S *head.* MORGAN *jumps in surprise when*

16

HARPO *swings the horseshoe over him.* HARPO's *grin fades when he sees* MORGAN. *He tries to get away, but* MORGAN *grabs him. Several* PEOPLE *come up, patting* HARPO *on the back, and congratulating* MORGAN.

PEOPLE *(ad lib)*:
Nice going, Stuffy!
You rode a great race!
Some jockey you got there, Morgan!
MORGAN *(forcing a smile—to the* PEOPLE*)*: Yes—he certainly is. *(He pats* HARPO *on the back. Then* LOUDLY, *so that the* PEOPLE *can hear)*: I'm proud of you, Stuffy! *(He puts his arm around him—*HARPO *looks at him in surprise)*

MORGAN *bows right and left as the* CROWD *cheers him, but holds on very tightly to* HARPO. *The* CAMERA TRUCKS WITH THEM *as they go through the* CROWD. HARPO *begins to puff up and smile, but suddenly his smile changes to fear, as* MORGAN's *hand begins to dig into his shoulder in an angry grip.*

The Stable *as* MORGAN *and* HARPO *enter the scene. There are still some* PEOPLE *around.* MORGAN *smiles brightly at the* PEOPLE, *who call out to him:* "Congratulations." "Great race!" *etc. As they pass, he roughly shoves* HARPO *inside.*

Interior, Stable
HARPO *is still wearing the laurel wreath. He gets to his feet as* MORGAN *enters. He goes to* HARPO *and twists the two ends of the horseshoe around* HARPO's *neck, almost strangling him.*
MORGAN: Didn't I tell you to throw this race? *(*HARPO *nods)* You little—*(He punches* HARPO *right in the face.* HARPO *straightens up, and his features set in a fixed grin. This infuriates* MORGAN*)* You've run your last race for me! *(He punches* HARPO *again.* HARPO *still grins)* If I ever catch you around here—I'll break your neck! *(He punches* HARPO *again.* HARPO *still grinning)* You're fired!

17

MORGAN *punches* HARPO *again, turns on his heel, and starts out of the stable.* HARPO *still has the set grin on his face. Suddenly, he falls forward and we realize that he has been out since the first punch. He topples against the lower half of the Dutch door which serves as an entrance to the stable.*

Cut to:
Exterior, Stable

The lower half of the Dutch door slams into MORGAN *as he is walking away. He turns around furiously. (Here we play the Dutch-door routine, which can only be indicated here.)* MORGAN *turns furiously through the open doorway. We see* HARPO *come to his senses. He starts to his feet grabbing the upper section of the Dutch door. It slams out of his hand and flies forward, catching* MORGAN *right on the head.* HARPO *lurches to his feet and accidentally kicks the lower part forward, again hitting* MORGAN. MORGAN *advances menacingly.* HARPO *backs away terrified. He suddenly grabs the top part of the Dutch door and throws it forward, catching* MORGAN *on the head again and knocking him off his feet.* HARPO *dashes out of the stable and down the row of stables.* MORGAN *picks himself up and starts after him. We see* HARPO *duck into another stable.*

Cut to:
Interior, Gil's Stable, *as* HARPO *rushes in.* GIL *is currying* HI-HAT. HARPO *flies in and dives headfirst into a pile of hay.* GIL, *confused by this sudden action, is about to haul* STUFFY *out and ask him what it's all about when* MORGAN'S VOICE *comes over the* SOUND TRACK.

MORGAN'S VOICE *(offscene)*: Come back here, you little . . .
At the sound of MORGAN'S VOICE, HI-HAT *reacts violently. He rears up,* WHINNIES, *and kicks.* GIL *grabs his head and tries to soothe him.*

GIL: Whoa, Boy!—whoa. . . .
MORGAN *appears in the stable entrance and* HI-HAT *reacts even more violently at sight of him.*

MORGAN: Have you seen that jockey of mine?

GIL *(trying to soothe the* HORSE *who is still rearing)*: No, Mr. Morgan. *(Then as* HI-HAT *grows more violent)* Whoa, Boy. *(To* MORGAN *as he advances looking for* HARPO*)* Keep back—you know how scared he is of you!

MORGAN *hesitates between coming in and looking for* HARPO *and the menace of the* HORSE.

MORGAN: You're sure Stuffy didn't come in here?

GIL *(frantic in his efforts to soothe the* HORSE*)*: No—I saw him duck around the corner. *(Then to* HI-HAT*)* Whoa, Boy—calm down.

The HORSE *turns around in his rearing and as* MORGAN *starts out,* HARPO, *from under the cover of the hay, launches out and gives him a swift kick.* MORGAN *flies out of the door, then picks himself up and looks back.*

MORGAN *(viciously)*: I should have plugged that nag when I owned him.

He exits. GIL *starts patting* HI-HAT *and soothing him, as he calms down.*

GIL: There, there, HI-HAT—he can't beat you any more.

HARPO *sticks his head out of the straw and shakes it vigorously, in agreement with* GIL—*then, with* HI-HAT *already calmed down, he jumps up on* GIL *and hugs him.*

GIL *(trying to disentangle* HARPO *from around his neck)*: Wait a minute!—what did you do to Morgan?

HARPO *grabs the swinging door and throws it to illustrate. He shrugs and smiles "That's all." Just then the door swings back and konks* HARPO *square on the head. As* GIL *helps him up, we hear on the* SOUND TRACK:

CHICO'S VOICE: Getta your ice cream. Tootsie-frootsie ice cream.

HARPO *looks offscene, signals his delight with a* HONK *of the horn, and starts out.* CHICO *is wheeling his wagon, as* HARPO *rushes into scene.*

CHICO: Stuffy!

They extend their hands, and HARPO's *hand goes right past* CHICO's *hand and into the ice-cream wagon.*

CHICO (*slamming the cover*): Get out of there! That was some ride you put up, Stuffy. Baby, I had five bucks right on the nose. I won sixty cents. (HARPO WHISTLES *and indicates he is through*) What's the matter? Who you ridin' tomorrow? (HARPO *lights match*) You're fired? (HARPO *nods affirmatively*) Oh—Morgan fired you— he wanted you to throw the race?

GIL (*entering*): Wanted Stuffy to be crooked?

CHICO: You know he's honest—(*But he is careful to move his wagon out of* HARPO's *reach*) He'sa honest—but you've gotta watch him a little. Hey, Gil, why don't you giva him a job riding Hi-Hat?

GIL: We can't afford a jockey—We haven't enough money to eat on ourselves.

CHICO: Eat, eat, eat! All the time eat! We don't have to eat, *I'll* eat—

    The SHERIFF *walks into scene, as* HIS VOICE *is heard on the* SOUND TRACK.

SHERIFF'S VOICE: Hey you!

GIL (*nervously*): Hello, Sheriff.

SHERIFF: Well—have you got the money for the feed bill?

GIL: Well—it's this way, Sheriff—

SHERIFF (*starting for the stall*): That's all I wanted to know! Now I'm taking the horse.

CHICO: Hey!—You can't taka Hi-Hat!

SHERIFF: Listen—you guys been stalling me for weeks. Either I get the money right now—or the nag goes with me.

CHICO: All right—I paya the bill (*He hands the* SHERIFF *a five-dollar bill*)

SHERIFF: Five bucks! The bill is a hundred and forty dollars!

CHICO: There is no hundred-and-forty-dollar bill!

GIL: Thanks, Tony—but it's no use. Give it back to him, Sheriff.

SHERIFF: Oh, no, this is better than nothing—

    (*He reaches up to put the money in his back pocket.* HARPO *sidles up to the* SHERIFF *and gets so close to him that the* SHERIFF *puts the bill into* HARPO's *pocket.* HARPO *hands the money around the* SHERIFF's *back to* CHICO. CHICO *hands the*

money to the SHERIFF, *the* SHERIFF *says, taking the money)*
Well, that makes ten. Have you got any more?
(He starts to put money in his pocket)
CHICO *(eyeing* HARPO*)*: Well, I'll let you know in a minute—
*(*HARPO *tries to repeat the same pocket business, but the* SHERIFF *gets the money in his own pocket. Nothing daunted,* HARPO *calmly reaches into the* SHERIFF's *pocket, gets the money and hands it to* CHICO. CHICO *triumphantly hands the money to the* SHERIFF*)*
I know I had five dollars!
SHERIFF *(impatiently)*: All right! Hurry up, have you got the rest of it?
The SHERIFF *has put his hand into pocket with bill and* HARPO *is at loss how to get it. He takes a piece of straw and surreptitiously tickles the* SHERIFF's *neck.* SHERIFF *slaps his neck, taking his hand out of his pocket.*
CHICO: We can't hurry, but we've got it.
This time the SHERIFF *puts the money in another pocket, but* HARPO *doesn't realize this, and reaches in the same pocket for the money. He goes way down and finally comes up with the* SHERIFF's *sock. The* SHERIFF *pulls up his trouser leg, and sees his sock is missing. He then sees* HARPO *and makes a lunge for him.* HARPO *goes out the stable door and the* SHERIFF *runs after him,* SHOUTING *dire threats.*
CHICO: Come on, we got to get some more money fast!
GIL: What's the use? I only bought the horse to make a flash for Judy, and now—*(He takes out the engagement ring and looks at it)* Well, this is going back—
CHICO: Sure it's going back to Judy. With Stuffy ridin' Hi-Hat you winna so much money you buy her a ring for every finger—
GIL: Boy, if I could only win a race! I'd like to show Judy!
CHICO: You show her, but first we gotta show the sheriff some more money—
GIL *(struck by an idea)*: I've got a tip on Sun-Up in the next race. Can't lose—
CHICO: Sun-Up? I got a tip on Sun-Up, too.

21

GIL *(disconcertedly)*: That's great!—but where'll we get the money to bet with?

CHICO: Don't worry about the money!—Come on, we go find a sucker.

> CHICO *leads* GIL *out, wheeling his wagon, the* CAMERA TRUCK- ING WITH THEM. *As they pass between a row of stalls, a* HORSE *is being led from one stall to another.* CHICO *goes right underneath the* HORSE'S *stomach with his wagon.*

Quick Dissolve to:

Groucho, *as he rushes up to the line at the betting booth and worms his way to the head of the line.*

MAN IN LINE: Hey you, get at the end of the line.

GROUCHO: What's that?

BUYERS: Get at the end of the line!

GROUCHO: You turn around the other way and *I'll* be at the end of the line. *(He prepares to place a bet)*

MRS. UPJOHN *(offscene)*: Yoo hoo, Doctor! Doctor Hackenbush! *(She enters)* Why in the world did you run away from me? I thought I'd never catch up with you.

GROUCHO: Neither did I! I must be out of shape.

MRS. UPJOHN: What were you doing at that window?

GROUCHO *(obviously stalling)*: I thought that was the public library. I was trying to get a bookie.

MRS. UPJOHN: Oh, oh, oh, there it goes again! That's what I want to see you about. *(She indicates a pain in her heart)*

GROUCHO: Whoa! Steady! Steady there! Whoa! Whoa! I'm afraid we'll have to put you out to pasture.

MRS. UPJOHN: But Doctor, it's my heart. My heart—it's right here.

GROUCHO: Emily, your heart is so big it's all over the place. Ah, Emily, isn't there room in there for me? All I ask is a little corner in your heart just big enough for me and my dogs.

MRS. UPJOHN: Oh, Doctor!

GROUCHO: Emily, I can't hide it any longer. I love you! *(He takes*

22

her hand) It's the old, old story, boy meets girl. Romeo and Juliet! Minneapolis and St. Paul! Oh, Emily, we could be so happy in a little house on the side of a hill.

MRS. UPJOHN: How romantic!

GROUCHO: When I come home from work, you'd slide down and meet me.

MRS. UPJOHN: Slide down?

GROUCHO: Just the days I work. It certainly wouldn't hurt you to slide one day a month, would it?

MRS. UPJOHN *(taking him by the arm)*: Come, Hugo, let's take a little walk and talk it over.

GROUCHO: I'll tell you what you do. You take a walk and I'll talk it over! Take a stroll over the rustic bridge.

MRS. UPJOHN: But the bridge is washed out!

GROUCHO: Well, it's got nothing on you. *(He tries to get away, but she takes him by the arm)*

MRS. UPJOHN: Hugo, now you come along with me.

> GROUCHO *casts a longing eye at the betting line, as* MRS. UPJOHN *drags him away, we see* CHICO *and* GIL *in background.*

Cut to:

Closer Shot—Gil and Chico

CHICO: Getta your ice cream—*(He overhears* ONE OF THE MEN *in line)*

MAN IN LINE *(to* PERSON *in front of him)*: I think I'll take a chance on Sun-Up.

> CHICO *winks at* GIL *and addresses* MAN IN LINE.

CHICO: Sun-Up hasn't got a chance, it's a fixed race—*(Confidentially)* Put your dough on Beatrice K.

MAN IN LINE: Say, thanks!

CHICO: Thatsa okay—Getta your ice cream—

GIL *(puzzled)*: I said Sun-Up was gonna win!

CHICO: Sure—thatsa why I tell him to bet on the other horse. If too many people bet on Sun-Up, the odds go down, and we don't

23

win as mucha money. (GROUCHO *rushes by.* CHICO *studies him for a moment*) I thick I founda my sucker!

CAMERA PANS WITH GROUCHO *as he rushes toward the betting window. He looks around apprehensively, getting across that he has eluded* MRS. UPJOHN. *The betting line has dwindled down to* TWO MEN, *and* GROUCHO *takes his place in line. The* MEN *quickly get down their bets, and now it's* GROUCHO'S *turn.*

GROUCHO: Two dollars on Sun-Up.

CHICO *comes into scene, pushing his ice-cream wagon.*

CHICO: Hey, you want something hot?

GROUCHO: Not now. I just had lunch. Anyhow, I don't like hot ice cream.

CHICO: Boss, I don't sell ice cream. That's a fake to fool the police. I sell tips on the horses. Want something good today?

GROUCHO: No, some other time. Run along, eh, I'm betting on Sun-Up. (*To* TICKET SELLER) Two dollars on Sun-Up!

CHICO (*tugging at* GROUCHO'S *coat*): Sun-Up is the worst horse on the track.

GROUCHO: I notice he wins all the time.

CHICO: That's just because he comes in first.

GROUCHO: I don't want him any better than first. (*To* TICKET SELLER) Two dollars on Sun-Up!

CHICO (*tugging at* GROUCHO'S *coat*): Suppose you bet on Sun-Up! What do you get for your money? Two to one!

GROUCHO (*pointing to board*): Two to one? It says on the board up there—Sun-Up ten to one.

CHICO (*derisively*): That's the time he went home last night.

GROUCHO (*looking at board*): Hey, that Lady Lou is quite a tramp. She didn't get home till eight to five.

CHICO: What do you say? One dollar and you remember me all your life.

GROUCHO: That's the most nauseating proposition I've ever had.

CHICO: Come on, Boss, you look like a sport.

CHICO *gets* GROUCHO *to walk away from the window, using the*

24

tip for bait. GROUCHO *is tempted, wavers for a second, finally falls and pays* CHICO *a dollar.*

GROUCHO *(examines the envelope)*: What's this?

CHICO: That's the horse!

GROUCHO: How did he get in here?

CHICO: Ice cream. Tootsie-frootsie ice cream!

GROUCHO *(reading the slip inside the envelope)*: Z–V–B–X–R–P–L—I had that same horse when I had my eyes examined.

CHICO: Ice cream. Tootsie-frootsie ice cream!

GROUCHO: Hey, Ice Cream, come over here. What about this optical illusion you just slipped me? I don't understand it.

CHICO: That's the name of the horse in code.

GROUCHO: What do you mean, code?

CHICO: Look in your code book. That will tell you what horse you got! Getta your ice cream!

GROUCHO: Hey, wait a minute. What do you mean—code book? I haven't got a code book.

CHICO: You no gotta code book?

GROUCHO: No, do you know where I can get one?

CHICO: Just by accident, I think I got one here. *(He takes a book out of the wagon)*

GROUCHO *(pointing)*: How much is it?

CHICO: That's free.

GROUCHO: Oh, thanks.

CHICO: Justa one dollar printing charge.

GROUCHO: Aw, give me one without printing. I'm sick of printing. *(He throws the book back)*

CHICO *(he rehands it to* GROUCHO*)*: You want to win, don't you?

GROUCHO: Yes, but I don't want to have the savings of a lifetime wiped out in five minutes.

CHICO: Come on, you look like a good sport.

GROUCHO *takes the book and reads*—MUMBLING.

Close on Chico *at the betting window.*

CHICO: Two dollars on Sun-Up.

Back to:
Scene

GROUCHO: Hey, Ice Cream, come here. I can't make head or tail out of this!

CHICO: That's all right! Look in your master code book. That will tell you where to look.

GROUCHO: What do you mean "master code book?" I haven't got any master code book.

CHICO: You no gotta master code book?

GROUCHO: No. Do you know where I can get one?

CHICO: Just by accident, I got one right here. *(He gets a book out of the wagon)*

GROUCHO: Certainly's a lot of quick accidents around here! *(Excitedly)* Just a minute. Is there a printing charge on this?

CHICO: No.

GROUCHO *(pleased; takes book)*: Thanks.

CHICO: Justa two dollars delivery charge.

GROUCHO: What do you mean, delivery charge. I'm standing right next to you.

CHICO: Well, for such a short distance, I make it a dollar.

GROUCHO: Couldn't I move over here and make it fifty cents? *(He moves over to* CHICO*)*

CHICO *(moves a couple of feet away)*: Yes, but I'd move over here and make it a dollar again just the same.

GROUCHO: Maybe I better open a charge account.

CHICO: You got some references?

GROUCHO: The only one I know around here is you.

CHICO: Thatsa no good! You'll have to pay cash!

GROUCHO: You know, a little while ago, I could have put two dollars on Sun-Up and avoided all this. *(He fumbles for his money)*

CHICO: And throw away your money!

GROUCHO *(reading)*: Z–V–B–X–R–P–L—the letter Z stands for J unless the horse is a filly.

CHICO: Ice cream, getta your tootsie-frootsie ice cream!

GROUCHO: Hey, Tootsie-frootsie, come over here. Is the horse a filly?

CHICO *(disinterestedly)*: I don't know. Look in your breeder's guide. Getta your ice cream!

GROUCHO: What do you mean, breeder's guide? I haven't got any breeder's guide.

CHICO *(dramatically)*: You haven't got a breeder's guide?

GROUCHO (SHUSHING *him)*: Not so loud. I don't want it to get around that I haven't got a breeder's guide. Even my best friends don't know that I haven't got a breeder's guide.

CHICO: I feel sorry for you, Boss, walking around without a breeder's guide. Why you're throwing your money away buying those other books without a breeder's guide. *(He is perfectly still)*

GROUCHO *(contemplates the situation)*: Where can I get one—as though I didn't know.

CHICO *(reaches for book)*: One is no good. You've got to get the whole set.

GROUCHO: All I wanted was a horse, not a public library. How much is it?

CHICO: One dollar apiece, or four for five.

GROUCHO *pays and gets the books.*

Cut to:
Close on Chico, *as he tears to the betting window again.*
CHICO *(to* TICKET CLERK*)*: Two dollars on Sun-Up.

Back to:
Scene
GROUCHO *(displaying original code sheet)*: This is the thing I started with. Now, I'm all set! ! Let's see! Z–V–B–X–R–P–L is Burns.

CHICO: That's right, Burns! That's the name of the jockey. Some days, they give you the names of the jockeys, instead of the horses." Find out who jockey Burns is riding and that's the horse you bet on. Just look in the book.

GROUCHO: I'm getting the idea all right. For a while I didn't get the hang of it *(He starts looking in book)*

CHICO: It's not that book! (GROUCHO *starts fumbling through*

27

another book) It's not that book! *(GROUCHO starts fumbling through another book)* It's not that book. No, you haven't got that book.

GROUCHO: You've got it, huh? *(Nodding his head)* It won't be long before I get it, will it?

CHICO *(nodding his head)*: Getta your tootsie-frootsie!

GROUCHO: I'm getting a fine tootsie-frootsing right here. That's the last book I'm buying. Here's a ten-dollar bill! Hurry up with the change.

CHICO: I ain't got no change. I'll have to give you nine more books.

GROUCHO *(as CHICO starts piling books all over him. When his arms are full, CHICO stacks them between his legs)*: You don't handle any bookcases there, do you? Say, am I dripping books down there?

CHICO *(indicating GROUCHO's knees)*: Close! Close!

GROUCHO: It's a good thing I brought my legs with me. What horse have I got?

CHICO *(reading)*: Jockey Burns is riding number one-five-two. Why, that's Rosie!

GROUCHO *(going to BOOKIE at window)*: Two dollars on Rosie!

BOOKIE: I'm sorry, sir, that race is over.

GROUCHO: Over? Who won?

BOOKIE: Sun-Up.

CHICO: That's my horse! *(He gathers up money from BOOKIE)* Thanks very much. *(He exits with money in hand)*

    GROUCHO *throws books in ice-cream wagon. He starts pushing cart offscene, calling "getta your tootsie-frootsie ice cream."*

                                             Fade out

Fade in:

Close Shot—a Girl's Hand, *handing over a small sheaf of memo slips to* JUDY'*s hand. As* JUDY'*s hand riffles the slips, we read.*

        "Mr. Stewart called at 11:00"

        "Mr. Stewart called at 11:05"

        "Mr. Stewart called at 11:10"

            etc.

Over this action comes the VOICE *of the* TELEPHONE GIRL.
TELEPHONE GIRL'S VOICE: Miss Standish—these calls came for you while you were out.
The CAMERA PULLS BACK, *revealing* JUDY *in the lobby of the sanitarium at the telephone desk.*
JUDY *(annoyed)*: Thank you.
She ceremoniously tears the slips in half and throws them in a wastepaper receptacle. The TELEPHONE GIRL *talks into the phone.*
TELEPHONE GIRL: Hello? . . . Mr. Stewart? *(She looks at* JUDY *quizzically)*
JUDY: I'm still out! *(She walks away,* CAMERA MOVING WITH HER. *She speaks to an intern)* Have you seen Doctor Hackenbush?
INTERN: Why, yes—He's over there. *(He points offscene.* JUDY *looks in that direction)*

Cut to:
Close—on Groucho *comfortably ensconced in a lobby armchair, with his feet resting on a very fragile jardiniere, reading a book, on the cover of which we see the title:* "WHAT TO DO 'TILL THE DOCTOR COMES." JUDY'S VOICE *is heard on the* SOUND TRACK.
JUDY'S VOICE: Doctor Hackenbush!
GROUCHO *guiltily jumps to his feet and hastily deposits the book in the jardiniere, as* JUDY *comes into scene.*
JUDY *(smiling)*: Doctor—may I have one of your pictures?
GROUCHO: Why . . . I haven't got one. I could give you my footprints, but they're upstairs in my socks.
JUDY *(smiling)*: But, Doctor, I want to announce your association with the sanitarium—we'll send your pictures to all the papers.
GROUCHO *(alarmed)*: The Florida papers?
JUDY: Yes. . . . It'll be wonderful publicity.
GROUCHO: Publicity? Oh, we mustn't have any of that, Miss Judy— you know, the ethics of my profession . . .
JUDY: But—we've *got* to get new patients!
GROUCHO: Well, after all, the old patients were good enough for your father. . . . *(Then, with supermodesty)* . . . anyhow, Miss

Judy—who wants to see my picture? I'm not a famous doctor—I'm just a simple man with horse sense—*(Suddenly catching himself)*

JUDY *(smiling)*: You're just being modest, Doctor—but we'll forget about the pictures. *(She puts her hand on his arm)* Remember—I'm depending on you . . . the success of the sanitarium is in your hands.

GROUCHO *(alarmed)*: But look, Miss Judy—suppose I were to tell you I'm not the doctor you think I am. . . .

JUDY: You're the only one that can help me—you've got to keep Mrs. Upjohn happy. *(She is struck by a sudden thought)* Why don't you take her to the water carnival tomorrow night? She'd love it!

GROUCHO: I don't know about that—but I'll tell you what I'll do. Have the stableboy put a saddle on Mrs. Upjohn and I'll ride her around the park a couple of times.

> JUDY *smiles and exits.* GROUCHO *crosses to the lobby desk and speaks to the* TELEPHONE GIRL.

GROUCHO: Have the florist send roses to Mrs. Upjohn—and put in a card from me—*(looking at the pretty* TELEPHONE GIRL*)* No—tell him to send the card to her, and keep the flowers for yourself.

> *The* GIRL *is busy answering the phone. She smiles at* GROUCHO.

TELEPHONE GIRL: Just a moment, Doctor Hackenbush! *(She speaks into the phone)* Yes, Mr. Whitmore, I've put through that long-distance call to the Florida Medical Board. *(*GROUCHO *reacts to this)* I'm doing the best I can! It ought to come in any minute!

> GROUCHO *takes this big and realizes he's in a spot.*

GROUCHO *(moving away)*: If that call's what I think it is, you'd better send the flowers to me at the depot.

> CAMERA MOVES WITH HIM *as he rushes across the lobby and ducks into an anteroom.*

Cut to:

Interior, Anteroom *as* GROUCHO *rushes to the phone.*

GROUCHO: Get me Mr. Whitmore.

Cut to:
Interior, Whitmore's Office
WHITMORE *(answering phone)*: Hello?

Cut to:
Interior, Groucho's Office
GROUCHO *(in falsetto voice)*: Here's your Florida call, Mr. Whitmore.

Cut to:
Interior, Whitmore's Office
WHITMORE: Okay—Hello?

Cut to:
Interior, Groucho's Office
GROUCHO *(in singsong manner of Southern telephone operator)*: Good-mornin'—Florida Medical Board—

Cut to:
Interior, Whitmore's Office
WHITMORE: I want the man in charge of records!

Cut to:
Interior, Groucho's Office
GROUCHO *(in GIRL'S VOICE)*: Record Department? Just a moment, Sugar—*(Now in* MAN'S VOICE—SINGING*)* In the blue of the night, vo-de-o-do! Record Department, Colonel Hawkins speaking—

Cut to:
Interior, Whitmore's Office
WHITMORE: Hello, Colonel Hawkins—I wired you for information about Doctor Hackenbush!

Cut to:
Interior, Groucho's Office
GROUCHO: Will you-all repeat that? I don't want you to repeat all of it, I just want you-all to repeat it.

31

Cut to:
Interior, Whitmore's Office
WHITMORE *(slightly annoyed)*: I'm trying to find out something about Dr. Hackenbush!

Cut to:
Interior, Groucho's Office
GROUCHO: I'm sorry, suh—there's a hurricane blowing down here, you'll have to talk a little louder!

Cut to:
Interior, Whitmore's Office
WHITMORE *(shouting)*: I WANT TO KNOW ABOUT DR. HACKENBUSH!

Cut to:
Interior, Groucho's Office *as* GROUCHO *kicks up the key to the Dictograph.*

Cut to:
Interior, Whitmore's Office *as the Dictograph* BUZZES. WHITMORE *rushes to it and flips up the key.*

Cut Back to:
Interior, Groucho's Office
GROUCHO *(into Dictograph)*: Hey, Whitmore, you'll have to cut out that screaming. The patients are complaining.

Cut to:
Interior, Whitmore's Office *as he flips the key and hurries back to the telephone.*

Cut Back to:
Interior, Groucho's Office
GROUCHO *(into phone as the Colonel)*: —and I hope, suh, that is the information you wanted.

Cut to:
Interior, Whitmore's Office
WHITMORE: I'm sorry—I didn't hear it. I was called to the Dictograph.

Cut to:
Interior, Groucho's Office
GROUCHO: What was that you said, suh?

Cut to:
Interior, Whitmore's Office
WHITMORE *(shouting)*: *I was called to the Dictograph!*

Cut to:
Interior, Groucho's Office
GROUCHO *(into Dictograph)*: Whitmore, one more yelp out of you and I'll have you thrown out of here!

Cut to:
Interior, Whitmore's Office
He glares at the Dictograph and hurries back to the phone.

Cut to:
Interior, Groucho's Office
GROUCHO *(into phone)*: —and I trust, Suh—that answers your question.

Cut to:
Interior, Whitmore's Office
WHITMORE: I'm terribly sorry, Colonel, I didn't hear you. . . .

Cut to:
Interior, Groucho's Office
GROUCHO: Well, I accept your apology.
A DARKY comes in with a mop and a pail to clean up the office. GROUCHO takes one worried look at him, not wanting to be overheard.

33

GROUCHO *(into phone)*: Pardon me a moment, suh—while I step out and free a slave. *(He puts his hand over the mouthpiece—to* DARKY*)* You can take the day off.

The DARKY'*s eyes light up and he bows out of the office.*
GROUCHO *(into phone)*: You'll have to speak a little louder!

Cut to:
Interior, Whitmore's Office
WHITMORE: *I want to find out something about Hackenbush!*

Cut to:
Interior, Groucho's Office
GROUCHO *(into Dictograph)*: Whitmore—this is the last time I'm going to warn you about that yowling!

Cut to:
Interior, Whitmore's Office
He slams down the key, and rushes back to phone.

Cut Back to:
Interior, Groucho's Office
GROUCHO: —and in conclusion let me say—

Cut to:
Interior, Whitmore's Office
WHITMORE: I'm sorry—what was that you said about Hacken-bush?

Cut to:
Interior, Groucho's Office
GROUCHO: You mean Dr. Hackenbush! Oh, no—he's not here.

Cut to:
Interior, Whitmore's Office
WHITMORE: I know he's not there. *He's here!*

Cut to:
Interior, Groucho's Office
GROUCHO: Then what are you bothering me for, Yankee? If he's there—ask *him!*

Cut to:
Interior, Whitmore's Office
WHITMORE: *But I want to know something about his Florida record!*

Cut to:
Interior, Groucho's Office
GROUCHO: Oh! His record! Well, I might say—*(His eyes fall on a plaque hanging on the wall.* DR. STANLEY's *picture is prominently displayed, and below it a tribute to him as a gentleman and a doctor.* GROUCHO *reads it verbatim, but substitutes the name of* HACKENBUSH *for* STANLEY) Dr. Hackenbush, M.D., P.H.D., and some mo' letters, whose great services to humanity and whose outstanding contributions to the field of medicine will be remembered forever. Only because of his untimely departure—*(He is flustered. The next words on the plaque are "from this earth")*

Cut to:
Interior, Whitmore's Office
WHITMORE: His departure?

Cut to:
Interior, Groucho's Office
GROUCHO: Yes—his depature from the sunny shores of Florida et cetera—et cetera—et cetera—And the charge is seventy-four dollars!

Cut to:
Interior, Whitmore's Office
WHITMORE: Are you sure you're speaking of Dr. *Hugo Z.* Hackenbush?

Cut to:
Interior, Groucho's Office
GROUCHO: Who?

Cut to:
Interior, Whitmore's Office
WHITMORE *(shouting)*: *Hugo Z. Hackenbush!*

Cut to:
Interior, Groucho's Office
GROUCHO: Who is calling him?

Cut to:
Interior, Whitmore's Office
WHITMORE: The Standish Sanitarium.

Cut to:
Interior, Groucho's Office
GROUCHO: That's where he works.

Cut to:
Interior, Whitmore's Office
He is now thoroughly riled.
WHITMORE: I know—I want to get some information as to his qualifications for the job.

Cut to:
Interior, Groucho's Office
GROUCHO: What job?

Cut to:
Interior, Whitmore's Office
WHITMORE *(shouting angrily)*: As head of the sanitarium!

Cut to:
Interior, Groucho's Office
GROUCHO: Who?

Cut to:
Interior, Whitmore's Office
WHITMORE *(bellowing)*: *HACKENBUSH!*

Cut to:
Interior, Groucho's Office
GROUCHO *(speaks into the Dictograph)*: Did you call me, Whitmore?

Cut to:
Interior, Whitmore's Office
WHITMORE *(shouts into Dictograph)*: No—you sap! *(He then shouts into phone)* Hello. . . !

Cut to:
Interior, Groucho's Office
GROUCHO *(into phone)*: When Hackenbush comes in, I'll tell him to phone you.

Cut to:
Interior, Whitmore's Office
He is beside himself with rage. He slams the phone down furiously, his mouth framing a curse. He starts angrily out of the room, as CHICO's *head appears in the window.*
CHICO: Hey! Are you the doc?
WHITMORE *(looking at him angrily)*: No!—And I'm not the information desk either! *(He starts for the door)*
CHICO *(calling after him)*: 'Atsa no way to get new customers. (*WHITMORE leaves* SLAMMING *the door. Alongside of* CHICO's *head comes* GIL's *and* HARPO's*)* Come on!
    HARPO *vaults over and lands into the room.* CHICO *starts to follow him.* HARPO *wanders around until he spots a mounted fish, which hangs on the wall. He eyes the fish avidly, takes out some salt and pepper from his pocket, and advances toward the plaque.*

Cut to:

Gil and Chico—at Window

CHICO *has climbed up to the sill.* GIL *stops him and remains outside.*

GIL: Wait a minute, Tony. We'll never get away with this. I don't look sick!

CHICO: How about Stuffy. Any guy who looks like him—must be sick! *(He takes* GIL's *arm)* Stuffy looks sick enough for both of you.

GIL: What good is that going to do me?

CHICO: You wanta see Judy, don't you? All right—They make Stuffy a patient, and tonight you sneak in the window and take his place!

GIL *(protesting)*: But Tony—!

CHICO: Listen, Gil—I fixa everything. You wait here, and I tella you how I make out. You leava it to me *(*GIL *shrugs.* WE PAN WITH CHICO *as he crosses the room to* HARPO. HARPO *is on a chair putting the last touch of salt and pepper to the fish, and preparing to cut the fish with a paper knife.* CHICO *grabs him)* Hey! Thatsa no good to eat! CHICO *pulls* HARPO *off the chair. The phone* RINGS. CHICO *quickly lifts the receiver off the hook so that the* RINGING *will not bring anyone into the room. Through the receiver we hear the* VOICE OF THE OPERATOR.

OPERATOR'S VOICE: Here's your Florida call!

HARPO *places his ear against the phone which lies on the table.*

CHICO *(grabbing phone)*: Hey! Thatsa not for you! *(A* MAN's VOICE *is heard over the phone impatiently saying, "Hello, Hello."* CHICO *decides to answer the call)* Hello?

MAN's VOICE: This is the Florida Medical Board. Regarding Dr. Hackenbush—

CHICO: Hacknapuss? I never heard of him.

MAN's VOICE: I want to tell you about him. Our records show that he is a veterinary—a horse doctor!

CHICO: I don't need a horse doctor! *(He turns to* HARPO, *after hanging up receiver)* Hesa crazy—calls up here for a horse doctor!

Come on, we go seea the doc! *(HARPO gets scared and pantomimes that he doesn't want any doctor to saw off his arm.* CHICO *continues reassuringly)* Aw, no—this is a nice doc. He's gonna give you a lot of beautiful nurses and all the food you can eat! *(HARPO still pantomimes his fear—*CHICO *trying to convince him)* It's plenty nice, Stuffy—ice cream—steak—beautiful nurses—everything I like!

> HARPO *weakens and they start out.*

Cut to:

Corridor—Camera Moves with Chico and Harpo *as they walk along the highly polished corridor where a "*QUIET PLEASE*" sign is prominently displayed.* CHICO *leads* HARPO *by the hand, and is annoyed when he hears the* SQUEAKING *of shoes.*

CHICO *(indicating sign)*: Hey! Be quiet! Taka your shoes off! *(HARPO does so, and* CHICO *leads him down the corridor again. Again the* SQUEAKING *is heard.* CHICO *looks at* HARPO'S *stocking feet and addresses him angrily)* Take those off too! *(HARPO takes off his socks revealing spats over his bare feet.* CHICO *again takes him by the hand as they tiptoe up the corridor. The* SQUEAKING *continues.* CHICO *looks at* HARPO'S *bare feet, and then at his own shoes. He takes a couple more steps and discovers that his shoes were* SQUEAKING *all this time. He* LAUGHS LOUDLY *at his discovery)* Thatsa some joke! It wasa me all the time.

> HARPO *joins in the* LAUGHING. *Puts on his shoes, and the two start up the corridor again. As they continue up the corridor,* HARPO *loses one of his shoes. As he goes to pick it up, he notices a very pretty* NURSE *crossing the hall in the opposite end, with a tray on which is a huge steak, a glass of milk, some ice cream, etc.* CHICO *has rounded a corner.* HARPO *quickly puts on his other shoe and races down the corridor toward the* NURSE.

Cut to:

Corridor Intersection

> HARPO *appears and looks in both directions for the* NURSE,

who has disappeared. WE FOLLOW HIM *as he pushes open a door and looks into a room. There he sees a tray of food alongside a* BRAT *who is having a tantrum, pushing the food away.*

Cut to:
Child's Room

HARPO *comes in and advances over to the tray of food. The* CHILD SLAMS *the tray angrily with her hand. Now* HARPO *tries to make her eat the ice cream. He scoops up a spoon and tries to eat some himself, but the* KID SQUAWKS. *The* CHILD *is holding a balloon on a stick. She hits* HARPO *with it, and the balloon comes off and collapses. The* CHILD *starts to* BAWL. *To shut her up,* HARPO *puts the balloon to his lips and tries to blow it up, but he inhales a deep breath and swallows the balloon. The* CHILD *starts to* BAWL. NURSE'S VOICE *is heard on* SOUND TRACK.

NURSE'S VOICE: Don't cry—Don't cry, Baby, I'm coming—
HARPO *alarmed, dives under the bed. The* NURSE *enters the room, accompanied by* TWO ORDERLIES.

NURSE *(to the* BRAT*)*: Now you're going to get a nice ride out to the sun porch! Here we go.

The ORDERLIES *roll the bed toward the door and as it moves away, we discover that* HARPO *is not on the floor beneath it.*

Cut to:
Shot under Bed

Here we see HARPO *hanging onto the springs, monkey fashion, getting a free ride. The* CAMERA PULLS BACK AND TRUCKS WITH THEM, *as the* ORDERLIES *roll the bed out into the corridor.* CAMERA FOLLOWS *as they push the bed past* CHICO, *who is looking around for* HARPO. *As the bed goes past* CHICO, HARPO HONKS *his horn. The* NURSE *and* ORDERLIES *look puzzled at one another.* CHICO *looks around, knowing from the* SOUND *of the horn that* HARPO *is near.* WE FOLLOW CHICO

40

as he opens a door and looks into a large office to see if
HARPO *is there.*

Cut to:

Interior, Groucho's Office

CHICO *looks around for* HARPO, *opening the door of a closet and peering in.* VOICES *are* HEARD *approaching the office.* CHICO *opens the door marked* "STERILIZATION ROOM," *and ducks in. The automatic door starts to close.* CHICO YELLS *for help, but the door* SLAMS *shut, and cuts off the sound of his voice. At this moment several* DOCTORS *and* NURSES *enter, with* GROUCHO'S SECRETARY, *all talking at once.*

FIRST NURSE: I must see Dr. Hackenbush!

A DOCTOR: Where is the Doctor? It's important.

WILMERDING: I have a case to discuss with him.

A door opens and GROUCHO *enters on a wheelchair pushed by an* INTERN.

GROUCHO *(as he gets out)*: Pick me up at five.

SECRETARY: Doctor, may I have your okay on this, please?

GROUCHO: I'm too busy! I'll put the "O" on now and come back later for the "K." *(To* NURSE*)* Get me the Turkish bath.

The NURSE *picks up receiver.*

GROUCHO *(to* WILMERDING*)*: Wilmerding, what time are you operating?

WILMERDING: One-thirty.

GROUCHO: When you're through with that knife, let me have it. I want to do some whittling.

NURSE: Turkish bath on the phone, Doctor.

GROUCHO: Hello, is that you, Gus? . . . This is Hackenbush. . . . Yeah, Doc! . . . Will you look in the steam room and see if my frankfurters are done? That will be all. *(To* NURSES *and* DOCTORS, *as he clears his desk)* Now, I'll have to ask you all to trot out of here—I've got work to do of the utmost importance.

DOCTORS *and* NURSES *exit hurriedly.* GROUCHO *opens the typewriter partition at the end of his desk, revealing, instead*

41

*of a typewriter, a pillow, and a sheet. He lies down on the pillow, throws the sheet over himself and prepares to take a nap. Suddenly, the door of the steam room flies open. Steam rolls out—*GROUCHO *takes one look and frantically picks up the phone.*

GROUCHO *(into phone)*: I hate to be a gossip—but I think the joint's on fire!

Suddenly, CHICO *is propelled out through the steam, looking very mildewed and wet. He reacts when he sees* GROUCHO *at the desk, but not half as much as* GROUCHO *does when he sees who it is.*

CHICO: Oh, so *you're* the doc!

GROUCHO: Yes. Remember me?—I used to be in the book business.

As he says this, he opens a bag and draws out several operating instruments, which he starts to sharpen on each other— CHICO *looks at him very worriedly.*

CHICO: Hey—Boss! I gotta something good for you today.

GROUCHO *(sarcastically)*: What are the odds?

During all this, CHICO *is backing away from* GROUCHO *and* GROUCHO *is approaching* CHICO.

CHICO *(protesting)*: No, no! . . . I bringa you a patient.

At this moment, the other door flies open, and HARPO *comes in* PLAYING *his flute.*

GROUCHO *(rushing to* HARPO*)*: Well!—you didn't get him here any too soon.

HARPO *holds back.*

CHICO: Hesa not gonna hurt you.

GROUCHO: Sit down and I'll snatch you from the jaws of death. *(He feels his pulse)* Either he's dead, or my watch has stopped. *(He reaches for a thermometer and shakes it off)* Here, flip this under your flapper. *(He puts it under* HARPO's *tongue.* HARPO *reacts)* That's it. Just take it easy. It didn't hurt, did it? *(*HARPO *pantomimes "yes" and then starts eating the thermometer)* Well, that temperature certainly went down fast. *(*HARPO *grabs a bottle of poison and takes a swig)* Don't drink that poison, that's four dollars an ounce. *(He starts adjusting his mirror headpiece)*

42

CHICO: I guess he's pretty sick, eh, Doc?

GROUCHO: We'll soon enough find out. *(As GROUCHO turns again to HARPO, HARPO stares at the mirror headpiece)* Hey, don't look at me—I'll look at you. You just look the other way.

HARPO *looks in the mirror and crosses his eyes.*

GROUCHO: Hey, what do you think this is, a peep show? That's rather a strange looking sight, isn't it? Huh? I don't know—I haven't seen anything like that in years. Outside of a museum you don't often encounter one of these. That's all desiccation along there. He's got about—I would say about a one per cent metabolism with an overactive thyroid and a glandular affectation of about fifteen per cent with no mentality at all. *(HARPO assumes a pose of supreme happiness and pride)* All in all, to sum it up briefly, this is one of the most repellent sights I've ever peered at.

CHICO *(laughing)*: Hey, Doc—you got the looking glass turned around. You're looking at yourself!

GROUCHO *(camping)*: I knew it all the time. That was a good one on all of us. I knew it every minute. Let's do it again some time. *(He resumes his professional manner and goes to HARPO)* Say "Ah." *(HARPO opens his mouth, but no sound comes out)* Ah! *(HARPO again opens his mouth)* Louder! Louder! *(This time HARPO opens his mouth, GROUCHO starts to run off)*

CHICO: What are you doing, Doc?

GROUCHO: I'm going to the ear doctor, I'm deaf. *(He returns to HARPO)* Well, there's one final test. *(He presses HARPO's stomach and a balloon comes out of HARPO's mouth. GROUCHO looks up just as the balloon disappears)* Say, am I stewed, or did a grapefruit just go past? *(He squeezes HARPO's stomach again—repeat balloon business)* If that's his Adam's apple, he's got yellow fever. *(Or, jaundice.) (He again squeezes HARPO's stomach and this time he grabs HARPO by the throat before the balloon disappears)* I got you that time.

CHICO: Look, Doc—he's got a blister on his tongue. No—he's a Ubangi.

GROUCHO: Well, just a minute. I'll get a hammer and ubangi that off. *(HARPO bows his head. CHICO points to it as GROUCHO returns)* Hey, look—it's swollen a lot, hasn't it? What is this wiry looking fungus?

CHICO: Some fungus, hey, kid? Hey, Doc—you're making a mistake. That's his head.

GROUCHO: If that's his head, *he's* making a mistake. *(*HARPO *has taken the balloon from his mouth, he lets the air out under his arms and squeals with glee. Stethoscope business. Apache dance and bull fight)* I can't do anything for him. This is a case for Frank Buck.

CHICO: Well, put him in a room till Frank Buck gets here.

GROUCHO: Shall we say a fifty-buck room, or would you like something better?

CHICO: We like something better, but we talk about the money tomorrow.

GROUCHO: Oh, no, you don't! It's cash on the line or out you go!

CHICO: You're making a big mistake. You could save money by using him for a guinea pig.

HARPO *starts* BEATING DRUMS *on the garbage pail.*

GROUCHO *(turning on him angrily)*: Why are you making that noise, with patients upstairs dying like rats in a trap?

CHICO: A year ago, he couldn't play a note.

GROUCHO: He's certainly holding his own. Listen, you guys— you've got to get out of here, I'm operating at eleven. *(To* CHICO*)* Have you got a knife in your pocket? *(He looks at his watch and then places it on desk)*

CHICO *(looking at watch)*: "Presented to Dr. Hugo Z. Hackenbush." Oh, so you're Hackenbush! I got a message for you. Somebody called up and said to tell you you're a horse doctor.

GROUCHO: Sh! Sh! Quiet!

CHICO: Well, he just told me to—*(It suddenly dawns on him)* Oh, so they don't know you're a horse doctor! Hey, Stuffy, he's a horse doctor!

CHICO WHINNIES; HARPO CLUCKS *his tongue and whips the desk with the stethoscope.*

CHICO: Well, I guess Gil's gonna be a patient now, eh, Stuffy?

GROUCHO: Now, listen boys, I'll admit it. You've caught me with my coat down. We'll have to get together on this thing. I'm open to any kind of a proposition.

CHICO: What will you give us to keep our mouths shut?

GROUCHO: I'll give you lockjaw. *(He sees* HARPO *drinking from poison bottle again)* Hey, you, you're going to get used to that poison and you won't be able to live without it. *(Turning to Chico)* You've got to get out of here. You can't hang around here. What are you going to do in a sanitarium?

CHICO: We can do as good as a horse doctor. I got an idea. Stuffy, what do you say we all move in?

HARPO *throws both of his shoes in the instrument cabinet.*

GROUCHO *(throwing out shoes and clock)*: Well, it's broke. Now I won't have to get up tomorrow. *(Sitting on desk)* Well, look, fellows, let's be reasonable. You know you can't stay here.

CHICO: I make you a proposition. You let my friend Gil Stewart stay here and we no say a word. He wants to see Judy, and—

While they're talking HARPO *jabs* GROUCHO *in the leg with a hypodermic syringe.*

GROUCHO *(not noticing* HARPO*)*: Well, the way it looks now, I haven't got a leg to stand on.

GROUCHO*'s leg gives way under him. Business of trying to get his legs straightened and walking with leg behind him.*

Fade out

Fade in:
Nurse Walking Along Corridor—Evening
*She is carrying a couple of large vases filled with flowers. As she passes a door marked: "*LINEN CLOSET*" a hand comes out, takes the flowers out of one of the vases without her noticing it and* CHICO *emerges from the linen closet and walks in the opposite direction from the* NURSE, *carrying the flowers. As the* CAMERA TRUCKS WITH HIM, JUDY *comes out of a room, and sees* CHICO.

JUDY: Hello, Tony—what are you doing here?

CHICO *(very sadly)*: I come to see a very sick friend. *(Dramatically)* Oh, boy . . . is he sick!

JUDY: That's too bad. Is it anybody I know?

CHICO *(shrugging his shoulders)*: Oh—itsa nobody you care for.

JUDY *(her curiosity aroused)*: Who is it?

CHICO: Oh—what do you care . . . itsa just Gil.

JUDY *(worriedly)*: Gil!—sick!—here? What's the matter with him?

CHICO: Well, Miss Judy—itsa dis way. He fella so bad because you never want to see him that the other night he walk all night in the rain and catcha double pneumonia.

JUDY: *What?* *(Then with a sudden thought)* But it hasn't rained here for weeks.

CHICO: I don't know about that. I'm not a doctor. Anyway, hesa very, very sick.

JUDY: Where is he?

CHICO: You comea with me.

Cut to:

Exterior, Gil's Room in the Hospital

GROUCHO *is coming out of the room as* JUDY *and* CHICO *hurry into the scene.*

JUDY: Dr. Hackenbush—what is it?—How is he?

CHICO *(meaningly and menacingly)*: Go ahead—you tell her Doc.

GROUCHO *(with a scowl at* CHICO*)*: Well, it's not much fun being kicked in the head by a horse.

CHICO *tries to motion to* GROUCHO *over* JUDY'*s shoulder but* GROUCHO *pays no attention.*

JUDY *(looking dubiously from* GROUCHO *to* CHICO*)*: A horse?— But Tony said he was caught in the rain.

GROUCHO *(trying to square himself)*: Yes—he got caught in the reins—the horse's reins.

JUDY *(growing more and more suspicious, to* CHICO*)*: You said he had double pneumonia.

CHICO: Well, he hada single pneumonia—but I tossa him double or nothing and he won.

JUDY *(her suspicions fully aroused, to* GROUCHO): May I see him, Doctor?

GROUCHO *(petting her on the shoulder as he opens the door for her)*: Be brave, Miss Standish—he may not recognize you. He didn't recognize the nurse—but of course he'd never seen her before.

JUDY *goes inside.*

Cut to:
Interior, Gil's Room—Dimly Lighted
  GIL *lies in bed all bandaged up. . . .* JUDY *peers in the door.*

Cut to:
Close Shot—Judy *as she considers a moment, anger in her eyes, then comes to a swift decision—her plan is made and she instantly swings into a tender Florence-Nightingale attitude, maintained throughout scene.*

GIL *(in a far-off ghostly voice)*: Who's there?

JUDY: Judy. . . .

GIL *(faintly)*: Come closer Judy. . . . I can't see you. *(pathetically groping with his hands as* JUDY *approaches)* Where *are* you Judy . . .

JUDY *(sitting on bed and taking his hand)*: Here, Gil . . . *(Gently pushing him back as he tries to sit up)* No, no, you mustn't exert yourself.

GIL *(nobly, going little-Eva-on-her-deathbed)*: *I'm* all right . . . *(He groans to disprove words)*

JUDY *(soulfully)*: Oh, you're so *brave,* Gil!

GIL *(a bit bewildered)*: Brave?

JUDY: Tony told me—*(Dramatically painting scene)* That horrible auto—skidding the corner, whirling upon an innocent child—and you risked your life—!

GIL *(playing up)*: I'll never forget—one awful moment—then everything went blank . . . *(Continuing . . . as* JUDY, *spurred on by his confirmation of the lie, nods to the waiting* INTERNS *who advance)* . . . but it doesn't matter . . . I'm here with you. . . . *(He*

47

reaches for her hand—gets the INTERN's *hand)* Could you stroke my head, Judy? *(Blissfully as the* INTERN *obliges)* Now I'm ready for anything! *(He reaches up to embrace* INTERN . . . *discovers mistake)* What's the matter? *(He yanks off bandage and gazes in bewilderment at the* INTERNS*)* What is this!

JUDY *(soothingly)*: Now, now, don't get excited! We're moving you, Gil—this dingy little room—! *(She glances about in scorn)*

GIL *(meaningly)*: . . . Home is where the heart is. . . .

JUDY *(firmly)*: But it isn't what you deserve . . . There should be air—and a view—no one knows how long you'll be here!

GIL *(with satisfaction)*: That's right! Weeks, months—

JUDY *(cutting him off)*: Years! *(Gesturing to* INTERNS*)* Handle him carefully, boys. *(She gives nod and look which accounts for the roughness that follows)*

GIL *(letting out yell as they twist and bounce him on to the stretcher)*: Hey! Take it easy!

JUDY *(reprovingly to* INTERNS, *with contradictory nod)*: Be gentle, boys!

GIL *(as more rough stuff ensues)*: I'm a sick man!

JUDY *(to* GIL *as* INTERNS *turn toward corridor)*: Just keep calm—remember your heart. . . . Everything's going to be all right!

Cut to:

Corridor *as* INTERNS *bounce the stretcher along.* JUDY *follows.*

GIL *(calling)*: Stay with me, Judy!

JUDY *(significantly)*: Don't worry, Gil—no patient has ever received the treatment you're going to get!

They have reached the end of the corridor. She signals to the INTERNS *and one of them opens a door leading to a chute—the table is tipped and* GIL *goes flying down the chute.*

Cut to:

Exterior, Sanitarium

GIL, *a mass of bandages, is sitting outside the sanitarium, looking up at a window at which stands* JUDY *with a grim look on her face.*

Fade out

Fade in:
Gil and Chico at Rail of Race Track
It is dusk. GIL *has his foot thrown over the top of the rail and is peering out, apparently following a* HORSE *running around the track.* CHICO *is just below him, holding a stop watch.*

Cut to:
Different Angle—Chico and Gil at Rail
In the background we see the home stretch. HARPO, *astride* HI-HAT, *is approaching the finish line.* CHICO, *as* HARPO *nears the finish line, looks down at his watch, then quickly slips it into his pocket—but it is evident from his expression that he is disappointed and only putting on an act to fool* GIL.

CHICO *(with mock bravado)*: Hey, 'atsa fine!—He just breaka the record.

GIL *(not fooled for a second)*: Let me see that watch! *(He holds out his hand for the watch)*

CHICO *(purposely misunderstanding—takes* GIL's *hand and shakes it warmly)*: You gotta some horse there!

GIL *glares at him, reaches in* CHICO's *pocket and takes out the watch—examines it.*

GIL: A mile in one-forty-five!—I thought so.

CHICO: Maybe the watch shesa slow.

GIL: It's not the watch.

During this discussion HARPO *has dismounted and led the* HORSE *up to* GIL *and* CHICO. HARPO *hangs his head sheepishly.*

GIL *(patting* HARPO*)*: It's not your fault, Stuffy . . . *(Putting his arm around the* HORSE*)* And it's not your fault, either—I guess we're both in the wrong business.

CHICO *(indignantly)*: Whata you talk—Hi-Hat hesa great horse!

GIL *(glumly)*: I can't understand it—I thought he was a natural. *(Then a little more hopefully)* If we only had enough money to train him properly.

CHICO: Hey—after you sing at the water carnival tonight—we have plenty of money.

GIL *(smiling)*: That is—if *my* tryout is okay.

CHICO *(adjusting* GIL's *muffler—confidently)*: Donta you worry, Gil—you're going to sing lika Carus'.

GIL *(to* CHICO*)*: I hope you're right. *(Then to the* HORSE—*with mock severity)* I'm singing for *you*—and I expect you to run for *me. (He looks at watch)* Cool him off, boys—I've got to go to rehearsal.

CHICO *(patting* HI-HAT*)*: Sure—and we puta the radio on in his stall so he can heara you sing.

  GIL *smiles and exits.*

CHICO: Come on, Stuffy—we giva Hi-Hat the once over light.

  They start walking away with the HORSE.

SHERIFF'S VOICE *(offscene)*: Hey—you!

Cut to:

The Sheriff

  The CAMERA PANS WITH HIM *as he walks toward the* BOYS. *He approaches them.*

CHICO *(nervously)*: Hello, Sheriff.

SHERIFF: I thought I told you guys not to take the horse out of the stable until I got the rest of my dough!

CHICO: We didn't—he just walked out and we followed him.

SHERIFF: I've warned you!—Now I'm taking the nag.

CHICO: Hey—you can't take that horse!

  HARPO *shakes his fists threateningly at the* SHERIFF, *who pushes him aside roughly, then takes the lead rope and throws it around* HI-HAT's *neck.*

CHICO: But, Sheriff—that horse belongs to Gil!

SHERIFF: Not now he don't.

  The SHERIFF *starts to lead the* HORSE *away.* CHICO *and* HARPO *look after him frantically.*

CHICO: Hey, Stuffy—we don't want to lose Hi-Hat . . . *(*HARPO *grabs his horn and waves it menacingly like a war club)* Okay, come on!

  HARPO *and* CHICO *sneak up behind the* HORSE. *Unseen by the* SHERIFF, *who is walking a few paces ahead,* CHICO *takes the rope off of* HI-HAT'S *neck and puts it on* HARPO. HARPO *jerks his head as the* HORSE *has been doing and the* SHERIFF, *not knowing the switch, keeps tugging the rope.* CHICO *leads* HI-HAT *out of scene. The* SHERIFF, *without looking around, gives a terrific yank on the rope and pulls* HARPO *right off his feet, sending him flying through the air. He bangs into the* SHERIFF, *knocking him down, with a loud honk of* HARPO'S *horn. The* SHERIFF, *amazed, looks around and takes in the situation.*

SHERIFF *(jumping to his feet)*: Stop in the name of the law!

As he starts to chase CHICO, HARPO *trips him up with the rope and he falls down.* HARPO *rushes to* CHICO *and jumps on the* HORSE.

SHERIFF: You'll get jail for this!

But the BOYS *gallop off.*

Fade out

Fade in:

Boxes—at Edge of Lake

The boxes on rafts are decorated for the water carnival and are filled with gay CROWDS *dressed in summer-evening attire.* CAMERA PANS ALONG *the row of boxes and* HOLDS *on one box in which we see* CHICO *and* HARPO *in evening clothes. They are slouched in the box, acting like big society. The* CAMERA PANS DOWN *and we see that the* BOYS *have ripped up several of the boards in the box, so that they can fish, and that fishing lines are attached to the ends of their canes. In a corner of the box is a string of fish which the boys have already caught. The* CAMERA PANS UP AGAIN *as an immaculately dressed* MAN *in the next box bows low to acknowledge an introduction.* HARPO *looks in that direction and, using the shiny seat of the* MAN'S *pants, he carefully adjusts his tie and quickly straightens his hair. At this moment, a distinguished-looking* MAN *and* WOMAN *come to this box and are surprised to see that it is already occupied by the* BOYS.

51

MAN *(haughtily)*: This is our box!

CHICO: Come on in—there's plenty of room.

Suddenly, the SHERIFF *appears, and his eyes light up at the sight of the* BOYS.

SHERIFF: I'll take care of this!

He steps between the MAN *and the* WOMAN, *enters the box, and the* CAMERA PANS DOWN *as he disappears into the water. As the* SHERIFF *disappears in the water,* HARPO *and* CHICO *kick the boards back in place, grab the fish, and jump to the the next box, then to a raft, then to a box—the* CAMERA TRUCKING WITH THEM. *As* CHICO *and* HARPO *jump to the next raft,* CHICO *notices* GROUCHO *at the table with* JUDY *and* MRS. UPJOHN. GROUCHO *is trying to make a spoon jump into a glass.*

CHICO *(grabbing* HARPO): Come on—I think we camp here.

GROUCHO *glares at the* TWO BOYS, *and* MRS. UPJOHN *looks amazed.* HARPO *immediately lifts the top off the chafing dish and warms his hands over the steam.*

MRS. UPJOHN: Who are these men?

GROUCHO *(pretending not to notice them)*: What men?

He gets back to his spoon trick, trying to avert MRS. UPJOHN'S *attention.*

GROUCHO: Now the object is, to make the spoon jump into the glass.

CHICO *(looking at chafing dish)*: I don't lika this. Let's have fish.

HARPO *pulls a fish out of his pocket and slams it on the table.*

MRS. UPJOHN: Hugo! Look what they're doing!

GROUCHO *(pretending to be engrossed in the spoon trick)*: I can't look now—I've got to concentrate.

On MRS. UPJOHN'S *line,* HARPO *dumps the crepe suzette into her open purse.* CHICO *has gathered up all of the condiments on the table and has started to put a little of each in the chafing dish.* HARPO *starts to clean the fish, scaling it with* MRS. UPJOHN'S *lorgnette.*

MRS. UPJOHN *(to* GROUCHO): Hugo! Do something! Call the police! Send those men away!

GROUCHO *(looking up from his spoon trick, and pretending to be surprised at seeing* CHICO *and* HARPO): Oh! Those fellows! *(To the* BOYS*)* Now look, boys—

CHICO *starts kindling the fire under the chafing dish. He breaks bread sticks and tosses in various inflamable objects.*

CHICO *(to* HARPO*)*: Itsa funny—A big town like this and they only gotta one *horse* doctor . . . Maybe it's a one-horse town.

HARPO *leans in front of* MRS. UPJOHN, *reaching across the table, and takes out a handful of sauerkraut and a frankfurter.* MRS. UPJOHN *looks at him in amazement as he puts the sauerkraut in his pipe and pats it down with the frankfurter.*

MRS. UPJOHN: Oh!—Oh! What are they doing?

GROUCHO: I think they're cooking my goose.

A WAITER *walks by with a tray of demitasses.* HARPO *grabs one of the tiny cups and swallows it, cup and all.*

JUDY *(worriedly)*: Doctor! You must do something!

GROUCHO: Well—*(He turns to* CHICO *and* HARPO*)*

HARPO *grabs the horn of plenty and squeezes out the filling on a cake which is on the table. He draws a horse's head and proudly shows it to* CHICO.

CHICO: Hey—Thatsa pretty sick-looking horse. I think he needs a *horse* doctor.

MRS. UPJOHN: I won't tolerate this another minute!

GROUCHO: Emily, I'm disappointed in you. You're turning out to be a first-class snob!

MRS. UPJOHN *(furiously)*: How dare you talk to me like that! !

JUDY *looks at* GROUCHO *and* MRS. UPJOHN *worriedly.*

CHICO *has finished his sauce and now adds more fuel to the fire. He adds several bread sticks, menus, hard rolls, etc,* HARPO *is finishing scaling the fish. He and* MRS. UPJOHN *look up as* GROUCHO *talks, and* HARPO *unwittingly*

GROUCHO: Oh,—I see. They're not good enough for you! Don't forget, you blueblooded Amazon—All men are created free and easy. Have you forgotten Jefferson's immortal words? I have. Say, I've even forgotten the music. Your

scrapes some sequins off MRS. UPJOHN's *sleeve, which is next to the fish. Now that he has scaled the fish,* HARPO *reaches in the fish's mouth and pulls out the backbone. He puts a paper napkin over this and when* GROUCHO *starts singing* "Johnny Comes Marching Home," HARPO PLAYS *the tune on the fishbone.* CHICO *salutes and stands at attention.*

grandfather wouldn't have been ashamed to mop up gravy with these peasants—of course, he'd have been glad to get any kind of a meal. We've come a long way since the Pilgrims landed on the rocks. We've come through muck and mire, rain and sleet, fire and theft, shot and shell, and we won't come back—I said we won't come back till "Johnny Comes Marching Home Again, Hurray, Hurray"—!

GROUCHO SINGS *the last few words, and brandishing a carving knife, marches up and down like a Civil War veteran.*

GROUCHO *(looking offscene):* Pull up another chair, boys—here comes the sheriff.

Cut to:

Shot of Sheriff *wringing out his clothes and looking off in the direction of the* BOYS.

Cut Back to:

Scene

CHICO: I don't think we wait for dessert!

HARPO *grabs the fish out of the pan. They start to run,* HARPO *turns back and hits the spoon which* GROUCHO *has been trying to spin into the glass. The spoon flies across the table and goes down* MRS. UPJOHN's *dress.*

MRS. UPJOHN: Doctor, oh! *(She clutches her heart)* My smelling salts! *(She reaches into her bag for smelling salts and takes out the crepe suzette)* I don't mind eating out of your hand, but when it comes to eating out of your handbag—!

GROUCHO *picks up a menu and looks at it.* JUDY *takes a napkin and wipes the crepe suzette from* MRS. UPJOHN's *hand.*

GROUCHO *looks past the menu and reacts at the sight of some-one.* CAMERA PANS *to show next table where* FLO MARLOWE *is giving* GROUCHO *the eye.*

He returns her glance and she waves to him. GROUCHO *teeters on his chair like a bashful boy and waves the menu at her.* GROUCHO *notices* MRS. UPJOHN *looking at him. He pretends to be swatting flies with the menu.*

FLO *leaves her table, casting a come-hither look at* GROUCHO.

GROUCHO *(rising)*: I'd better go get a fly-swatter.

MRS. UPJOHN: But those are raisins.

GROUCHO: Well—I'll get a raisin-swatter.

There is a ROLL OF DRUMS, *the* MUSIC *begins and the lights start to dim.*

MRS. UPJOHN: Hugo—the show is starting.

She grabs GROUCHO's *arm—he slumps into his chair greatly annoyed.*

Cut to:

Flo *in the semi-darkness, she steps off the raft.* WHITMORE *is standing at the edge of the* CROWD *on the shore. Everyone is looking toward the lake.* WHITMORE, *without averting his gaze, speaks to* FLO.

WHITMORE: Nice going, Flo—You've got him hooked!

FLO *(smiling)*: I was always lucky with brunettes.

The music swells to a CRESCENDO. *The* CAMERA PANS *around to take in the set. The water curtain descends revealing the number.* GIL *goes into his song. Early in the number he discovers that he is near* JUDY's *table. He* SINGS *his song to her, but she turns away.* GIL *finishes the song. The production number begins.*

(Possibly a cut during the number reveals CHICO *and* HARPO *perched on the high-diving springboard watching the number, safe from the* SHERIFF.*)*

Cut to:

Audience *as they give the production number a warm round of* APPLAUSE.

Cut to:

Flo, *returning to her table to get her wrap.* CAMERA MOVES BACK *to show* GROUCHO'S *party at the next table.* JUDY *and* MRS. UPJOHN *are looking toward the lake, and* APPLAUDING. GROUCHO *has his back turned to the lake and is loudly* AP-PLAUDING *with his eyes on* FLO.

MRS. UPJOHN *(still applauding)*: Isn't it beautiful?

GROUCHO *(looking at* FLO*)*: It's the prettiest number *I've* ever seen.

FLO gives GROUCHO *a come-hither look and strolls away.* GROUCHO *darts a look at* MRS. UPJOHN APPLAUDING *the number, and sneaks out of the box and follows* FLO.

MRS. UPJOHN *(to* JUDY—*not noticing* GROUCHO'S *departure)*: I'm so glad we came! It's been so impressive—Hasn't it, Hugo? *(She turns and is amazed to discover that* GROUCHO *has disappeared. She looks around for him, and catches a glimpse of him disappearing in the crowd)* Hugo! Hugo!

She hurries after GROUCHO, *with a murderous look in her eye and exits—as* GIL *appears in the background.* GIL *steps onto the raft where* JUDY *is sitting alone.*

JUDY *(turning—annoyed)*: What are you doing here?

She rises and starts to go. GIL, *to stop her, pushes the raft with his foot and it goes out into the lake.*

JUDY: Gil—stop that!

At that moment the MUSIC *starts for* GIL'S *reprise and the spotlight falls on the* GIRL *in the boat whom* GIL *had sung to previously. The* GIRL *is very flustered being alone and no* GIL *to sing to her. Suddenly* GIL'S VOICE *starts to* SING *and the spotlight picks him up as he goes into the second chorus, with the indignant* JUDY *forced to share the spotlight with him. Loud* APPLAUSE *at the song's end.* GIL, *with a mischievous smile, takes* JUDY'S *hand and forces her to take a bow with him. At first she holds back, furious, realizing the hundreds of eyes that are on her, then yields. More* APPLAUSE—*they bow again . . . then* GIL *waves the spotlight away and the raft is left in semi-darkness. The water curtain rises, concealing them from the* PEOPLE *on the shore.*

JUDY: Well, I hope you're satisfied.

GIL: Umm—I think the act could stand a little polishing. You've got to give them more personality in the second chorus—but a couple of weeks on the road and we'll wow 'em. Stewart and Standish—songs and patter—why we're a cinch for forty weeks. And then we'll put the baby in the act—What do you think?

JUDY: I think you're crazy!

GIL: Crazy? Why, kids are always sure fire!

JUDY (bitingly): Now that you've succeeded in making a complete fool of me—would you mind putting me ashore?

GIL: Aw, come on, Judy, where's your sense of humor?

JUDY: I never had much use for practical jokes.

GIL (with a wry smile): You mean—like giving a fellow a free ride down a laundry chute? (JUDY smiles in spite of herself) Judy!

JUDY (trying to be serious): Yes.

GIL: Do you mind if I touch you?

JUDY: What?

GIL: I just want to make sure that it's true. You smile—you laugh—Judy, you're human.

JUDY: Can't you ever be serious about anything?

GIL: I'm terribly serious about you, Judy. Why do you suppose I took this job?

JUDY (weakening a bit): Well—why did you?

GIL: I did it for Mrs. Upjohn—I'm madly in love with her.

They both laugh.

JUDY: You fool!

GIL: We've missed a lot of fun together.

JUDY: I know, but I've been so worried. (Hopelessly) Bills—notes—Morgan won't wait—

GIL: Morgan?

JUDY: He took over the notes and if we can't pay—(She makes a helpless gesture)

GIL (soberly): So that's it. (Rising; firmly) I think I'll go and interview that gentleman.

JUDY: I'm afraid there's nothing we can do.

GIL: Something's *got* to be done, and whatever it is I'm going to do it.

JUDY: Gil!

GIL: Yes?

JUDY: Do you mind if I touch you?

GIL: What?

JUDY: You're frowning—you're serious—Gil, you're human!

GIL *smiles at her as he starts propelling the boat by means of an oar or a pole.*

Cut to:

Chico and Harpo, *perched on the springboard, looking at the* BOY *and* GIRL.

CHICO: Hey! Look at that. Judy liksa him!—Thatsa swell!

HARPO *is carried away by the love scene they are viewing, snuggles up to* CHICO *(and perhaps takes his hand).*

CHICO *(pushing him away): (He spouts some indignant Italian phrase.)*

Suddenly they are aware of the springboard shaking a bit. They look around.

Cut to:

Ladder

The SHERIFF *is climbing up to get the* BOYS.

Cut Back to:

Chico and Harpo *as they edge away from the* SHERIFF *until they come to the end of the springboard. They climb over and hang by their hands. The* SHERIFF *reaches over to grab them, and the* BOYS *let go, dropping onto a box which is directly below the springboard. As they drop, the springboard catapults the* SHERIFF *over the water curtain, and he splashes into the lake.*

Cut to:

Chico and Harpo *in the box. They get to their feet, and jump ashore.*

CHICO: Come on, we gotta hide!

They rush away running past the bandstand, where the MARIMBA ORCHESTRA *is now* PLAYING. *They turn the corner at the edge of the stand, and they come to a door which opens onto the* MUSICIANS' *room. A few* MUSICIANS *are loitering outside, smoking cigarettes, etc. They are dressed in typical outdoor band uniforms, with gold buttons, etc. The* TWO BOYS *exchange looks and duck into the dressing room.*

Cut to:

Interior, Dressing Room *as* CHICO *and* HARPO *enter. The* MUSICIANS *are* TUNING UP, TALKING *amongst themselves, etc.* CHICO *and* HARPO *sneak behind a row of lockers. They are smiling confidently, when the* SHERIFF'S VOICE *is* HEARD *at the doorway.*

SHERIFF'S VOICE: Hey, buddy!

The confident smile fades from CHICO's *and* HARPO's *faces. In a nearby locker we see two band uniforms. As they start to reach for them—*

Cut to:

Sheriff, in Locker Room

The MUSICIANS *are streaming past him on their way to an open door which leads to the platform.*

SHERIFF: Do you mind if I dry out in here?

MUSICIAN: Go ahead!

The SHERIFF *stops short as he sees* CHICO *and* HARPO *follow the* MUSICIANS *onto the platform. The* BOYS *are buttoning up the uniforms which they have put on over their clothes. The* SHERIFF *looks at them suspiciously, not quite sure that they are his men. As the* BOYS *go through the door to the platform,* TWO MEN *in their underwear rush out from behind the lockers.*

MEN *(ad libbing)*: Somebody stole my uniform! Where's my suit?

The SHERIFF *reacts to this. His suspicions are confirmed. He makes a beeline for the door, but* CHICO *and* HARPO *are too fast for him. The* SHERIFF POUNDS *on the door and starts away furiously.*

59

Cut to:
Other Side of Door

CHICO *and* HARPO *are* LAUGHING *and slapping each other on the back, for having outwitted the* SHERIFF. *Suddenly the orchestra platform starts to rise.*

CHICO: Hey! Let us out!

The platform comes into view about ten feet up so that the SHERIFF *cannot reach the* BOYS. HARPO *and* CHICO *are quite confused. The* AUDIENCE APPLAUDS. HARPO *tentatively steps forward to the conductor's station and takes a bow.* CHICO *goes to the only vacant instrument, the piano.*

Cut to:
Orchestra Platform—Audience's Angle

The SHERIFF *rounds a corner, and looks suspiciously at* HARPO *and* CHICO. HARPO *sees the* SHERIFF, *and edges away to the side of the platform, where there is a vine growing up the latticework. Pretending to be inspecting the sheets of music on the piano, he reaches over and picks three caterpillars off the vine. He uses one for a mustache, and the other two for eyebrows. The effect is not unlike the appearance of the* ORCHESTRA LEADER *from whom Harpo stole the uniform.*

Confident that his disguise is complete, HARPO *goes to the rostrum and* RAPS *his baton for silence.*

Cut to:

Violinist *as he presses his bow on the strings of his violin, and is bewildered to discover there is no hair on the bow.* WE PAN OVER *to* CHICO *who is next to him, at the* PIANO. CHICO *has used the hair for a long flowing white mustache.*

Cut to:
Harpo

He nods at the audience and just then the caterpillars go to work, crawling up his cheek, etc. (Intercut to SHERIFF, *re-*

acting and finally getting wise to the disguise.) He sits down and menacingly waits. HARPO *gives the orchestra the downbeat and the* MUSICIANS *start* PLAYING.

HARPO *uses the various gags of leading an orchestra. The* VIOLINIST *motions him away.* HARPO *shows his union card, and is allowed to remain. He* RAPS *for attention and this time the* ORCHESTRA *goes into a number.* HARPO *tries to keep the* CELLIST *from using tremolo, then his hand starts shaking and he scratches himself. He grabs the* CELLIST's *bow and starts scratching viciously. He directs* CRESCENDOS *and* DIMINUEN-DOS *with the greatest of pride and the* PLAYERS *follow his directions. The* ORCHESTRA *starts* PLAYING *a classical number.*

Cut to:
Chico, at Piano
He works into his specialty number. At the conclusion of his number, he takes a bow. He keeps bowing as he backs up toward the rear of the platform. The SHERIFF *starts around the side of the platform to grab* CHICO, *should he attempt to escape at the rear.* CHICO, *in taking a last bow, stumbles over a railing behind him, and topples onto the awning at the back of the platform. He rolls down the awning and lands on his feet. The* SHERIFF *starts after him, but* CHICO *has too much of a head start, and quickly disappears in the* CROWD. HARPO *seeing this, attempts to get away via the awning, but the* SHERIFF *whirls around and blocks his way, standing below. Just then the platform starts down and* HARPO *knows if he goes to the ground floor, he'll be nabbed. He quickly pushes a button. The platform comes up as* HARPO *dashes to the piano to start a number. He starts to* PLAY *a classical number in most discordant fashion. He becomes so worked up over his artistry that he* POUNDS *the keys with his fists and feet. (Maybe he stops and the platform starts down again. He resumes and it goes up.) He beats hell out of the piano and gradually, the*

instrument falls apart. In the end, all that's left are the strings in the shape of a harp. HARPO *stands them in an upright position and goes into his harp specialty.*

At the conclusion he takes a bow and, noticing that the platform is sinking, he decides to play another number. He twirls the piano seat around to adjust it. When he sits on it, it whirls around and throws him into the lake, as the SHERIFF *executes a take-em.*

Cut to:

Exterior, Pavilion

GROUCHO *and* MRS. UPJOHN *are looking toward the lake, obviously watching* HARPO.

GROUCHO: There goes our cook after some more fish.

MRS. UPJOHN *(looking toward the pavilion)*: Oh, Hugo—I'd love to dance—but, do you think my heart can stand it?

GROUCHO: If I can stand it, anything can.

They go into the pavilion, CAMERA TRUCKING WITH THEM, *and start dancing.* GROUCHO *spots* FLO *dancing with a* MAN. *She gives him the eye.*

GROUCHO *(disguising his voice, he shouts)*: Change your partners!

He leaves MRS. UPJOHN, *rushes to* FLO, *and then starts doing solo trucking steps;* MRS. UPJOHN *comes up to him indignantly.*

MRS. UPJOHN: I'm surprised at you.

GROUCHO: Oh, so you didn't know I could truck?

MRS. UPJOHN *goes into his arms, and he is forced to dance away with her.*

Another Angle

GROUCHO *and* MRS. UPJOHN *dancing.* FLO *in the background looks at him petulantly.* GROUCHO *dances over to her.*

GROUCHO: Change your partners!

He grabs FLO *and this time they go into a hot rumba.* MRS. UPJOHN *looks on bewildered.*

MRS. UPJOHN: Hugo!

The number changes to minuet time. GROUCHO *leaves* FLO *and wheels around to* MRS. UPJOHN.

GROUCHO *(grabbing her hand)*: I was just getting around to you. You're just the minuet type.

They go into a minuet.

MRS. UPJOHN: Hugo, I'm disappointed in you. To think of you dancing with that strange woman!

GROUCHO: Well, don't think of it. Think of me dancing with you. *(He takes her in his arms.* FLO's PARTNER *has reclaimed her.* GROUCHO *maneuvers it so that he and* MRS. UPJOHN *are right beside* FLO *and her* PARTNER. *As they dance,* GROUCHO SPEAKS *over* MRS. UPJOHN *to* FLO) I'm crazy about you . . . *(Looking at* FLO) Nothing will ever come between us again. If you only knew how lonely I get—night after night in my little room at the sanitarium—*room four-twelve.*

MRS. UPJOHN *(a-twitter)*: Perhaps I *could* come in and say goodnight to you.

GROUCHO: Yes—we could have a midnight snack—a nice little steak between us.

FLO *nods that it will be okay and dances away.*

MRS. UPJOHN *(coyly)*: Why, Hugo . . .

GROUCHO: Oh—you *would* stay up until midnight—that's the way you follow doctor's orders. I told you to get to bed by ten. *(He gives her a little shove)* Now skip along—and don't forget to brush your teeth.

Cut to:

Exterior, Pavilion as FLO *and* WHITMORE *walk out.* WHITMORE *sees* MORGAN *standing nearby and steps next to him, casually taking out a cigarette.* MORGAN *offers him a light. The* MEN *speak quietly without looking at each other.*

WHITMORE: Worked like a charm.

GIL *appears in the scene and looks for a moment at the* TWO MEN. MORGAN *and* WHITMORE *immediately affect a casual manner.*

WHITMORE: Thanks for the light, Mr. Morgan.

He strolls off to FLO. GIL *comes up to* MORGAN.

GIL: Hello, Mr. Morgan.

MORGAN (*cordially*): Hello, Stewart—you were okay, boy. You can start singing at the casino tomorrow—but I'll pick your leading lady for you.

GIL: Oh—you mean Miss Standish. Well—you know how it is. . . .

MORGAN (*sarcastically*): Yeah—I hope you'll be very happy.

GIL: Look, Mr. Morgan—I want to talk to you about that. If you'll give Miss Standish a little more time, I'll make good on those notes somehow.

MORGAN (*with a sarcastic laugh*): *You*? Why you haven't even got the cash to take care of a horse.

GIL (*earnestly*): You've *got* to give us more time.

MORGAN: Listen, Stewart—I hired you as a singer, not as a business adviser.

GIL (*flaring up at his tone of voice*): I guess you don't *need* any advice on this deal—it looks like you've worked it out pretty well.

MORGAN: What are you getting at?

GIL: Oh nothing—except that you and Whitmore seem to hit it off pretty well—and I was just thinking. . . .

MORGAN: Singers shouldn't think—it's bad for their health.

GIL (*furiously*): If you're pulling any fast ones—you're not going to get away with it!

Without GIL *seeing it,* TIP *and* BEEF, *at a signal from* MORGAN, *have walked up behind him.*

MORGAN: Here's one fast one for you!—You're fired!

GIL: Okay—and don't bother about paying me for tonight—I'll take it out in trade.

He aims a blow at MORGAN. TIP *grabs his arm.* BEEF *grabs him and the* TWO MEN *give him the* "bum's rush," *sending him spinning into a clump of bushes.*

GIL (*rubbing his chin*): Well—that's the shortest job I ever had: one verse and two choruses.

Cut to:
Road, at Side of Lake

WHITMORE *is helping* FLO *into a wheelchair which is propelled by a* MAN *on a bicycle at the rear of it.* WHITMORE *gets in beside her. The* ATTENDANT *starts to put the robe around them. Just as he has tucked in the robe and starts back to mount the seat—from around a bush comes* HARPO, *the* SHERIFF *close in pursuit.* HARPO *sees the bicycle, jumps on it, and starts pedaling. The* ATTENDANT *is thrown down and the* SHERIFF *trips over him.*

Cut to:
Traveling Shot—Flo and Whitmore, *in the wheelchair with* HARPO *bicycling.*

Flo and Whitmore in Chair, with Harpo
Listening Carefully
FLO *(suspiciously)*: Say—just why are you so anxious to frame this Hackenbush?
WHITMORE *(covering up)*: I told you—we're just playing a little joke.
FLO *(more suspicious than ever)*: Listen, Whitmore—you and Morgan aren't the playful type. *(Then threateningly)* Come on—let's have it—*or I walk!*
WHITMORE *(deciding to break down)*: Well, as long as Mrs. Upjohn keeps Hackenbush in the sanitarium, her trustees will put up the cash—but once he's out . . .
FLO *(furious)*: So that's it! You and Morgan get the joint and all I get is fifty bucks. *(She starts to get up)* Let me out of here.
WHITMORE *(frantically)*: Now wait a minute, Flo—I'll give you an extra hundred.
FLO *(holding out her hand)*: Okay! Give!
WHITMORE: Not yet! I want to make sure you're in that room when I bust in with Upjohn.
FLO: Listen, toots . . . I'll be in that room if I have to pull a sit-down strike . . . *(She laughs scornfully)* And be sure to knock first!

Cut to:
Harpo on Bicycle, *very upset by the plot he is overhearing and so absorbed that he does not notice a bump in the road. The*

65

bicycle goes over the bump, throwing HARPO *off the seat and* WHITMORE *and* FLO *start down a slight incline, angrily gesticulating and ad-libbing:* "What are you doing?" "Stop!" "Let us out!" *etc. The chair with the empty bicycle reaches the bottom of the incline and turns over.* FLO *and* WHITMORE *pick themselves up angrily.*

Cut Back to:

Harpo, *running wildly in the direction of the lake. At the side of the road which overlooks the lake and links the sanitarium and the casino, he stops and* WHISTLES. *A* DOG *comes toward him, thinking he has been called.* HARPO *motions him away and* WHISTLES *again. Another* DOG *comes up.* HARPO *motions him away impatiently and* WHISTLES *again. He is surprised to hear several answering* WHISTLES. *He goes in the direction of the sounds,* CAMERA MOVING WITH HIM, *and we see* CHICO *playing blindman's buff with half a dozen* GIRLS *from the carnival. The* GIRLS *are* WHISTLING *to get* CHICO's *attention—when he goes toward them, they elude him, amid much* GIGGLING. *As* HARPO *rushes in, the* GIRLS *rush out.* CHICO *blindfolded, hears* HARPO *WHISTLING. He grabs* HARPO *and kisses him.* HARPO's *horn* HONKS. CHICO *tears off blindfold and sees* HARPO. *He is enraged.*

CHICO *(furiously)*: What do you want? *(*HARPO *indicates* HACKEN-BUSH*)* Looking for Buffalo Bill? *(*HARPO WHISTLES "No." *Indicates* HACKENBUSH *again, and starts the* GROUCHO *walk)* Oh!—Doctor Hackenbabush! *(*HARPO WHISTLES *and nods "Yes." Shakes hands with* CHICO*)* *(*HARPO *then pantomimes curves)* Doctor Hackenabush gotta snake? *(*HARPO *shakes head "NO," and* WHISTLES. *Makes more curves)* Oh! Gotta apple dumpling? *(*HARPO *gives big* WHISTLE. WHISTLES DOCTOR HACKENBUSH, *then makes curves on two sides)* Thatsa no apple dumpling! *(*HARPO *pulls up pants leg, and shows bare leg and runs his hands over leg)* Oh! It's a woman! *(*HARPO *nods "Yes," and again they shake hands.* HARPO WHISTLES *and stamps twice)* Oh! Shesa gotta wooden leg! *(*HARPO *indicates*

"No," *stamps and* WHISTLES*)* Shesa gotta woodpecker? *(*HARPO *gives a big* WHISTLE *in disgust. He puts his hand to his head)* Hesa gotta headache? *(*HARPO WHISTLES *"*No,*" and starts again)* Doctor Hackenabush—thersa woman—*(*HARPO *nods again)* Oh! The woman—she knock on the door. *(*HARPO WHISTLES *happily, and indicates this is correct)* All right! Whatsa the woman gonna do? *(*HARPO *now tries to get across that* GROUCHO *is being framed by the dame, and goes into the wildest gestures possible. This builds up to his fainting in* CHICO*'s arms)*

Dissolve to:
Interior, Groucho's Living Room at Sanitarium
   As scene FADES IN GROUCHO *is dancing to strains of the "*Blue Danube." *There is a* KNOCK *on his door.*
GROUCHO: Yes?
FLO: It's Miss Marlowe.
GROUCHO: Just a minute, fruitcake. *(The spraying perfume routine—spraying everything in sight)* Come in.
FLO *(entering)*: Oh, Doctor, thank you!
GROUCHO: Thank yo! Do you like gardenias?
FLO: I adore them! How did you know.
GROUCHO: I didn't, so I got you forget-me-nots. One whiff of this and you'll forget everything. Shall we sit down?
FLO: Thank you.
GROUCHO: Thank yo!
FLO *(as* GROUCHO *holds chair for her)*: Thank you.
GROUCHO: Thank yo!
FLO: You're such a charming host!
GROUCHO: The Hackenbushes are all like that. Would you like a short beer?
FLO: Nothing, thank you.
GROUCHO: Thank yo! *(He sits at table)* Ah, Miss Marlowe, I've dreamed of this moment. For days I've been trying to see you, and I still don't seem to be making the grade. *(He loses sight of her behind huge bouquet of flowers)* Have you got a periscope? *(Peer-*

ing in among the flowers trying to see FLO*)* A quiet evening alone with you! What more could anyone ask? *(He can't see her for the flowers)* Did you sneak out of here? Oh, there you are! *(He perches up on back of chair)* Isn't this too, too, devastating? Do you mind carving? I can't reach the steak from here. *(*KNOCKING *heard at door.* GROUCHO *glares at door, annoyed.* FLO *looks at her wrist watch, expecting it is time for* WHITMORE. GROUCHO CALLS *out)* This room is unoccupied.

He turns back with a smile to FLO *and she gives him a come-hither glance. More* KNOCKING *is heard. The door opens and* CHICO *and* HARPO *enter.* GROUCHO *and* FLO *are each annoyed, but for different reasons.* HARPO *and* CHICO *advance into the room,* HARPO*'s eyes glued on the* GIRL. *They pause about ten feet inside the door.*

CHICO: Hey, Doc, can you see us?

GROUCHO: If I can't there is something wrong with my glasses.

He waves to HARPO *and* CHICO *to beat it, sits down on the chair, beams on the* GIRL, *expecting the other two to leave. Instead,* HARPO, *who has been leering at the* GIRL, *indicates to* CHICO *her curves, with gestures.*

CHICO *(under breath, to* HARPO*)*: Is that the girl? *(*HARPO *quickly nods "Yes." He rubs his hands)* We go to work on her.

They hurry down toward the GIRL *and* GROUCHO. GROUCHO *and the* GIRL *hear them, turn, and look annoyed.*

CHICO *(stopping at* FLO*'s chair, puts arms around her. She pulls back)*: Ah, signorina, gentile, è bella di statura—*(Which should mean, "Ah, lady, you have a beautiful figure.")*

He grabs her, she struggles. CHICO *jumps into her lap.* GROUCHO *gets to his feet on his chair in a protesting manner.*

CHICO *(arms around* FLO*)*: Oh, baby, you look good to me. *(He mauls her; she struggles, but he holds her tight)*

GROUCHO *(resenting* CHICO*'s actions)*: Wait a minute! I thought you came to see me.

CHICO *(holding the struggling* FLO*)*: I can see you from here.

He goes to work on her again. She struggles and tries to shove him off. HARPO, *looking on with wild eyes, sees how annoyed she is and decides to help; he jumps onto* CHICO's *knees, then pulls up his right trouser leg and pats it invitingly for* GROUCHO *to come and sit on his knee.*

GROUCHO *(still standing on the chair)*: Oh, no, not for me—three men on a horse!

FLO *(pushing them off and jumping up indignantly)*: What's the meaning of this?

She moves quickly around to GROUCHO *who hops off his chair and meets her just back of the table.* GROUCHO *pats her hand reassuringly.* CHICO *and* HARPO *stand facing them, disappointed that* GROUCHO *is siding with the* GIRL.

CHICO: She's in with Whitmore, Doc. She's trying to frame you.

GROUCHO *(holding her hands)*: I wouldn't mind framing her. A prettier picture I've never seen.

He gives her the ge-ga eye, as HARPO *and* CHICO *scowl.*

FLO *(giving* GROUCHO *the "works")*: Thank you.

GROUCHO: Thank yo!

FLO *moves toward her chair at the table, giving* HARPO *and* CHICO *a triumphant stare as she passes them.* GROUCHO *follows and pushes the chair under her.*

FLO *(sitting)*: Thank you!

GROUCHO *(leaning on his elbow on table, back of her chair)*: Thank yo!

CHICO *leans over, cups his hand to* GROUCHO's *ear and* YELLS *loudly:*

CHICO: I'm tellin' you in secret, Doc, she's outta to get you!

GROUCHO *(resenting this, moving toward* CHICO *threateningly)*: What do you mean, she's out to get me?

FLO *(jumping to her feet)*: This is the worst insult I've ever had in my life.

GROUCHO: Well, it's early yet.

     (Or)

It's only eight o'clock.

FLO *(faking her attitude—to* GROUCHO*)*: I'm leaving!—(HARPO *and* CHICO *react, pleased.* HARPO *spies her wrap across the room and dashes across to get it)*—I'm certainly not going to stay here with these men!

She gives them a dirty look and turns to get her wrap. HARPO *has it, holding ready for her, and nearly smothers her with it, gets it around her neck and gives it a good yank, choking her. She struggles to get loose while* HARPO *tries to push her toward the door to get rid of her.* CHICO *runs to the door and holds it open for her exit.* GROUCHO *hurries to her rescue.*

GROUCHO *(jumping into the thick of it)*: Hey! *(To* FLO, *as he reaches for wrap)* You're not leaving!

He jerks the wrap off of her. Half of it comes away in his hand, leaving a piece around her shoulders. She reacts. GROUCHO *indicates the* TWO BOYS. HARPO *picks up the piece of fur that* GROUCHO *tosses aside.*

GROUCHO: They're leaving! *(*GROUCHO *glares at* HARPO *and* CHICO *and goes toward them)* Now, listen, boys. You've got her all wrong. This is my aunt from Detroit. She's come to talk over some old family matters.

CHICO: I wish I had an aunt that looked like that!

GROUCHO: Well, take it up with your uncle! *(He moves toward* FLO, *who is again seated at the table)*

CHICO *(calls to* GROUCHO*)*: Hey, Doc, you're playing with fire!

GROUCHO *(crossing back toward* CHICO*)*: I noticed you didn't mind being scorched.

CHICO *(backing toward door as* GROUCHO *advances, still trying to warn* GROUCHO*)*: I got fire insurance.

GROUCHO: You better get accident insurance!

With this he practically shoves CHICO *out the door. By this time* HARPO *has arrived near door with* FLO *carried by her arm over his back. She gets to her feet and gives him a sudden push out of the door.* GROUCHO *quickly reaches out, grabs the knob and shuts the door.*

GROUCHO *(while shutting door)*: How do you like those bruisers trying to chisel in on me!

FLO, *adjusting her clothes, is moving toward the chair at the table again.* GROUCHO *gets an idea, turns back to the door and turns the key in the lock, then comes toward* FLO.

FLO *(standing by chair.* GROUCHO *enters and seats her)*: Thank you.

GROUCHO: Thank yo!

He goes around to his chair and sits down, beams across the table at FLO. *She beams back.*

FLO: How about a little Scotch?

GROUCHO *(quickly picking up large water glass and holding it toward* FLO, *as though she had bottle)*: How about a big Scotch? *(Then realizing she wants him to order some)* All right, I'll order some. *(He gets up and starts for phone on table at left side of room)*

FLO *(as he crosses)*: Thank you.

GROUCHO *stops and comes back toward the table and bows elaborately.*

GROUCHO: Thank yo! *(He goes back to the phone, picks it up)* Will you have the bellhop hop up with some hop Scotch? *(He hangs up phone and turns back toward table. To* FLO*)* I'll flip you to see who pays for it.

He sits down and beams across the table at the GIRL. *There is a* KNOCK *on the door and the* SOUND *of keys opening the lock.* CHICO *and* HARPO *enter, dressed as* BELLBOYS. *There is a big master key ring around* HARPO's *neck or arm.* CHICO *carries a tray with glasses of Scotch and Seltzer bottle, and highball glasses.*

GROUCHO *(sarcastically commenting to* FLO *as he crosses toward them)*: You certainly can't complain about the service around here.

He picks up the Scotch and a highball glass and starts to pour whisky into the glass. HARPO *picks up the Seltzer bottle, shakes it, and squirts it toward glass. It flies all over the tray and on the* PEOPLE. FLO *jumps to safety.*

GROUCHO: Hey, just fill the glass, not the room!

He and CHICO *duck back toward the sofa, to miss the Seltzer.*

The Seltzer bottle gets locked. Business of HARPO *trying to stop it. It squirts toward* GROUCHO *and* CHICO *and they duck up toward table.*

71

CHICO: I'm tellin' you, Doc—*(Still intent on saving* GROUCHO*)* I've got proof she's no good.

GROUCHO *is putting glass on table.* HARPO *turns the bottle upside down, and the Seltzer hits* GROUCHO *on the other side of the table.*

GROUCHO *(as he ducks down,* CHICO *close to his elbow)*: Have you got waterproof? *(They land under the table on hands and knees)*

CHICO *(under table with* GROUCHO*)*: Doc, you better get her out of here. *(Water hits them under table)*

GROUCHO *(starting to crawl on all fours)*: If he keeps this up she'll float out.

CHICO *crawls after him.*

CAMERA MOVES WITH THEM.

CHICO: If you don't float her out we'll have to bail you out.

The water again hits them. Apparently this brings GROUCHO *to a decision. He leaps to his feet,* CHICO *following him.*

GROUCHO: Boys, I think you're right. This is no place for a man who hasn't been in the Navy. Let's all get out.

He puts an arm around each of the BOYS' *shoulders and hurries with them toward the door.* HARPO *and* CHICO *are delighted, thinking* GROUCHO *has gotten wise and is getting away in time.(*HARPO *perhaps tosses the Seltzer bottle back of him, unnoticed by* GROUCHO*, in* FLO'S *direction)*

At the door GROUCHO *pauses just long enough for the* OTHER TWO *to go out ahead. He follows just far enough to get hold of the door knob, pull the door shut. Then he starts toward* FLO*, who is moving toward the table, shaking the water out of her dress.* GROUCHO *gets an idea, hurries back to the door and shoots the bolt, unnoticed by* FLO*. He hurries down to* FLO *who stands in front of chair, waiting for him to seat her.*

FLO *(as* GROUCHO *slides chair under her)*: Thank you!

GROUCHO *(prancing to other side of table)*: You take it. *(He almost collapses table. Fiddling with food)* Tomato juice?

FLO: Thank you.

GROUCHO *takes can of tomato juice out of soup tureen.*

GROUCHO: Have you got a can opener? *(He looks for one and finds it)* Here it is.

He starts to open can as clock STRIKES *eight.* FLO *reacts and reaches for his hand, draws him to her as she rises.*

FLO: I'm really not hungry. Couldn't we just sit over here? *(Indicating settee, drawing* GROUCHO *toward it)* I want to be near you. I want you to hold me. *(She holds him)* Oh, Doctor, hold me! Hold me closer, *closer!*

GROUCHO *(getting his arms around her)*: If I hold you any closer, I'll be in back of you!

FLO: Oh, Doctor, you're so comforting.

GROUCHO: We Hackenbushes are all like that. Shall we sit down and bat it around?

FLO: Thank you!

GROUCHO: Thank yo!

He sits and she sits in his lap. Business of GROUCHO *looking for her on the couch beside him, then discovering her in his lap.*

GROUCHO: You're either nearsighted or near-seated.

(*Or*)

Are you a little near-seated?

There is a vigorous KNOCKING *on the door.* GROUCHO *keeps* FLO *on his lap. She puts her arms around him, ready for the discovery.*

GROUCHO *(reassuringly)*: Don't worry. They can't get in. *(*FLO *gets closer to him; cuddles)* I've bolted to door.

FLO *reacts—she didn't want the door locked.*

The door suddenly bursts in and falls to the floor. CHICO *enters with painter's ladder, pails, and wallpaper supplies, dressed in painter's coveralls.* HARPO *follows in, with all of the same paraphernalia, knocking down a table by the door with the leg of his ladder. They have buckets of paste and* HARPO *is carrying a paste bucket on his head.* CHICO *sets his ladder down, between the couch and the door.* FLO *jumps up and glares at both of them as* HARPO *takes his ladder to the opposite side of the couch.*

CHICO: We come to hang the paper.

73

GROUCHO (*still seated*): Why don't you hang yourselves?

FLO: If you think you're going to get rid of me you're crazy!

She flounces herself back on the couch beside GROUCHO.

CHICO (*starting up his ladder—to* HARPO *on other side, also starting up his ladder*): That's right, Stuffy. You work on that side and I'll work on this side. We'll meet on the ceiling.

HARPO *nods "yes" and dips brush in paste bucket he is wearing on his head.* CHICO *puts paste on the wall with a huge brush.*

GROUCHO: You'll meet on the gallows is my prediction!

HARPO *takes dripping brush from the pail on his head, steps on back of couch and his foot lands on* FLO's *hair, pinning her to the couch. She struggles to free her hair.* CHICO *lets the first roll of paper unroll in front of* GROUCHO.

GROUCHO (*sticking his head out from behind paper*): End of the first act! There will be a short intermission. No necking in the lobby.

HARPO *is sopping paste on the wall over* FLO, *who is struggling to release her hair from under his foot.* CHICO *lets another roll of paper unroll in front of* GROUCHO.

GROUCHO (*sticking his head out between the two strips of paper*): I must be a citizen. I just got my second papers.

HARPO *now lets a roll of paper unroll. Then both* HARPO *and* CHICO *cut loose on the papering and pasting.*

FLO (*struggling under paper*): I want to get out of here.

GROUCHO (*breaking through for a second*): Too late. The ice is forming. (*More paper covers them. He peeps out*) Look out and see if there are any penguins.

HARPO *steps on* FLO's *head with his other foot. She is covered with wallpaper but makes violent heavings under the paper.* FLO *suddenly struggles out and socks* HARPO *in the stomach. He caves over and dumps paste on her from the bucket on his head. She stumbles back, fighting to get the paste out of her face.* CHICO *comes down his ladder and follows her.*

CHICO: So you're going to stay, huh?

FLO (*struggling to wipe her eyes*): Yes, I am!

CHICO *flips more paste on her face and figure. A good plop of it goes in her mouth.*

CHICO: So you won't get out?

FLO *(sore as hell, trying to get paste out of her mouth)*: No, I won't.

All during this she has been backing up to dodge the paste CHICO is flipping on her. She is driven to the corner. Paste from CHICO's brush flies onto the wall back of her. HARPO comes down his ladder and throws a roll of paper at the wall, it sticks and unrolls, dropping in front of FLO. CHICO quickly starts to paste the paper on her, HARPO throwing more rolls, which stick where they land and unfurl down in front of FLO.

GROUCHO *(coming out from under paper, from sofa, covered with pieces of paper; looks around)*: Where's my girl? *(He sees the boys working on her. She is mostly covered by this time. He jumps toward them, YELLING)* Hey, cut that out!

HARPO *and* CHICO *suddenly stop—so does* GROUCHO, *as they hear:*

Angle—Down Hallway, a Good Ways from Groucho's Door

CAMERA MOVING AHEAD—MRS. UPJOHN, *in very huffy mood, is walking along with WHITMORE.*

MRS. UPJOHN *(in loud and angry voice)*: If he's got a woman in his room, I'll discharge him!

WHITMORE *is well pleased with himself.*

Angle—Inside Room

The THREE BOYS *react to what they have just heard.*

GROUCHO: Unless I'm mistaken I'm fired!

(*Or*)

I hear the voice of unemployment!

He moves toward the table as CHICO *throws a bucketful of paste on the wall above and the paper covering FLO. HARPO begins to bombard the wall with rolls of paper and CHICO begins a wild pasting in, using two brushes.*

GROUCHO *yanks the tablecloth off the table without dis-*

75

*turbing the dishes and pins (or ties) it around himself in a
funny manner.*

HARPO *is about to throw another roll of paper at the wall.
He has his arm raised over his head and the paper drops to
the floor back of him and rolls out in the foreground toward
the* CAMERA. *He turns to run after it when it starts to reroll
and chases him back toward the ladder and up the ladder, in
a frightened manner. He leaps up to the top of the ladder and
onto the shelf above him.*

GROUCHO *has started to do a little fancy papering of his own
as* MRS. UPJOHN *and* WHITMORE *enter the room.* HARPO *goes
berserk and tries to paper himself on the wall.*

MRS. UPJOHN *and* WHITMORE *quickly look around and
react to the activity they see. Then* MRS. UPJOHN *remembers
what she came for and realizes there is no woman in the room.*

MRS. UPJOHN *(to* WHITMORE; *indignantly)*: There's no woman
here!

WHITMORE *looks surprised, then seeing the papers draped
over the couch moves quickly to it, tears the paper aside, revealing that no one is there.* HARPO *leans forward and the
bucket drops off his head, almost hitting* WHITMORE. *Some
of the paste splashes on him and nearly hits* MRS. UPJOHN.
They jump back and react to the danger.

GROUCHO *then pretends to see* MRS. UPJOHN *for the first
time and approaches.*

GROUCHO: Ah, this is indeed a pleasure. Won't you take a bucket
and join us? *(To* HARPO *and* CHICO *in "head-waiter" manner)*
Paper for two more!

This is ignored by HARPO, *who is papering over the cuckoo
clock. He climbs up on the vase on the shelf.* HARPO *dips the
brush into his hair, forgetting that the bucket is gone. He dips
it in so vigorously he almost knocks himself out.*

CHICO *is still papering* FLO *to the wall.*

MRS. UPJOHN *(to* WHITMORE, *a little sharply)*: I think you have
made a mistake!

HARPO *realizes he is out of paste,* WHISTLES *to* CHICO *and gestures that he wants paste tossed up to him.*

The following action and dialogue runs concurrently:

CHICO *runs over to foot of* HARPO'*s ladder, tosses the paste bucket up to* HARPO, *who dips his brush in it while it is on the fly. He slathers the paste on the wall over and under the cuckoo clock; then slaps a piece of paper on the wall, letting it hang down over the clock.* HARPO WHISTLES *for a second dip of paste.* CHICO *tosses the bucket up toward him.* HARPO'*s foot slips inside the vase and he knocks the bucket with the brush, causing it to hurtle out and land upside down on* WHITMORE'*s head.*

WHITMORE: But, Mrs.—

MRS. UPJOHN (*to* GROUCHO, *graciously*): Pardon us for intruding, Hugo. I'll see you at dinner.

She sails from the room. WHITMORE *is about to follow her when he thinks he sees* FLO *moving under the paper in the corner. Before he can be sure, the paste bucket covers his head.*

WHITMORE *throws the bucket aside and tries to wipe the paste from his face.* CHICO *runs him out of the room.*

GROUCHO *comes forward and shakes hands with the* TWO BOYS.

GROUCHO: Boys, you saved my bacon.

HARPO *has regained his balance on the shelf as the bird in the cuckoo clock breaks through the paper: It* "CUCKOOS."

HARPO *swats it with his paste brush and it disappears.* HARPO *gets another piece of paper over the clock.*

FLO *is fighting her way out of the paper. Again the cuckoo bird breaks through the paper and* "CUCKOOS." HARPO *takes a kick at it with his foot with the jar stuck on it. He loses his footing and slips off the shelf to the ladder, and slides down the ladder, landing on the floor on his seat and shoots out across the room in this sitting position.*

FLO *has extricated herself and has now reached the* BOYS, *who are in front of the couch by this time. She starts in on them, sore at them and plucking gobs of paper off her face and hands.*

FLO: I'll get even with you! Of all the dirty, low-down snakes!

GROUCHO *(crossing in front of her toward table)*: Thank yo!

FLO *starts to storm out of the room.* CHICO *drops a roll of wall paper so that it hangs back of her.* HARPO *dashes in with a big brush, full of paste, and swipes it on the paper, sticking it to* FLO's *rear end, like a long wedding train. She rushes out angrily.*

CHICO *and* HARPO *shake hands over their victory.*

Fade out

Fade in:

Interior, Sanitarium Lobby—

Close on Telephone Message Slips *in* JUDY's *hand. The hand shuffles the slips and we read:* "MR. STEWART CALLED AT 10:00." "MR. STEWART CALLED AT 10:05," *etc.*

WE PULL BACK *to reveal* JUDY *angrily reading the messages at the phone desk.*

TELEPHONE GIRL *(pleased with herself)*: —but I told him you were out.

JUDY *(trying to suppress her annoyance)*: Well, from now on, put his calls right through.

GIL *has come up from behind* JUDY *during the above line. He smiles and takes the phone slips from her hand.*

GIL *(handing slips to* TELEPHONE GIRL*)*: Better make a note of that. I've just about run out of nickels.

JUDY *(embarrassed)*: Oh, hello.

GIL *(with mock feeling)*: I'll miss that phone booth. It was sort of like home to me.

JUDY *smiles embarrassedly, and leads* GIL *away,* CAMERA MOVING WITH THEM.

JUDY: Gil—how did you make out with Mr. Morgan?

GIL: Hmm—he was a little tougher than I figured.

JUDY: Well, we're going to be a little tougher than *he* figured. Gil— I think we'll make a go of it. Business is improving and if it keeps up, we're sure to get the money from Mrs. Upjohn's trustees.

GIL: But you said, last night—?

JUDY: This morning I had a long talk with Mr. Whitmore, and he told me there's nothing to worry about. He's going to take care of everything.

They have walked onto the veranda, CAMERA MOVING WITH THEM. GIL *stops and turns to* JUDY.

GIL: Not if I can help it! (JUDY *looks surprised*) Judy—that guy's not on the level.

JUDY: Nonsense! He worked with my father for years.

GIL: Well, he's working with Morgan now.

JUDY: Why, that's impossible!

GIL: You think so? Well, last night when I went to see Morgan—

Interior, Groucho's Room

HARPO *is alone in the room, at the foot of the bed, tensely waiting. He* WHISTLES, *looking through a door which leads into the next room.* CHICO'S VOICE *is* HEARD *from offscene.*

CHICO'S VOICE: All ready!

HARPO *takes a large round mahogany ball from the top of the bedpost, crouches in the position of a bowler, and lets fly through the door leading into the next room. He rushes after the ball, the* CAMERA TRUCKING WITH HIM *into the next room. The ball goes crashing into ten objects—milk bottle, ginger-ale bottles, vases, shoes, etc.—lined up against the door of the living room in the manner of tenpins.* CHICO *jumps out of the way like an alley-boy as the ten objects go crashing to the floor.* (NOTE: *The living room is still in somewhat of a shambles from the paper-hanging scene of the night before.*)

CHICO (*scoring on the wallpaper*): Hey—'atsa strike—Two more strikes and you're out!

HARPO *nods proudly, grabs the ball and goes rushing back into the bedroom, the* CAMERA TRUCKING WITH HIM. *He spits on his hands, rubs them together and prepares for the next bowl. Then he lets the ball fly. Once again the* CAMERA TRUCKS WITH THE BALL *and just as it about reaches the objects, which* CHICO *has stood up again, the door opens and* GROUCHO *appears. The ball hits him in the knee and he falls down together with the ten objects.*

CHICO *(to* HARPO—*looking at the ten objects and* GROUCHO *lying there)*: Hey!—You got eleven that time!

GROUCHO *(rising)*: Well—that's the end of my knee-action. *(He straightens out his leg)*

In the open doorway, GIL *appears—rushes in.*

GIL: Hey, Doctor—we're in a jam! *(He closes the door behind him)*

GROUCHO: No news is good news—so don't tell me about it.

GIL: There's a Dr. Steinberg here—he claims you're a fake!

GROUCHO: He does—eh? Well, if I weren't a fake, I'd sue him. *(Then indignantly)* Who is this Dr. Steinberg?

GIL: He seems to be a real doctor—but I suspect he's in with Whitmore. *(Then eagerly)* You've got to hurry! He's examining Mrs. Upjohn.

GROUCHO *(hurrying toward his bedroom)*: I'll say I have to hurry!— I'm hopping the next banana boat!

GIL: But, Doctor—wait a minute!

The CAMERA TRUCKS WITH GROUCHO AND GIL *as they go into the bedroom.* GROUCHO *looks in amazement at* HARPO, *who has preceded them into the bedroom.* HARPO *is slashing open the mattress and taking out a huge bundle of straw.*

GROUCHO: If you're looking for my suitcase—it's *under* the bed.

HARPO *pays no attention to him, takes the straw and starts for the closet. In the meantime,* GROUCHO *has reached for his suitcase under the bed.* HARPO *opens the closet and there stands* HI-HAT, *whom he proceeds to feed.*

GROUCHO *(with a start of amazement)*: I'll never be able to get that in this little bag.

GIL *(in amazement)*: It's Hi-Hat!

CHICO: Sure—Stuffy hida him here last night. *(Patting STUFFY on the back, while HARPO looks bashful and modest)* Thatsa very smart—the sheriff never look for Hi-Hat here.

GROUCHO: No—but suppose they look for me here. *(Then dropping his bag)* Never mind the bag—I'll send for my clothes later. *He starts for the door. GIL stops him.*

GIL: You can't go, Doctor. If you run out where will Judy be?

GROUCHO: She won't be in jail and that's where I'll be—Besides, what can I do?

GIL: You've *got* to break this examination up somehow!

GROUCHO: Not today I don't!

GIL *(angrily)*: What are you—a man or a mouse?

GROUCHO: You put a piece of cheese down there—and you'll find out.

CHICO: Hey, Doc—you can't leava Judy in a fix like that!

HARPO *comes up and rubs* GROUCHO's *sleeve pleadingly.*

GROUCHO *(softening)*: All right—*(Then threateningly—to* CHICO *and* HARPO*)* But you boys keep out of this. You stay here while I go down and dangle from the gallows. *(Striking a dramatic pose)* It's a far, far better thing I do than I have ever . . . *(In his dramatic intensity, he does not notice where he is going. He starts for the closet door and bumps into* HI-HAT*)* Oh, I beg your pardon!

As he goes out of the room—

Dissolve to:

Interior, Examination Room

MRS. UPJOHN *is seated on an examination table,* WHITMORE *and* STEINBERG *stand beside her.* STEINBERG *has a stethoscope on her heart.*

MRS. UPJOHN: Well, Doctor—you hear that murmur?

STEINBERG *(shakes his head)*: Just as I thought—your heart is in excellent condition.

WHITMORE: You see, Mrs. Upjohn, I was right about Dr. Hackenbush.

MRS. UPJOHN: I can't understand it. He told me that my—
GROUCHO *rushes in.*

GROUCHO: Emily, it's four o'clock. You know you should be up on the roof taking your sunbath. Come along.

MRS. UPJOHN: No. no!—I want you to meet Dr. Leopold X. Steinberg.

GROUCHO: As soon as the sun goes down. Come, Emily.

MRS. UPJOHN: No, no, Hugo—Dr. Steinberg has a few questions he would like to ask you.

GROUCHO: I have a few questions I'd like to ask him! Steinberg, what do you do with your old razor blades?

WHITMORE: Dr. Hackenbush, Professor Steinberg has examined Mrs. Upjohn and he finds her in perfect health.

MRS. UPJOHN: You've been saying that I'm sick, Doctor.

GROUCHO: You're on your last legs.

STEINBERG: Nonsense, she's as healthy as any woman I ever met.

GROUCHO: Steinberg, you don't look as though you ever met a healthy woman.

WHITMORE: This is very vital to Mrs. Upjohn. We must decide which diagnosis is correct. Proceed, Dr. Steinberg.

STEINBERG *(taking her hand)*: Now, we will see—

GROUCHO: Take your hands off her. *(To* MRS. UPJOHN*)* A fine doctor! *(To* STEINBERG*)* Don't you know you're not supposed to touch a patient without sterilizing yourself? *(To* MRS. UPJOHN*)* You don't see me running an examination like that.

WHITMORE: No—that's true. And I think it would be very interesting to see just how Dr. Hackenbush does conduct an examination.

MRS. UPJOHN: Splendid! Splendid! Show them, Doctor.

STEINBERG: Yes—yes—*(To* WHITMORE*)* This should be very instructive.

MRS. UPJOHN *(expectantly)*: Well, Doctor—

GROUCHO *(stalling—not knowing where to begin)*: Well—I'll be very glad to, but I haven't got my sphygmomanometer with me.

STEINBERG: It's right here, Dr. Hackenbush.

GROUCHO: It's changed considerably since I was a boy.

STEINBERG: Well, proceed—

GROUCHO (*stalls*): Well, in a case like this, there's always the danger of infection. (*He goes to washbasin and starts washing hands à la Men in White*) In case you've never done it, this is known as washing your hands. (*He discovers he has been washing with his wrist watch on. He takes the watch off, puts it on the table. STEINBERG eyes it. GROUCHO takes the watch and drops it in the water*) I'd rather have it rusty than missing. You'll go a long way before you see prettier drippings than these.

STEINBERG: Why sterilization? After all, this is not an operation, you know.

GROUCHO: Not yet it isn't but I may get hot and operate on everybody in the joint, including you.

MRS. UPJOHN: Come, come, Doctor, I'm ready.

GROUCHO: Mrs. Upjohn, I guess I know my business. Of course, that's just a guess on my part. (*Or:* "of course, this is not my business") But at any rate, I know a thing or two about cleanliness. That's more than I can say about this mountain goat standing here. Steinberg, aren't you a fugitive from a mattress? And please don't point your beard at me. (NOTE: *may use last sentence in other place*)

WHITMORE: Come, come, Doctor!

GROUCHO: We'll proceed immediately. (*Drying his hands*)

WHITMORE: Ah—at—(GROUCHO *plunges his hands in the water again*) Dr. Hackenbush, you've already washed your hands!

GROUCHO: Well, I haven't brushed my teeth yet. (*He starts brushing teeth*)

MRS. UPJOHN: Doctor, unless you proceed immediately—

CHICO'S VOICE (*over public-address system*): Calling Dr. Hackenbush! Calling Dr. Hackenbush! Go to Room Six-sixty-six. The patient, she's got a bad case of St. Vitus's dance.

GROUCHO (*as he starts to walk across*): Pardon me! I've got to go up and dance with a patient.

WHITMORE (*stopping him*): Some other doctor can attend to that.

GROUCHO: This is an errand of mercy. I must go.

There is a sound of a scuffle coming over the radio. We hear CHICO *YELLING* "Ouch—Let go," *etc.*

CHICO'S VOICE: Never mind, Dr. Hackenbush. That dance is over. The patient decided to sit it out.

Over this is heard HARPO'S HORN *over loud-speaker.*

GROUCHO: Come out of that box and fight like a man.

He stops in his tracks. Realizing that he can't stall any longer, he turns to MRS. UPJOHN.

GROUCHO: Now, Mrs. Upjohn—we'll proceed with the examination. I want you to take your arms, not too slowly, let them wave through the air with the greatest of ease. *(Working his outstretched arms up and down like an eagle)*

MRS. UPJOHN: Like that, Doctor?

GROUCHO: Not too swiftly! Fine.

MRS. UPJOHN: How long do I have to do that, Doctor?

GROUCHO: Just until you fly away.

CHICO *and* HARPO *enter, dressed in white caps, gowns, and sterilization masks—*HARPO *turns his back to audience, disclosing Standard Oil (or Coca-Cola) sign on his gown.* HARPO *does allez oup gag to* STEINBERG. CHICO *crosses and indicates for him to stop.*

GROUCHO *(aside)*: I don't know what I'd do without you two, but I'd like to try sometime.

WHITMORE: Dr. Hackenbush, tell me, where did these two men come from?

GROUCHO: I don't know. They must have crawled out of a test tube. I've never seen them before.

CHICO *(crosses to* STEINBERG*)*: I'd like to introduce myself, I'm Dr. Steinberg.

GROUCHO: You're Dr. Steinberg? Then this man's an impostor.

WHITMORE: Nonsense, I know this is Dr. Steinberg.

HARPO *steals and presents card to* STEINBERG.

STEINBERG *(reads card)*: "Dr. Steinberg"!

GROUCHO: Probably all sprung from the same family. Dr. Steinberg, permit me to introduce my friends and colleagues. Dr. Steinberg, this is another Dr. Steinberg. *(HARPO bows, bending over backward)* Dr. Steinberg and Dr. Steinberg and Dr. Steinberg. One is the original. I don't know who is Dr. Steinberg. Are you Dr. Steinberg?

MRS. UPJOHN: Doctor—Doctor, I'm waiting. What do you want me to do now?

GROUCHO: Take a deep breath. I want you to exhale and inhale simultaneously. *(As CHICO engages STEINBERG in conversation, HARPO has poured soap bubbles into STEINBERG's pipe with a syringe)* Hey, Steinberg, you'd better send for a plumber, your pipe is leaking.

HARPO does a Chevrons gag, then allez oups STEINBERG, then goes into skating routine.

MRS. UPJOHN: What a strange intern!

GROUCHO: They're hard to get this time of year.

WHITMORE: Dr. Hackenbush isn't going to continue with the examination. Professor, may we have your diagnosis, please.

STEINBERG: Perhaps you'd like to read—

GROUCHO takes gloves, then accepts copy of diagnosis and tears it up.

GROUCHO: I wouldn't touch that—not the kind of work I do. What do you know about medicine? You stand there and call yourself a quack. You don't know the first thing about bacteriology *(medicine)*. Steinberg, if you were twenty years older, I'd take you outside and slap the daylights out of you.

(Business of getting tangled up in gloves?)

MRS. UPJOHN: I'm so embarrassed.

HARPO does book business. GROUCHO crosses, takes book away, tears out page.

GROUCHO: Don't read that book. One look in there is equivalent to two years in Paris.

WHITMORE: Dr. Steinberg, do you remember your diagnosis?

STEINBERG: Perfectly. To begin with, her pulse is absolutely normal.

GROUCHO: *(A line to be gotten)*

STEINBERG: You take her pulse. Take her pulse.

85

GROUCHO (to HARPO): Take her pulse.

HARPO *steals* MRS. UPJOHN'*s purse.*

MRS. UPJOHN: My purse! My purse!

GROUCHO: He doesn't spell very well.

STEINBERG: Her pulse!—her pulse!

MRS. UPJOHN (*taking* GROUCHO'*s and* CHICO'*s hands*): Come, come, gentlemen!

GROUCHO: You shouldn't have touched us. Now we're all unsterilized.

He and CHICO *walk to basin,* SING "Down to the Old Mill Stream" *as they wash and do daisy chain.*

MRS. UPJOHN: Well, I must say I've seen quicker examinations.

GROUCHO: Maybe, but you've never seen a slipperier one.

STEINBERG: Well, gentlemen, I hope you're ready to proceed.

WHITMORE: Doctor, what do you expect to do next?

CHICO: The next thing I think we do is wash our hands.

They wash their hands again, this time HARPO *drinking water out of the basin, wiping his hands on* STEINBERG'*s coat,* GROUCHO *on* HARPO'*s, and* CHICO *on* GROUCHO'*s apron.*

GROUCHO: Nurse! Sterilization!

THREE NURSES *enter with gown for each of the* BOYS. HARPO *embraces his* NURSE *as she is helping him on with his apron. In so doing, her dress comes off.*

GROUCHO: Just put the gown on, not the nurse.

During the laugh, HARPO *does an allez oup to* STEINBERG *and* MRS. UPJOHN. CHICO *lies flat on the floor, acrobat-fashion and* GROUCHO *stands on his desk, gazing off in the direction of the* NURSE *through a stethoscope.*

MRS. UPJOHN: Doctor—Doctor! Please pay attention to me.

GROUCHO: One at a time, Mrs. Upjohn.

(*Or*)

You'll have to get in line.

STEINBERG: This is insane absolutely.

MRS. UPJOHN: Oh, dear! Oh, dear!

GROUCHO: How is it, a dame like that never gets sick?

MRS. UPJOHN: But I am sick.

DR. STEINBERG: Ach, this is ridiculous. I prove it to Dr. Hackenbush now—Put the patient in a horizontal position. I'll examine her.

HARPO *puts the table in a horizontal position, then jerks the lever so that* MRS. UPJOHN'S *feet fly up in the air.*

MRS. UPJOHN: I can't stand this excitement. What are you doing?

HARPO *places sign* "MEN AT WORK" *on* MRS. UPJOHN'S *heels.* GROUCHO *takes it off and throws it away.* HARPO *grabs the paste jar and starts to lather* MRS. UPJOHN. CHICO *follows with an instrument to shave her.* CHICO *or* HARPO *puts a hot towel on her.* GROUCHO *shines her shoes.* HARPO *gives her a manicure.*

STEINBERG: Stop that nonsense! Let's have an X-ray.

WHITMORE: The X-ray.

CHICO: X-ray! X-ray!

HARPO *selling paper. Phone* RINGS. CHICO *goes to answer it.*

WHITMORE: I'm going to call the police.

(*Or*)

GROUCHO: Don't touch that phone. It hasn't been sterilized.

CHICO *throws the phone into basin.*

RADIO (*announcing*): Attention, please! Ambulance call at First and Main! Ambulance call at First and Main!

Instead of AMBULANCE FADE OUT, *at this point, we will go into sterilization gags with the* BOYS *sterilizing everything in the room. Finally, when* HARPO *accidentally turns the sun lamp on the sprinkling system, he almost causes a complete inundation of the room. At this point the* HORSE *will come into the room and we*

Fade out

Fade in:

Close Shot—Wash Line *with* HARPO'S, CHICO'S *and* GROUCHO'S *clothes, with their hats on top of them. A blanket on which is written* "HI-HAT" *also hangs on the line. The* CAMERA PANS *over to a dilapidated barn in a sylvan setting.*

Dissolve to:
Interior, Barn

Seated on the straw in attitudes of utter dejection are GIL *and the* THREE BOYS. HI-HAT *is in an improvised stall in a corner of the barn.* GIL *is fully clothed and the* THREE BOYS *are wrapped in horse blankets.* CHICO, GROUCHO, *and* HARPO *are huddled together, their heads leaning on their right arms. They sit there for a moment in silence, then almost automatically they shift their heads to their left hands all in unison. Another moment of silence and the* THREE BOYS *shift again, only this time* GROUCHO, *in the middle, goes in the opposite direction and gets his chin cupped in* CHICO's *hand.* CHICO's *chin gets in* HARPO's *hand and* HARPO *leans, but there is no hand to support him and he goes falling over. The* THREE BOYS *glare at each other.* GIL *suddenly gets up with a gesture of despondency and walks to the window. The* BOYS *look at him sympathetically.*

GIL: Well, I certainly messed things up for Judy.

GROUCHO: *You* messed things up! I suppose my fine Italian hand had nothing to do with it!

During the ensuing conversation the BOYS *pull in the line, see their clothes are dry, and start to get dressed.*

CHICO: Hey—you gotta no Italian hand. It was me who did it.

GIL *(turning to the window)*: No, boys—it was nobody's fault but mine.

HARPO WHISTLES *and points accusingly to himself in indicate that it was his fault.*

GROUCHO: Listen, I don't want any more argument. It was my fault.

CHICO: Well, maybe it was your fault.

HARPO *agrees with* CHICO *and points accusingly at* GROUCHO.

GROUCHO *(indignantly)*: Oh!—it was my fault eh? That's the thanks I get! I give you the first shower you've had in years and you turn on me like a snake in the grass!

They hear someone approaching.

CHICO *(in a hoarse whisper)*: The Sheriff!

The BOYS *rush for cover. As* HARPO *starts away, we discover that the coat he put on is still attached to the line.* HARPO *starts running in mid-air. In a moment the clothespins come loose from the coat and* HARPO *is dropped to the ground. The moment his feet touch the ground, they are going so fast that he runs smack into the wall, almost knocking himself out.*

The door opens and JUDY *enters. She is carrying blankets. She looks around disappointedly as she sees the barn is deserted. She slowly turns around. The heads of the* BOYS *start to pop up.* GIL'*s head emerges first and he gets up and goes toward her.*

GIL *(in amazement)*: Judy . . . !

The BOYS *all emerge from their hiding places.*

JUDY *(approaching the* BOYS*)*: I brought you these blankets—I thought it might be cold living out here. *(She looks around the barn and unconsciously her face falls as she sees the dismal surroundings)*

GROUCHO *(following her gaze—with a forced attempt to cheer her)*: It isn't much, but we call it "barn."

During this, GIL *has been watching* JUDY *with a strained and unhappy look. He goes toward her.*

Cut to:

Two Shot—Gil and Judy

GIL *(bitterly)*: Remember me, Judy—the man who was going to fix everything for you?

JUDY *(softly)*: You did your best, Gil.

GIL *(sarcastically)*: Yes—and our best is none too good . . . in fact, it's rotten.

JUDY: It's pretty difficult to save a sinking ship.

GIL: Not for me, it isn't. . . . I can always plug a couple of holes in the side and make it sink faster. You ought to stick to me, Judy—I'll bring you luck!

JUDY *(with a smile)*: I'm sticking. *(GIL takes her hand, too moved to say anything)* Gil—the sanitarium doesn't matter any more. You were right—I've been taking things too seriously. It's better this way—Now I can have fun—I won't be tied down—I can relax and really laugh. *(And with that she bursts into tears)*

GIL *(putting his arm around her)*: Judy—darling!—please!

CHICO: Sure—don't cry, Miss Judy—we feela bad, too—but we laugh—see? *(Then aside to* STUFFY*)* Go on, laugh, Stuffy!—laugh!

HARPO *has a broad set grin on his face and tears are streaming down his cheeks. Now* CHICO *starts to cry.* GROUCHO *gives a forced unnatural* LAUGH, *then looks scared.*

GROUCHO: Where did that come from?

GIL *(drawing* JUDY *to her feet)*: Come on, Judy—it can't be that bad. *(Then leading her to the door, pointing to the* DARKIES *who are lolling about)* Look at them—they've got the right idea: If things look bad today—they just laugh it off and wait for tomorrow.

As he says this, the CAMERA TRUCKS WITH THEM *as they go out of the barn. Sprawling around the outside of the barn are a number of* COLORED BOYS *with jugs and various other improvised musical instruments, the* MUSIC *of which has come softly underneath the preceding scene. As* JUDY *and* GIL *emerge, we* CUE INTO *the* SONG, *"Tomorrow Is Another Day." On the last chorus,* GROUCHO, CHICO, *and* HARPO *join in. At the end of the number, there is* APPLAUSE *offstage. The* BOYS, GIL, *and* JUDY *turn and there stand the* SHERIFF, MORGAN, *and and* MORGAN'S TWO HENCHMEN.

GROUCHO *(looking at the* SHERIFF *and* MORGAN*)*: I think I'll sit this one out.

He makes a dash for the door at the far end of the barn with CHICO, HARPO, GIL, *and* JUDY *after him. They open the door and there stand* TIP *and* BEEF. GROUCHO *quickly closes it.*

SHERIFF *(addressing* GROUCHO, CHICO, *and* HARPO*)*: You're under arrest—all of you!

GROUCHO *(indignantly)*: Look here, my good man—you've got nothing on me . . . My skirts are clean!

MORGAN *(drawing a paper out of his pocket)*: Oh yeah . . . ? *(Waving the letter under* GROUCHO's *nose)* Well, the Florida Medical Board doesn't seem to think so!—Horse doctor—eh! *(To* SHERIFF—*raising his voice)* Put them all under arrest!

HI-HAT, *at the sound of* MORGAN'S VOICE, *rears up and kicks out violently.* GIL *quickly rushes* JUDY *to safety.*

JUDY *(amazed and frightened)*: What's—what's happening?

GIL *(sheltering her)*: It's Hi-Hat—every time he sees Morgan he acts up.

HI-HAT has practically gone crazy—he is romping around the stable, kicking everything in sight. The BOYS, the SHERIFF, and MORGAN are ducking under his hoofs, which are coming like bullets from all sides.

MORGAN *(just missing a hoof)*: I'll fix that nag!

He draws out a pistol. GIL sees it, quickly pushes JUDY outside the door and makes a flying leap for MORGAN—knocks him down, and grabs the pistol, which he throws through the window.

Suddenly HI-HAT starts for a huge window above the door. He takes a terrific leap through the open window with HARPO hanging onto his tail—both of them go out the window.

CHICO: Hey—look at that horse jump!

The SHERIFF and MORGAN pick themselves up. MORGAN WHISTLES and TIP and BEEF come rushing in.

MORGAN: Come on!—get 'em!—all of 'em!

The SHERIFF, MORGAN, TIP, and BEEF advance menacingly on GIL, CHICO, and GROUCHO. We now have a free-for-all which is to be worked out on the set with dialogue to accompany the business—probably ending up with the BOYS running into the feed stall, the FOUR HEAVIES chasing them in and getting locked in themselves. Then CHICO and GROUCHO pull a rope and hay, feed, etc., comes down over the HEAVIES. Details of this to be worked out with props on hand. The BOYS rush out of the barn. JUDY is waiting outside, trembling. GIL quickly grabs her—they run away from the barn. Suddenly GIL stops and looks off.

GIL *(in excitement)*: Look!—Look at Hi-Hat!

Cut to:

Long Shot—Hi-Hat, *with HARPO in the saddle. He is galloping madly away, jumping fences, walls, hedges, etc., with fantastic ease.*

91

Cut Back to:

Group *as they watch* HARPO *riding* HI-HAT *from the crest of a hill.*

CHICO: Say!—I never saw a horse jumpa like that.

GROUCHO: We'd better all get on him—maybe he can jump bail.

They start moving out of the scene, as we

Cut to:

Long Shot

HARPO *still jumping over fences. He rounds a corner straight toward a twenty-four-sheet announcing in large letters:*

> COMING SATURDAY
> THE GRAND STEEPLECHASE
> SPARKLING SPRINGS TRACK

Below the caption is a picture of horses jumping over a fence. HARPO *and* HI-HAT *go straight for the poster and go through it, clearing the fence painted in the poster.*

Fade out

Fade in:

Long Shot—High Angle

Stables in foreground—saddling stalls—parade ring—grandstand—clubhouse, etc., in background. CROWDS *around paddock waiting for the horses—looking over the* HORSES, *etc. It is a scene of great activity and we get across that it is the day of the big steeplechase.*

Dissolve to:

Angle—Entry Board—of Horses—with Added Starter, Hi-Hat

Dissolve to:

Angle of Row of Stables

MORGAN *and* WHITMORE *are hurrying along, looking in each stable as they go—The* CAMERA TRUCKING WITH THEM.

MORGAN: They're not pulling any fast ones on me—Hi-Hat's not running in this race.

WHITMORE: But Hi-Hat isn't a jumper—

MORGAN *(peering in another stall)*: He was doing plenty of jumping in that barn last night.

WHITMORE *(disparagingly)*: But he can't beat *your* horse.

MORGAN *(grimly)*: I'm not taking *any* chances. My bank roll is riding on Galahad, and that's not all . . . if Hi-Hat should win, Stewart'll give the money to that girl and then we can kiss the sanitarium good-by.

The SHERIFF *enters the scene with* TIP *and* BEEF.

SHERIFF: Well, Morgan—you've got nothing to worry about— Hi-Hat's not on *this* track.

MORGAN: Good . . . and see to it that he doesn't *get* on. Put men at every gate. *(Then threateningly)* If that nag slips by you—it means your job!

MORGAN *turns abruptly and with* WHITMORE *goes toward observation barn.*

Cut to:

Angle—Entrance of Observation Barn as HORSES *led by* GROOMS, *followed by* TRAINERS, STABLEBOYS, *etc., come out.* MORGAN *and* WHITMORE *fall in with* SIR GALAHAD *and exit—others continue to file out of stable.*

Cut to:

Angle—Over Top of Saddling Barn *of string of* HORSES *being led from the observation stable on way to saddling stable.*

Cut to:

Closer on Groucho—in Tree (or a more amusing hiding place), *viewing the scene. Now that the* HORSES *are being led to the saddling stable, he gives a signal. He puffs vigorously on a cigar, and sends up a cloud of smoke. With the aid of his hat, he gives Indian fire signals.*

Cut to:

Chico—in an Amusing Hiding Place, *looking intently offscene,* *in order to catch the signal from* GROUCHO. *He in turn gives a signal in a gag—way to be devised.*

Cut to:

Harpo, *hiding behind a hedge, close to a refreshment stand, disguised as a gardener. He is clipping the hedge with shears. He gets the signal from* CHICO. *Still clipping the hedge, he reaches out with the shears and cuts the strings of several balloons tied to a refreshment stand. As the balloons soar aloft—*

Cut to:

Judy, *standing at the second-floor window of a small building— perhaps a small hotel. She sees the balloons go skyward, and now she gives her signal, dropping out of the window an apple she is eating. We see the object fall on the top of an ambulance parked on the street below. On the side of the ambulance is a sign:*

SPARKLING SPRINGS RACE TRACK

AMBULANCE

Cut to:

Interior, Ambulance, *where we see* HI-HAT *and* GIL. (GIL *is dressed in the outfit of an intern) He hears the object drop on the ambulance and starts saddling the horse.*

Cut to:

Groucho—in Hiding Place

    CHICO *and* HARPO *join him—he is looking through his binoculars toward the entrance gate.* CHICO *and* HARPO *crowd to him and try to peep through glasses, etc.* GROUCHO, *annoyed, breaks binoculars in half and gives glass to each.*

GROUCHO: Keep me posted, boys.

(Or)

If you can't see . . . *(Indicating his spectacles)* I'll break *these* in half.

94

Cut to:

Long Shot—Through Groucho's Binoculars, *of entrance gate, as ambulance drives through.*

Cut to:

Groucho, Chico, and Harpo

GROUCHO *(lowering binoculars)*: They're in. . . . *(Boys are overjoyed)*

CHICO *(to* HARPO*)*: Okay, Stuffy, go to it.

GROUCHO *(to* HARPO*)*: Ride'em, cowboy—or we'll be heading for the last roundup.

HARPO *nods and leaves.*

CHICO *(to* GROUCHO*)*: Come on, Doc, we geta reserved seats. *(They start away.)*

Cut to:

Road to Saddling Stalls

The HORSES *are being led. At this moment,* GIL *comes driving up in the ambulance (*JUDY, *maybe dressed as a nurse, is seated beside him). They are forced to stop the ambulance and wait for the string of* HORSES *to pass.* GALAHAD *is led past the ambulance by the* TRAINER *at whose side walks* MORGAN, *etc.* GIL *pulls his cap still lower and huddles in the driver's seat—* JUDY *lowers her head, so as not to be seen by* MORGAN. *They give a sigh of relief as* MORGAN *walks by without paying any attention to them.* SHERIFF *and a couple of* DEPUTIES *enter.*

SHERIFF *(to* MORGAN*)*: No sign of them yet, Mr. Morgan.

MORGAN: Well, there'd better not be or you know what—
On MORGAN'*s line, we—*

Cut to:

Angle—Ambulance

Hell breaks loose as HI-HAT *is kicking against the side of the ambulance—all eyes turned toward ambulance. Finally the force of the kicking knocks loose the sign:*

95

SPARKLING SPRINGS RACE TRACK
AMBULANCE

The sign falls off, revealing underneath, the wording:
STANDISH SANITARIUM
The SHERIFF *and* MORGAN, *etc., see and react to this. The*
MEN *exchange a knowing look.*

MORGAN *(gives* SHERIFF *a dirty look)*: All right, Sherlock—take a look in this ambulance.

The SHERIFF *and* DEPUTIES *dash toward the ambulance, where* GIL *has been trying to quiet* HI-HAT *through little window, back of driver's seat—*JUDY *warns him they are coming.* GIL *then tries to make a getaway with ambulance, but too late— the* SHERIFF *and* HIS MEN *are upon him—*GIL *prepares to resist* SHERIFF, *reaching for gun.*

SHERIFF *(warning)*: Take it easy, Stewart, or you'll be riding in the *back* of the ambulance.

DEPUTIES *grabbing* GIL—*he struggles.*

JUDY *(appealing to* GIL*)*: Gil, that won't do any good.

SHERIFF *(to* JUDY*)*: Hop out of there, lady—I'm taking possession. *(To* DEPUTIES*)* You boys keep on searching for those other mugs and I'll put this—*(Indicating ambulance)*—under lock and key. *(He puts* GIL *in ambulance and locks door)*

Cut to:

Angle—Chico and Groucho, *getting comfortably settled in some out-of-sight place to watch race. They hear* HARPO's *alarming* WHISTLE.

CHICO *(worriedly)*: Stuffy!

They look down. HARPO *enters and* WHISTLES *wildly. A* MAN *comes by,* HARPO *grabs his high hat and throws it away— then dashes away himself, with the* MAN *in pursuit.*

CHICO: Hi-Hat's gone! *(*BUGLE *blows)* Hey—they're-a gonna start the race.

GROUCHO *(firmly)*: They won't start this race until we find Hi-Hat. *They exit.*

Angle—Saddling Stall

HORSES *are being walked around and then led into stalls to be saddled.*

Cut to:

Close Angle—Chico, *carrying box of axle grease and a stick, crawls through buses at end of stalls unnoticed by* ATTENDANT *on gate—he slips into end stall, which is empty. In the adjoining stall, a* HORSE *is being saddled—he gets a chunk of grease on the stick and flips it under saddle as same is being placed on* HORSE's *back—he then sneaks out.*

Cut to:

Angle—Where Board Dropped Off of Ambulance

HARPO *enters, finds board, puzzled, he starts looking in ridiculous places.*

Cut to:

Angle—Parade Ring

HORSES *being led around,* OWNERS *and* JOCKEYS *stand in groups, talking:* MORGAN *is discovered with his* JOCKEY. TIP *and* BEEF *in background.*

MORGAN *(to* JOCKEY*):* Listen, Son—you're riding to win . . . and I don't care what you do as long as the judges don't see you doing it.

JOCKEY *nods knowingly.*

As BUGLE *sounds, calling* JOCKEYS *to mount—as they do so the saddles start slipping, throwing the* JOCKEYS *to the ground, etc.*

There is great confusion—the grease is discovered.

MORGAN *(to* TIP *and* BEEF*):* Those mugs are around here somewhere. *Find them!*

TIP *and* BEEF *rush out.*

Cut to:

Ambulance, *being driven by* GIL—SHERIFF *(and maybe a* DEPUTY*) seated alongside of him.* JUDY, *unnoticed, is trailing.*

Cut to:

Angle—Parade Ring

They are just finishing resaddling.

Cut to:

Bugler

He puts the bugle to his lips for the fanfare. Not a note comes out. Instead, the BUGLER *is amazed to see a series of soap bubbles flow out from the horn—we see* HARPO *slipping away. An angry* OFFICIAL *rushes in and gives* BUGLER *dirty look.* BUGLER, *bewildered, examines horn.*

OFFICIAL *(yells to* JOCKEYS*)*: Mount your horses! *(And then to* MAN *in red coat, mounted, who leads the* HORSES *onto track)* Hurry up!

The MAN *reacts—the* OFFICIAL *hurries out of scene.*

Cut to:

Close Angle—Man in Red Coat—*reveals it is* CHICO—*as he straightens and shoots a quick glance toward high-wide hedge which surrounds parade ring. We* PAN DOWN *to reveal a* MAN *tied and gagged, half-submerged in the top of hedge—*GROUCHO *is reclining on hedge nearby—has half nelson on* MAN, *who is muttering angrily through gag.*

GROUCHO: You're the dullest conversationalist I've ever listened to.

MAN *glares at him.*

Angle—in Front of Grandstand

CHICO, *leading the* HORSES *past the stand, is almost at the gateway which leads into the stands.*

Cut to:

Morgan's Box

WHITMORE *and* MRS. UPJOHN *are seated in the box—*MORGAN *is entering. He looks offscene at the track and reacts.*

MORGAN: Where's he taking those horses?

98

Cut to:

Long Shot—From Morgan's Angle

CHICO *wheels around and starts leading the* HORSES *directly toward the gateway to the stands.*

Cut to:

Gateway

GROUCHO *appears and swings open the gateway, allowing* CHICO *and about* THREE OTHER HORSES *to follow him in.* . . . *Then, before the* OTHER HORSES *can get through, he quickly shuts the gate. There is great confusion among the* SPECTATORS *at the gateway—they cannot understand this strange procedure.*

MAN IN CROWD *(to* GROUCHO*):* What did you open that gate for?

GROUCHO *(indignantly):* Did you ever see a horse open a gate by himself?

(Or)

They've got as much right to see that race as you have.

(Or)

(To GUARD*)* Get me a saddle. . . . If they're going to sit in the grandstand—I'm going to get out there and run.

By this time, CHICO *and another* HORSE *are up a few steps into the grandstand—*ATTENDANTS *are rushing toward them—there is much confusion. During this,* CHICO *starts to get off his* HORSE *as the* POLICE *begin to hem in on them.*

Cut to:

Harpo—High Up in the Grandstand

He sees CHICO *being pursued and registers his apprehension. At the same time, over the public-address system comes the announcement:*

VOICE: Will the jockeys please hurry to the starting line.

HARPO *becomes more worried. He turns and passes a huge fan which nearly blows his head off. His face lights up as he gets an idea. Pulling the lever beside the fan, he adjusts it to high speed—a gust of wind comes out and blows the hats off the nearby* SPECTATORS.

99

Cut to:

Section of Spectators—Shooting toward Track

A few hats come sailing into scene—and now the wind picks up the toppers of all those sitting in this section. In a moment, hundreds of hats are sent sailing onto the track.

Cut to:

Harpo

He is gleeful—he rushes to the next fan and throws the lever— the same action results, when the wind hits the next portion of the grandstand. HARPO rushes to a third fan and in a moment there is a veritable cyclone in progress.

Cut to:

Angle—over Morgan's Box

The hats are blowing toward MORGAN's box. MORGAN, MRS. UPJOHN, and WHITMORE turn around and take in the scene. Their hats naturally blow off too, and they have great difficulty in holding on to the box as fox furs, derbies, bonnets, etc., of all sizes and description, hit them squarely in their faces.

Cut to:

Judges' Stand

The dignified JUDGES are greatly confused as more hats go sailing by the stand and fall all over the track.

A JUDGE *(into telephone)*: Turn off those fans!

Cut to:

Angle—Near Rail

PEOPLE are fighting to get out onto the track to retrieve their hats. OFFICERS are attempting to hold them back. GROOMS are picking up the hats and throwing them back to the CROWD. Of course, nobody is successful enough to get his own hat back again.

(1) A FAT MAN ends up with a size five hat.

(2) A SKINNY MAN gets one that covers his ears.

100

(3) A Lady *ends up with a derby.*

(4) And a Tramp *makes away with a beautiful pearl-gray topper.*

Through all this, a Voice *is coming over the loud-speaker, pleading with the* People *to stay off the track so that the race may start.*

Cut to:
The Starting Line
    The Horses *are at the starting line. It looks as if they will be off in a second.*

Cut to:
Medium Full Shot—Near Tunnel
    People *are still scrambling for hats. One* Man *looks off, saying:*
Man: Never mind the hats. Down in front, they're starting the race!
    He puts a pair of binoculars to his eyes and looks offscene. At this moment, automobiles start streaming into the track and the tunnel is completely packed with them.

Cut to:
Judges' Stand
    The dignified Judges *are reacting to this unprecedented sight.*

Cut Back to:
Cars, *as they continue to pour into the track. The* camera pans *down the long line of cars and picks up* Groucho.
Groucho: Free parking! . . . Just leave your car—we'll park it for you!
    The camera continues to pan *down the line of cars to the outside gates—here we find* Chico *with a huge sign which reads:*

Free Parking

    Chico *is having a little argument with* One of the Drivers.

CHICO: That'll be ten cents.

DRIVER: But the sign says "free parking." What's the ten cents for?

CHICO: That's the tax.

At this moment a couple of COPS *rush into the shot.* CHICO *jumps up on top of the car and starts jumping from one car to the other,* CAMERA PANNING WITH HIM. *He is joined shortly by* GROUCHO, *who is also being pursued. The two continue to climb over, under, and through cars. They run toward the grandstand.*

Cut to:

Cars on Track

OFFICERS *and* DRIVERS *are trying to get the cars out—*HORNS *are blowing, motors are racing, fenders are being smashed, etc.*

Cut to:

Harpo, *alongside a beer wagon loaded with kegs. He sees something offscene and* WHISTLES *loudly.* GROUCHO *and* CHICO *rush across the scene pursued by* OFFICERS, TIP, BEEF, *and* DEPUTIES. HARPO *releases a peg at the rear end of the truck which holds the kegs in place—they roll out between* CHICO *and* GROUCHO *and their* PURSUERS. *This stops the* OFFICERS *and* OTHERS *momentarily, giving* GROUCHO *and* CHICO *a chance for a getaway. Some of the* OFFICERS *turn their attention to* HARPO—OTHERS *continue after* GROUCHO *and* CHICO *—the rest rush to stop the beer kegs from rolling all over the place.*

Cut to:

Track *as beer kegs roll into scene.* TRACK OFFICERS *do their best to stop them. One uniformed* OFFICER *in the foreground succeeds in halting one keg—as he starts to roll it back in place the bung comes out and the beer squirts in all directions.*

Cut to:

Flash of Morgan, Reacting

(This is not an essential cut but perhaps it will be shot for protection.)

102

Cut to:

The Ambulance, *driving along a country road. The* SHERIFF *turns a corner, and right in front of him he sees an overturned car, a* GIRL *sprawled out on the ground beside it. Her dress is torn, and dirt is smeared over her face. The* SHERIFF *brings the ambulance to an abrupt halt and rushes over to the* GIRL. *One look tells him that he must take her to a hospital. He rushes back to the ambulance, opens the door.*

SHERIFF: Get that horse out of there! Give me that stretcher!

GIL *hurriedly backs* HI-HAT *out of the ambulance, and hands the stretcher to the* SHERIFF. *The two of them rush to the* GIRL. GIL *sees that the girl is* JUDY; *he is just about ready to utter a yell when* JUDY *gives him a wink, which is unnoticed by the* SHERIFF.

SHERIFF: Come on—we've got to get her to a hospital right away!

They put her on the stretcher and rush back to the ambulance.

SHERIFF *(as they place her in the ambulance)*: You'd better stay in the back with her.

The SHERIFF *closes the door on* GIL *and* JUDY, *and rushes around to get in the driver's seat. As he does so, the back door opens and* JUDY *and* GIL *hop out very quietly. In a moment the* SHERIFF *gives the ambulance the gun, and with the siren wide open, he tears down the highway, with* GIL *and* JUDY *waving a fond farewell to him.* GIL *rushes over to the side of the road and gets* HI-HAT, *and with* JUDY *starts back in the direction of the track, as we—*

Cut to:

Track—at Starting Line

The HORSES *are all lined up. The* STARTER *has the flag in the air. Suddenly he gives the signal and the* HORSES *are off. We hear a tremendous* "They're off!" *from the stands.*

Cut to:

Morgan's Box

WHITMORE: They're off!

MORGAN: At last. *(He puts his binoculars to his eyes)*

Cut to:

The Horses—Approaching the First Turn

CHICO *and* GROUCHO *straighten up from behind the outside rail. They quickly move a section of the fence across the track. The* HORSES *thunder down to the first turn and now there is nothing for them to do but go straight off the track into the fields. The* JOCKEYS *try to pull them up, but to no avail.* CHICO *and* GROUCHO *are jubilant.*

Cut to:

Judges

They are burning with rage—ad libbing: "What sort of race is this?" *etc.*

Another one is TALKING *into the phone, giving instructions;* "Announce a false start!" *etc., etc.*

Cut to:

Harpo, Outside of the Track

(How HARPO *gets outside of the track hasn't yet been devised—the following suggestions have been made:)*

(1) HARPO *is sitting on a high fence watching the race when he hears the announcement* "False start." *He throws up his arms in glee and falls backward over the fence and out of the track.*

(2) TIP *and* BEEF *have caught* HARPO *and they throw him out of the track.*

As HARPO *picks himself off the ground, he shakes himself— suddenly he sees something,* WHISTLES, *and starts running.*

Cut to:

Gil and Judy—on the Road Outside of Track

They are standing beside the track-sprinkling wagon. GIL *has just switched one of the team of* HORSES *and is harnessing* HI-HAT *in its place.* HARPO *rushes up and indicates his joy.*

GIL: Stuffy!—what are you doing out here?

HARPO *pantomimes that he was kicked out of the track.*

JUDY: Have we still got time?

HARPO *nods.*

GIL: Come on—we've got to work fast.

At this moment the DRIVER *of the sprinkling wagon comes out of a store and reacts at the sight. He rushes to the wagon and climbs into the seat.*

DRIVER *(to* GIL, *who is standing by* HI-HAT*)*: Get away from that horse—he don't like strangers!

The DRIVER *heads for the track.* GIL *and* JUDY *look hopelessly at* HARPO, *but he is equal to the occasion. He runs after the wagon, climbs up the back and lets himself into the tank.*

Cut to:
Track

HORSES *are being led back onto the track from the fields into which they galloped.*

Cut to:
Gate of Track

The sprinkling wagon is driven through and has stopped in front of a fire hydrant inside the track. The DRIVER *connects up the hose and starts filling up the tank.* HARPO *finally pops out of the top of the tank as the water spills over. The* DRIVER *looks at him in stark amazement, too bewildered to move.* HARPO *jumps to the driver's seat and drives off toward the track.*

Cut to:
Starting Line

The HORSES *are being lined up, ready for the start.*

Cut to:
Harpo on the Wagon, *dashing madly onto the track.*

Cut to:
Morgan's Box

He is looking offscene in amazement.

MORGAN: What the . . .

The SHERIFF *rushes up.*

SHERIFF *(breathlessly)*: Hi-Hat—he got away from me!

Cut to:
Harpo

He leaps from the driver's seat to HI-HAT'S *back and, as he gallops along, he unhitches the wagon and goes hell-bent for the starting point.*

Cut to:
Morgan's Box

He turns furiously on the SHERIFF.

MORGAN: I'll say he got away! *(Then, as the* SHERIFF *looks in open-mouthed amazement)* Well, *do* something—stop him! !

The SHERIFF *rushes off.*

Cut to:
Starting Line

The HORSES *are now lined up and almost ready to go. The* STARTER *holds the flag ready to give the signal.* PAN OVER TO CHICO AND GROUCHO, *who are behind a hedge.* GROUCHO *is whirling a lasso, ready to throw it over the* STARTER'S *head. Suddenly* CHICO, *whose head is below the lasso, sees something—his eyes light up—he jumps erect with a* YELL *of delight.*

CHICO *(jumping up)*: Stuffy . . . !

He jumps right into the loop of the lasso, as GROUCHO *starts in amazement, the lasso tightening around* CHICO'S *neck, almost choking him.*

Cut to:
Starting Point

The STARTER *lowers the flag as a signal for the* HORSES *to start. They leap away just as Harpo comes up and he is off to a flying start.*

106

Cut to:
The First Hurdle
HARPO *is on the inside.* Several HORSES *make the jump as* HARPO *gallops up.* HI-HAT *wheels at the hedge and swings back his head facing in the direction from which he came. Other* HORSES *in background clear the hedge.* HARPO *reaches into his blouse, pulls out a large picture of* MORGAN *and holds it in front of* HI-HAT'S *eyes.* HI-HAT *rears up frightenedly, wheels around, and leaps over the hedge as if he'd been stung.*

Cut to:
Angle—Groucho, Chico, Judy, and Gil in a
Hiding Place in the Stands
They are CHEERING *wildly:* "It worked!" "It's in the bag!" *etc.*

Cut to:
Traveling Shot—Angle—Harpo on Hi-Hat
The first jump is in the background. HARPO *reaches back to place the photo into his blouse—but he has really tucked it under his arm.* HI-HAT *overtakes some* HORSES *and passes them.* HARPO *leans low, urging* HI-HAT *on—in doing so, he raises his arms and, unnoticed by* HARPO, *the picture flies away.*

Cut to:
Groucho, Chico, Judy, and Gil in Their Hiding Place
They are panic-stricken to see that HARPO *has lost the photo.*
JUDY: He's lost Morgan's picture!
GIL: That means we're sunk.
GROUCHO *(struck by a sudden idea)*: Not unless Morgan has lost his voice. *(He turns to* CHICO*)* Tony—your work has just begun.
As the OTHER THREE *look at him questioningly—*

Cut to:
Long Angle—Race, *approaching the second jump, which is some distance away.*

Cut to:

Closer Traveling Angle—Harpo *in about the sixth position. He reaches for the picture as the hedge looms up. It's gone! He frantically searches in his blouse, looks all around for the picture, almost falls off the* HORSE.

Cut to:

Angle—Morgan's Box

The loud-speaker over which the race is being described suddenly is cut off.

WHITMORE: Something has happened to the loud-speaker.

MORGAN *is intently watching the race through his glasses and doesn't answer.*

Cut to:

Angle—Second Hurdle—Traveling Shot of Harpo *who is in a panic. He tries feverishly to egg* HI-HAT *on and force him to make the jump.*

Cut to:

Morgan's Box

He is intently watching the race through binoculars. CHICO *sneaks up alongside of him, a microphone in his hand—he reaches up and snatches the binoculars away from* MORGAN.

CHICO: Hey—how are they doing?

MORGAN: Give me those glasses!

During MORGAN's *line,* CHICO *has shoved the microphone in front of him and his* VOICE *is carried out over the public-address system.* MORGAN *lunges for* CHICO, *but misses—then looks around.*

MORGAN *(calling)*: Oh, it's you—you greasy little crook. . . .

Cut to:

Angle—Near Amplifiers

GROUCHO, JUDY, *and* GIL *are looking anxiously off at the race, as* MORGAN's VOICE *booms over the amplifier.*

MORGAN's VOICE: Tip! . . . Beef!

Cut to:
Angle—at Second Hurdle
 HARPO *is working on* HI-HAT, *who has started to slow up.*
MORGAN'S VOICE *reaches them.*
MORGAN'S VOICE *(over amplifier)*: Grab that guy and get those
other mugs, too!
 HI-HAT *halts as though a buzzer had hit him, then leaps for-*
ward, clears the hurdle, and races madly on.

Cut to:
Angle—at Amplifier
 GROUCHO, JUDY, *and* GIL *cheer to see the plan work.*
GROUCHO: Hold the fort—I'm off for the front-line trenches. *(He*
dashes off).

Cut to:
Angle—Morgan's Box
 CHICO *rushes out pursued by* COPS.

Cut to:
Angle—Grandstand
 SPECTATORS *watching the race,* CHEERING *their choices.*
GROUCHO *races into scene, sees something off, ducks into a*
corner—and CHICO *runs into scene pursued by* COPS.
GROUCHO *(shouting to* CHICO*)*: Signals—sixteen . . . twenty-two . . .
thirty-four . . . pass!
 Without stopping, CHICO *hurls the microphone to* GROUCHO.
GROUCHO *catches it deftly. As he runs with the mike, a* COP
grabs for him.
GROUCHO *(indignantly)*: No fair—interference.
 He sidesteps the COP *and ducks away into the* CROWD.

Cut to:
Angle—Race, *at a point where there are no hurdles in sight.*
 HARPO *overtakes* GALAHAD. MORGAN'S JOCKEY *slashes* HI-HAT
across the face with his whip. HI-HAT *rears and almost throws*

HARPO, *but* HARPO *regains his balance—he goes after* GALAHAD *with murder in his eyes.*

(NOTE: *This dirty work takes place in a spot where brush shields it from the* JUDGES' *stand.*)

Cut to:
Angle—Morgan's Box
> *He lowers his glasses—looks anxiously toward* JUDGES' *stand, and* WHISPERS *to* WHITMORE.
MORGAN: I hope the judges didn't see that.
> *In the background, we see* GROUCHO *sneaking toward Morgan's box.* GROUCHO *comes up to* MORGAN *with the microphone.*
GROUCHO *(very coyly)*: Mr. Morgan—would you like to tell the radio audience what a heel you are?
MORGAN *(furiously)*: Get away from here!

Cut to:
Angle—at Hurdle
> HI-HAT *reacts as* MORGAN'S VOICE *comes over.*
MORGAN'S VOICE: Listen to me—you horse doctor . . .
> HARPO *clears the hurdle.*

Cut to:
Morgan's Box
> GROUCHO *running away with the microphone.*
GROUCHO *(into mike)*: Goodnight, folks. . . . We'll be with you again at the next hurdle.
> *A few* POLICEMEN *make a grab for* GROUCHO, *but he successfully escapes them.*

Cut to:
Track
> *Here we* HOLD *for further shots of the race.*

Cut to:
Groucho and Chico, in Stand
> CHICO *has a hot dog in his hand and* GROUCHO *is holding a*

DOG *who is trying to snatch the sausage. We see the microphone tied to the* DOG'S *back.* CHICO *hurls the hot dog offscene—*GROUCHO *lets go the* DOG, *who goes tearing after it.*

Cut to:
Morgan's Box
He is surrounded by his HENCHMEN, *the* DEPUTIES, *etc. The
hot dog lands in the box at his feet. The* DOG *rushes into the
box after it, almost upsetting* MORGAN.
MORGAN *(yelling angrily)*: Get out of here you mutt!
He takes a kick at the DOG—*it snaps.*

Cut to:
The Hurdle
MORGAN'S VOICE *comes over the scene.*
MORGAN'S VOICE: Ow-w-w—he bit me!
HARPO *and his* HORSE *clear the hurdle.*

Cut to:
Grandstand
The SHERIFF *runs into scene, stops short and* SHOUTS.
SHERIFF: Joe! Mac! . . . Come over here! Hurry up!
*The microphone is lowered into scene on a wire. As the micro-
phone goes into the* SHERIFF'S *pocket—*

Cut to:
Groucho and Chico *on the runway underneath the roof of the
grandstand. We see that they are lowering the microphone on
the wire. The* BOYS *exchange a look as they let the wire drop,
to give plenty of slack.*

Cut to:
Morgan's Box *as the* SHERIFF *and the* DEPUTIES *come into scene.*
SHERIFF: Those guys won't get in here again, Mr. Morgan.
MORGAN: If they do . . .

111

Cut to:

Race *as* MORGAN'S VOICE *comes over the loud-speaker.*

MORGAN'S VOICE: I'll have you bounced out so fast you won't know what's going on!

> HI-HAT *clears the hurdle, but* HARPO *loses his balance. He is thrown forward, flies over* HI-HAT*'s head, landing on his feet on* TWO RIDERLESS HORSES. *He plunges ahead with a foot on each horse, like a Roman charioteer.*

Cut to:

Morgan's Box

> *The* SHERIFF, *still standing guard, notices the wire dangling from the microphone in his pocket. Puzzled, he reaches into his pocket—when suddenly the microphone is yanked out of scene.*

Cut to:

Chico and Groucho, *frantically pulling in the slack wire. The microphone comes into scene. The* SHERIFF *scrambles after it. As he lunges for the* BOYS, *they pull the wire across the aisle. The* SHERIFF *trips over the wire, which gives the* BOYS *a head start on him and they make a getaway.*

Cut to:

Track

> HARPO *is still riding the* TWO HORSES *in charioteer fashion.* HI-HAT *is several lengths behind him. (We* HOLD *here on* HARPO *for whatever suspense gags we want.)*

Cut to:

Morgan's Box

> MORGAN, WHITMORE, TIP, *and the* OTHERS *are intently watching the race. Suddenly,* MORGAN *drops out of scene right through the floor of the box.*

Cut to:

Storeroom Beneath Morgan's Box *as* MORGAN *falls into scene. He hits the flooring with a thud and is knocked unconscious. We see* CHICO *standing on a stepladder with a saw in his hand and we get across that he has sawed a hole in the floor of Morgan's box.*

Cut to:

Morgan's Box

The OCCUPANTS *of the box ad lib:* "What happened to Morgan?" "He fell through the floor." "It's those mugs again."

SHERIFF: Let me at them *(He starts letting himself through the hole in the floor)*

Cut to:

Storeroom

GROUCHO *has placed a barrel on a table or some other object so that the barrel is right under the hole. We see the feet of the* SHERIFF *come through the hole in the floor, and hear a* YELP *of rage from the* SHERIFF *as he lands in the barrel. His head and shoulders are sticking above the floor and he is helpless to move.*

CHICO *goes to* MORGAN, *who is lying prostrate.* MORGAN *is out cold.*

CHICO *(holding a microphone in front of* MORGAN*)*: Wake up! Say something!

GROUCHO *(coming up)*: The dirty double-crosser!—he knocked himself out!

The BOYS *make frantic efforts to revive* MORGAN, *slapping his face, pouring water on him, etc. Finally he comes to and looks around.*

MORGAN: Where am I?

GROUCHO: You're too far away from the microphone.

MORGAN *wheels around, grabs* CHICO.

MORGAN *(taking a poke at* CHICO*)*: You asked for it!

113

Cut to:

Track *as* MORGAN'S VOICE *comes over the loud-speaker.*

MORGAN'S VOICE: I'm going to lick the tar out of you!

HARPO *is just about approaching a hurdle, standing up on the* TWO HORSES. *The* HORSES *start to spread and poor* HARPO *is about to do a split.* HI-HAT, *having heard* MORGAN'S VOICE, *comes to the rescue. He comes racing between the* TWO HORSES, *jumps, and picks up* HARPO *in mid-air—both of them clearing the hedge and landing comfortably on the other side.*

Cut to:

Storeroom

MORGAN *aims a blow at* CHICO. GROUCHO *konks* MORGAN *on the head with the microphone, knocking him out again.* FOOT-STEPS *are heard offscene, and ad-lib lines from the* SHERIFF, TIP, *and* BEEF. "They're in here." "Open the door!" *etc.*

As the door flies open, the MEN *pour into the storeroom,* CHICO *and* GROUCHO *jump onto the table or box, kick the barrel away, and climb through the hole in the floor.*

Cut to:

Morgan's Box *as the* BOYS *climb up.* MRS. UPJOHN *is the lone occupant—she reacts in amazement as* GROUCHO *appears.*

MRS. UPJOHN: Where is Mr. Morgan?

GROUCHO: He's down there with the rest of the rats.

(Or)

MRS. UPJOHN: Hugo—what are you doing down there?

GROUCHO: If you see my shadow—it means six more weeks of winter.

(Or)

MRS. UPJOHN: Hugo—what are you up to?

GROUCHO: I'm up to my vest—but if you give me a hand, I'll pull through.

(Or)

Emily—you look much better since I stopped taking care of you.

114

Cut to:
Angle—Race
> GALAHAD *and* HI-HAT *fighting it out for the lead—more rough tactics from* GALAHAD'S JOCKEY.

Cut to:
Morgan's Box
> MORGAN, WHITMORE, *the* SHERIFF, *etc., enter the box.* MORGAN *looks badly beaten up. (One of the* DEPUTIES *can pull a chair or a board over the hole in the floor.)*

MORGAN *(looking at the race)*: He's still in the lead—come on, Galahad!

Cut to:
A Position Near Top and Edge of Grandstand
> *(The following scenes are* INTERCUT *with* SHOTS OF THE RACE.*)*
> GROUCHO *and* CHICO *are watching the race, as* HARPO *approaches the last jump, the water hazard.*

CHICO *(excitedly)*: Hey—only one more jump . . . we gotta get to Morgan.

> GROUCHO *points in the direction of* MORGAN'S *box with his microphone which he holds in his hand.*

GROUCHO: Take a look at that . . .

Cut to:
Overhead Shot—Morgan's Box—
From the Angle of Groucho and Chico
> *The box is entirely surrounded by a cordon of* COPS, *including the* SHERIFF, TIP, *and* BEEF—*the place is thick with them.*

Cut Back to:
Groucho and Chico
GROUCHO: We'll get to Morgan, but we may have to join the police force.

CHICO *(desperately)*: We *got* to do it for Miss Judy.

GROUCHO *quickly puts the microphone into his lapel and sits on the rail which slopes down to the bottom of the grandstand where* MORGAN's *box is located.*

GROUCHO *(insultingly)*: You know—it'll be just my luck to be put in the same cell as you.

And with that, he starts to slide. CHICO *gets the idea and jumps on behind him. They both start sliding down the rail, the* CAMERA TRUCKING WITH THEM. *En route,* GROUCHO *passes a* FAT WOMAN *with a large chrysanthemum in her dress—he grabs it, as the* FAT WOMAN *reacts, and quickly puts the chrysanthemum on the microphone, concealing it from view. They arrive at the bottom and go hurtling off at terrific speed right into the center of the box. The* COPS, MORGAN, WHITMORE, *and* MRS. UPJOHN *all go into a heap. There is mad confusion.* GROUCHO, *lying almost on top of* MORGAN, *shoves the chrysanthemum into his face.*

GROUCHO: Smell . . .

MORGAN: Get off-a me! . . . Get off-a me!

Cut to:

Angle—at Last Hurdle

HI-HAT *and* GALAHAD *approach the jump. The following line is* HEARD *over the loud-speaker.*

MORGAN'S VOICE: Get that flower out of my face—or I'll kill you!

The HORSES *take the jump together.* GALAHAD'S JOCKEY *prods* HI-HAT *with the butt end of his whip. As a result of this both* HORSES *fall into the water hazard on the other side of the hurdle.*

Cut to:

Morgan's Box

EVERYONE *is stunned at seeing the* HORSES *fall.*

CHICO: Stuffy—get up! . . . Get up!

The COPS *try to drag them away, but the* BOYS *hang onto the railing.*

116

Cut to:
Track

HARPO *and the other* JOCKEY *have remounted (on the wrong* HORSES, *though none of our characters are aware of this. Mud covers the numbers of the horses). and they start galloping into the home stretch. It is a driving finish with* GALAHAD'S JOCKEY *roughing up* HARPO. *The gallop down the home stretch is* INTERCUT *with the following action in Morgan's box.*

Cut to:
Morgan's Box

The BOYS *are still linked around the rail . . . fighting has now become fast and furious. No sooner do the* COPS *get* CHICO'S *and* GROUCHO'S *hands off the rail than they take a foot-lock on it with their feet.* MORGAN *is trying to watch the race.*

MORGAN: Come on, Galahad—get going! Atta boy—faster . . . faster . . .

GROUCHO *pops up in front of* MORGAN, *blocking his vision.*

GROUCHO *(looking through the opposite end of Morgan's binoculars)*: All I can see is snakes' eyes.

MORGAN *(in a rage—pushing him away)*: You'll get life for this!

He climbs up on a chair. Simultaneously, CHICO *kicks the chair out from under him and* MORGAN *falls down right on his pratt with a howl of rage.* GROUCHO *twists around to look at the race, still holding on to the rail for dear life. Suddenly a worried look comes over his face.*

GROUCHO *(to* CHICO*)*: Hey—it isn't working . . . Galahad's ahead!

CHICO: Maybe Morgan's voice is changing.

MORGAN *has now lost all patience—he takes one of the clubs away from the* COPS *and is just about to bang on* GROUCHO'S *hands when* MRS. UPJOHN *enters the battle.*

MRS. UPJOHN: Don't you *dare* hit Hugo!

She launches at MORGAN *with her parasol and knocks him away from* GROUCHO. *The fighting grows faster and furiouser—* MRS. UPJOHN *laying right to left with her parasol.*

117

Mrs. Upjohn *(yelling)*: You let Hugo alone!

She takes a vicious swipe at Whitmore *or* Morgan, *misses him, and hits* Groucho.

Whitmore *(ducking)*: Look out!

Groucho: Now try hitting me, Emily—and maybe you'll get Morgan.

Chico *at this point bites the* Sheriff's *hand. The* Sheriff *lets out a* cry *of rage.*

Groucho: Nice work, Tony—he'll probably get hydrophobia. *(During all this excitement,* Morgan *has kept* yelling *the following threats, which should be* spotted *as we need them.)*

Morgan *(to* Mrs. Upjohn, *as she hits him)*: Why, if you weren't a woman . . . *(To* Chico, *as he tries to help the* Cops *disentangle him)* Get your hands off there! *(To* Groucho*)* Just wait until after this race. . . ! *(To the* Sheriff*)* Come on—*do* something . . . get them out of here!

(During all the above we intercut *with the actual race as indicated before.)*

Cut to:

The Finishing Line

as the mud-covered Horse, *ridden by* Morgan's Jockey *beats out* Harpo *on his* Horse *by a nose. Over the* sound track *comes the noise of wild* cheering.

Cut to:

The Box

Morgan *and* Whitmore *are jumping up and down like maniacs.*

Morgan *(pushing his way through the* Crowd*)*: Let me out of here!

He and Whitmore *rush out of the scene.* Groucho *and* Chico *cease all efforts to fight with the* Cops—*their faces are studies in grim dejection.*

Groucho *(to the* Sheriff—*sadly)*: What are your rates on a double room in your jail?

118

CHICO (*even more sadly*): Never mind about us—what about Miss Judy?

Cut to:
Judy and Gil—at Loud-speaker
> GIL *sadly turns away as he sees* MORGAN'S JOCKEY *cross the line ahead of* HI-HAT.

JUDY (*bravely*): Hi-Hat put up a great race, Gil.

Cut to:
Judges' Stand *as the winning* HORSE *rides up with the other* HORSES *following.* HARPO'*s head is hung in mortification.* MORGAN *and* WHITMORE *rush into the scene.* MORGAN *dashes up to what he thinks is* GALAHAD.

MORGAN: Good old Galahad. . . .
> *At the sound of* MORGAN'S VOICE *the mud-stained* HORSE *rears around, lashes out with his hind feet, and kicks* MORGAN, *who goes flying right into* WHITMORE—*both of them landing in a heap. At the same time the* JOCKEY *goes right over the* HORSE'*s head and lands on the track.*

Cut to:
Harpo, *his face reacting. He jumps off his* HORSE—*starts* WHIS-TLING *madly and pointing at the mud-stained winner. With his hands, he quickly scrapes away the mud . . . a large hunk of it goes right into* MORGAN'*s face just as he is about to rise. (Possibly another hunk goes into the* JOCKEY'*s face.) We suddenly see the number on the* HORSE *and realize that the* JOCKEYS *have changed* HORSES *and that* HI-HAT *is really the winner.*

Cut to:
The Box
> *Everybody is looking in amazement. Suddenly* GROUCHO *and* CHICO *let out wild* YELLS *of excitement.*

CHICO: Itsa Hi-Hat!

GROUCHO (*to* SHERIFF): Cancel that reservation.

They tear loose from SHERIFF *and the* POLICE *and dash toward* JUDGES' *stand.*

Cut to:

Judy and Gil

GIL'*s head is still turned away.* JUDY'*s face is filled with wonder, as she looks toward* JUDGES' *stand.*

JUDY (*with excitement—grabs* GIL'*s arm*): Come on—I want to put the wreath on the winner.

GIL *thinks she has lost her mind—then stands rooted, as he realizes; she yanks him from scene.*

Cut to:

Chico and Groucho on Track, *rushing toward* JUDGES' *stand. They pass* MORGAN *and* WHITMORE. *As* GROUCHO *passes,* MORGAN *is being helped to his feet by* WHITMORE—*practically unconscious.*

GROUCHO (*passing by* MORGAN): You yelled a mighty fine race, Morgan.

CHICO *has rushed up to* HARPO—*trying to embrace him.*

CHICO (*to* HARPO): Hey, Stuffy—'at wasa some race.

GROUCHO (*coming up*): Yes . . . I haven't seen so much mudslinging since the last election.

Cut to:

Judy and Gil, *running onto the track. The* CAMERA PANS WITH THEM *over to* HI-HAT *and the* BOYS. HARPO *is up on* HI-HAT *now.* GIL *throws his arms around the* HORSE. JUDY *is handed a floral wreath, which she puts on* HI-HAT'*s neck.*

HARPO *climbs down off of* HI-HAT—*removes saddle and tosses the sweat blanket over the* HORSE. *The proud* GIL *and happy* JUDY *start leading the* HORSE *toward the stable.*

GROUCHO (*very important*) *walking alongside of* HORSE *as* MRS. UPJOHN *comes rushing up to him.*

MRS. UPJOHN: Hugo . . . !

120

GROUCHO: You put up a nice fight, Emily—why didn't you tell me you were a welterweight?

Just then there is a wild SHOUT *offscene of* "Hallelujah"*—and as the* HORSE *starts moving toward the stable with* CHICO *and* HARPO *on one side;* MRS. UPJOHN *and* GROUCHO *on the other; and* JUDY *and* GIL *leading the* HORSE*—from behind the group, come streaming in from both sides a* CROWD *of* NEGROES *whom we saw in the barn . . . their pockets and their hands stuffed with money. As the* CAMERA TRUCKS WITH THE *Group leading the* HORSE *and followed by the* NEGROES*—we go into the final musical finale.*

Fade out

The End

THE FILM

Fade in:
Exterior, Railroad Depot—Sparkling Springs Lake—Day
Medium Shot—Depot
A PORTER *steps off the train;* PASSENGERS *follow.*

Medium Long Shot—Train Station
PASSENGERS *move toward a row of snappy-looking buses that belong to Morgan Enterprises, and one beat-up station wagon that belongs to the Standish Sanitarium.*

Medium Shot—Tony (Chico)
He CALLS *to* PEOPLE *as they pass by the Standish Sanitarium station wagon, ignoring him.*
TONY: Free bus to the sanitarium. This way to the Standish Sanitarium. Standish San—Standish San—This—this way to the Standish—Standish—free bus! Free bus! Standish Sanitarium!

Medium Shot—Passengers
They board the buses to the Morgan Hotel.

Medium Close-up—Tony
TONY: Free bus to the sanitarium. *(He gestures toward his empty station wagon)* Just got room for a few more!

Medium Shot—Tony
He stops a well-dressed MAN *in a Panama hat.*
TONY: Sanitarium?
MAN: No. Race track.
TONY: Hey, you don't want to go to the races. You're too sick.

125

Medium Close-up—Man

MAN: I'm going to the races!

Medium Close-up—Tony—*shooting over the* MAN's *shoulder.*

TONY: All right. You want something hot in the fifth race? *(The* MAN *gives him a dirty look which* TONY *ignores as he turns to the* OTHER PEOPLE)* Sanitarium? Bus to the sanitarium! Standish Sanitarium!

Close-up—Judy

She is a beautiful young girl, standing by the Standish Sanitarium station wagon. TONY *joins her.*

TONY: Free bus to the sanitarium.

JUDY: It's no use, Tony. If business keeps up like this, I'm afraid I'll have to drive the station wagon myself.

TONY: Oh, no, Miss Judy. You can't fire me.

Two Shot—Judy and Tony

They are next to the station wagon.

JUDY: But what if I can't pay your salary?

Close-up—Tony

TONY: That's different. You don't have to pay me, but you can't fire me.

Two Shot—Judy and Tony

JUDY *is in the station wagon.*

JUDY: Oh, Tony, you're sweet.

TONY *(he closes her door)*: Yeah. And don't worry, Miss Judy. I'm gonna get some customers if I have to make them sick myself. *(He gets in the driver's seat)*

JUDY: Oh, Tony, I'm afraid we need more than customers. You don't understand—I owe a great deal of money—far more than I can ever pay.

TONY: Let me see—who do I know that's rich? Hey, how about that big, strong sick woman at the sanitarium?

126

JUDY: You mean Mrs. Upjohn?

TONY: Yeah, that's the one! She'd be glad to lend you the money.

JUDY: Oh, no.

TONY: Oh, she's rich! Why, last week she gave me a dollar tip!

JUDY: She did once offer to help, but it doesn't seem right to borrow from the patients.

TONY: All right, we make her a partner.

JUDY: Oh, Tony!

TONY: Hey, we gotta hurry before she changes her mind. *(He closes the station-wagon door) (See film still 1.)*

Dissolve to:
Exterior, Standish Sanitarium
The station wagon pulls up in front of a Victorian mansion.

Dissolve to:
Interior, Sanitarium, Main Floor
Long Shot—Judy and Tony
They enter.

TONY: Go ahead, Miss Judy.

Two Shot—Tony and Judy

TONY *(whispering)*: There's Mrs. Upjohn now.

Medium Shot—Mrs. Upjohn and Dr. Wilmerding
MRS. UPJOHN *is a stout dowager;* DR. WILMERDING's *back is partially to* CAMERA.

DR. WILMERDING: But, Mrs. Upjohn—

MRS. UPJOHN: Now, there's no use talking any more, Doctor! I'm leaving! *(She turns to go)*

Long Shot—Judy and Tony in the Foreground; Mrs. Upjohn and Dr. Wilmerding in the Background
They are at the front desk of the sanitarium.

MRS. UPJOHN *(offscreen)*: Mr. Whitmore, I want my bill made out at once!

JUDY *turns and walks toward* MRS. UPJOHN.

127

Medium Shot—Front Desk—Mrs. Upjohn and Mr. Whitmore
He is the business manager of the sanitarium. JUDY *enters.*
WHITMORE: Just as you say, Mrs. Upjohn.
JUDY: What's the matter, Mrs. Upjohn?
MRS. UPJOHN: It's no fault of yours, my dear.

Three Shot—Judy, Mrs. Upjohn, and Dr. Wilmerding
MRS. UPJOHN: It's the doctor! The idea of telling me I'm perfectly well when I know I'm on the verge of a nervous collapse. Good-by, Judy dear. *(She clasps* JUDY's *hands)*

Medium Shot—Judy, Mrs. Upjohn, Dr. Wilmerding, and Whitmore
MRS. UPJOHN *(she hurries up the stairs)*: Have the boy come up and get my bags, please.

Two Shot—Judy and Dr. Wilmerding
JUDY *is heartbroken;* WILMERDING *is frustrated, but resigned.*
JUDY *walks across the room.*

Close-up—Tony
He looks sadly at JUDY.

Medium Long Shot—Judy
She hurries out of her room and into her office.

Interior, Office
Medium Long Shot—Gil
GIL, JUDY's *boy friend, is standing in a set of French doors as* JUDY *enters.*
JUDY: Gil! Oh, Gil! *(She runs to him)*

Two Shot—Gil and Judy
They embrace. She is on the edge of tears.
JUDY: I'm glad you're here?
GIL: What is it, honey?
JUDY: Hold me tight. I'll be all right. *(She cries)*

128

GIL: Come on, honey, tell me.

JUDY: It's Mrs. Upjohn—she's leaving.

GIL: Oh, let her leave! Say, I have something here worth a hundred Upjohns! *(He pulls a paper out of his jacket)*

JUDY: You don't understand—I'm going to lose this place!

GIL: No, you're not. That's what I'm trying to tell you. Honey, from me to you, with love!

Medium Close Shot—Gil and Judy

GIL *hands her an official-looking paper.*

JUDY: Your radio contract! You've got it! *(She reads)* "Gelding—out of Honey Lamb by Blue Bolt—two year—Hi-Hat"—*(To* GIL*)* Why, Gil, this doesn't make sense!

GIL: It's a horse, honey, a race horse.

JUDY: Perhaps I'm awfully stupid, but what do we want with a horse?

GIL: Now wait till I tell you. Horse wins race—owner wins money —owner gives money to girl he loves—girl saves sanitarium. Why, it's very simple!

JUDY: Very simple. But what happens if horse loses race?

Close-up—Gil—*shooting over* JUDY's *shoulder.*

GIL: Oh, but he can't lose. He's a wonder! I picked him up for a song. Only . . .

Close-up—Judy

Shooting over GIL's *shoulder, his back to the* CAMERA.

GIL: . . . fifteen hundred dollars.

JUDY: Fifteen hundred dollars?

Two Shot—Gil and Judy

GIL: Um-hmm.

JUDY: Why, Gil, that's all the money you had in the world!

GIL: Well, I still have my job singing at the casino.

JUDY: Now, Gil, you return that horse at once, and get your money back. You've got to go on with your music—your career!

129

GIL: Judy, you need money fast—more money than I could make in ten years of singing.

JUDY: I don't care! I want you to be a great singer, not a race-track tout!

GIL: Oh, wait a minute! That isn't fair!

JUDY: Are you going to return that horse?

GIL: I can't do that. I just bought him!

JUDY: You mean you don't want to. You'd rather bet on a horse than on yourself!

GIL: Of all the ungrateful people! *(He turns away from her and walks toward the French doors)*

JUDY: Well, what have I got to be grateful for? You've thrown away your career on a long shot, and gambled away our happiness! Here, take your horse! *(She hands him the contract)*

GIL: All right! *(He leaves through the French doors)*

JUDY: And I hope you're very happy with it!

Interior, Main Floor, Lobby
Medium Shot—Tony
He looks through a door into the lobby.

Medium Shot—Stairway—Mrs. Upjohn and Dr. Wilmerding
MRS. UPJOHN *and a series of* BELLBOYS *come down the stairs.* WHITMORE *joins them.*

MRS. UPJOHN: I'm going to someone who understands me. I'm going to Dr. Hackenbush.

DR. WILMERDING: Dr. Hackenbush? Why, I've never heard of him. Has he a sanitarium?

MRS. UPJOHN: The biggest in Florida . . .

Close-up—Tony
He hears her mention DR. HACKENBUSH *and snaps his fingers: an idea*

MRS. UPJOHN *(offscreen)*: That's what he told me. Of course, I was never there.

Three Shot—Dr. Wilmerding, Mrs. Upjohn, and Whitmore

MRS. UPJOHN: Hugo—Oh, I mean Dr. Hackenbush—always insisted on treating me in my home. Why, I didn't know there was a thing the matter with me until I met him.

Exterior, Sanitarium
Medium Shot—Tony and the Bellboys
   TONY *watches them carry* MRS. UPJOHN'S *luggage. He runs after the* FIRST BOY *and takes* MRS. UPJOHN'S *bags.*

Long Shot—Tony and the Bellboys
   TONY *leads the series of* BELLBOYS *back into the sanitarium. (See film still 2.)*

Medium Shot—Lobby—Tony and the Bellboys
   TONY *leads the* BELLBOYS *past* DR. WILMERDING *and on upstairs.*
   TONY: Excuse, please. We're sure getting a lot of new customers since they heard Dr. Hackinapuss is coming.
   MRS. UPJOHN: Did you say Hackenbush?
   TONY: Yes, ma'am.

Medium Shot—Mrs. Upjohn, Whitmore, and Dr. Wilmerding
   (See film still 3.)
   MRS. UPJOHN: I wonder if that could be the same one? Where does he . . .

Medium Close-up—Tony
   MRS. UPJOHN *(offscreen):* . . . come from?
   TONY: Where's your Hackinapuss come from?

Medium Close-up—Mrs. Upjohn
   MRS. UPJOHN: Palmville, Florida.

Medium Close-up—Tony *(See film still 4.)*
   TONY: That's the one! *(He goes upstairs after the* BELLBOYS*)*

Medium Shot—Mrs. Upjohn, Whitmore, and Dr. Wilmerding

MRS. UPJOHN *(very excited)*: Why—! Why—Judy! *(She hurries to* JUDY*)*

Two Shot—Judy and Mrs. Upjohn

MRS. UPJOHN: Judy, why didn't you tell me Dr. Hackenbush was coming here?

JUDY: Dr. Hackenbush—? *(She turns to look for* TONY*)*

Medium Close Shot—Tony

He comes downstairs, looking innocent.

MRS. UPJOHN *(offscreen)*: Oh, I'm so excited!

Two Shot—Mrs. Upjohn and Judy

TONY *hurries to the door. (He is on his way to try and find* DR. HACKENBUSH*)*

MRS. UPJOHN: Judy, why don't you make him chief of staff? He'd do wonders for the sanitarium. With Dr. Hackenbush in charge, I might help you financially. I don't say I will, but I might. *(She turns to leave;* JUDY *watches her, hopeful)* Oh, Mr. Whitmore, have my bags sent right up. I'm staying! *(*JUDY *runs to her office)*

Interior, Office
Medium Shot—Tony

He's sitting at the desk writing. JUDY *enters.*

JUDY: Who's Dr. Hackenbush?

TONY: I don't know. But if she wants a Hackinapuss—she gonna get a Hackinapuss!

Close-up—Telegram Blank

TONY *writes*:

> Dr. Hackenbush's Sanitarium
> Palmville, Florida.
> Come up and . . .

Dissolve to:
Close-up—Sign

DR.
HACKENBUSH'S
SANITARIUM
FOR
SMALL ANIMALS
AND HORSES

Dissolve to:
Interior, Hackenbush's Sanitarium
It's a barn.

Medium Shot—Dr. Hackenbush (Groucho)
CAMERA PANS DOGS, CHICKENS, DUCKS, *and their* FRIENDS.
We hear animal SOUNDS *in the background.*
HACKENBUSH *(offscreen)*: Inhale—exhale—inhale—
The CAMERA STOPS *on* DR. HACKENBUSH. *He's leaning over a*
HORSE, *examining it.*
HACKENBUSH: Inhale—*(He comes up from under the* HORSE,
smoking his cigar)
HANDY MAN *(offscreen)*: Here's a telegram . . .

Medium Shot—Handy Man and Hackenbush
HANDY MAN *hurries in with a telegram.*
HANDY MAN: . . . for you, Doc. *(He hands it to* HACKENBUSH,
whose stethoscope is still in his ears)
HACKENBUSH: What does it say?
HANDY MAN: Well, it goes on to say that—How should I know?
HACKENBUSH *(reading)*: "Come up and take care of Mrs. Upjohn.
Stop . . ."

Close-up—Hackenbush *(See film still 5.)*
HACKENBUSH *(reading)*: "You can write your own ticket. Stop.
Come at once Standish Sanitarium." *(Remembering)* Mrs. Upjohn!

133

Ah, Emily—she never forgot that hayride! *(He raises his eyebrows and slouches off past the* HANDY MAN*)*
HANDY MAN: Don't Mrs. Upjohn know you're a vet?

Medium Shot—Hackenbush *(See film still 6.)*
HACKENBUSH: No. She's so in love with me she doesn't know anything. That's why she's in love with me. *(The* HANDY MAN *comes over and helps him on with his coat)*
HANDY MAN: Well, they can throw a horse doctor in jail for treatin' people.
HACKENBUSH: Yes—they can throw a horse doctor in jail for not paying his rent, too. *(His arm won't go into his sleeve—he tries to force it)*
HANDY MAN: Something there—
HACKENBUSH: So what have I got to—

Close-up—Sleeve of Hackenbush's Coat
The HANDY MAN *takes a* PUPPY *out of the sleeve.*

Medium Shot—Handy Man and Hackenbush
HACKENBUSH *grabs his cane and medical bag and heads for the door, his stethoscope still in his ears. He reacts to a horse* WHINNY *offscreen, goes back to the* HORSE, *opens his bag, takes out a huge pill and feeds it to the* HORSE.
HACKENBUSH: Take one of those every half mile. And call me if there's any change.

Dissolve to:
Interior, Conference Room of Sanitarium
Three Shot—Morgan, Whitmore, and Judy
The sanitarium's MEDICAL STAFF *is in the background.* JUDY *is looking over a contract.*
JUDY: But, Mr. Morgan, if I sign this, it means I turn the sanitarium over to you today!
MORGAN: That's right, Miss Standish. And I'll give you five thousand dollars.

Close-up—Judy
JUDY: But the notes aren't due. I've got almost a month.

Two Shot—Whitmore and Morgan
MORGAN: Miss Standish, this place has been losing money steadily.
You'll never be able to pay.

Three Shot—Whitmore, Morgan, and Judy
MORGAN: If you wait, I'll take it over and you won't get a cent.
WHITMORE: As your business manager, Judy, I strongly advise
you to take Mr. Morgan's offer. *(He offers her his pen)*
JUDY: Oh, but you're forgetting about that doctor Mrs. Upjohn
recommended. Surely with him in charge, we'll be able to pay
Mr. Morgan.
WHITMORE: Oh, Judy, are you going to take the advice of a
hysterical patient?
MORGAN: Now look here, Miss Standish—
MRS. UPJOHN *(offscreen)*: Judy!

Medium Close Shot—Mrs. Upjohn
She bursts into the room excited. CAMERA PANS *her to* JUDY
and WHITMORE.
MRS. UPJOHN: Judy, he's here! He's here!
JUDY: Why, who's here?

Close-up—Mrs. Upjohn
MRS. UPJOHN: Dr. Hackenbush!

Medium Shot—Mrs. Upjohn, Judy, Morgan, and Whitmore
MORGAN: Are you going to sign that or not?
JUDY: Uh—no.
MRS. UPJOHN: Of course, she's not going to sign it!
JUDY: Why, I have a month—I can at least try this new doctor.
MORGAN *(grabbing the contract from her)*: You're going to wish
you'd taken that check! *(He leaves and* WHITMORE *follows)*

135

MRS. UPJOHN: Well!
WHITMORE: Mr. Morgan, Mr. Morgan!

Two Shot—Morgan and Whitmore

They stand in the doorway.
MORGAN: You fixed that all right!
WHITMORE: How did I know that old battle-ax was going to butt in? But don't worry, I'll get to work on this new doctor.
MORGAN: Work fast!

Medium Shot—Mrs. Upjohn and Judy

The MEDICAL STAFF *is still standing at attention in the background.*
MRS. UPJOHN: Don't let them bully you, my dear. With Dr. Hackenbush in charge, I'm sure my trustees will let me help you.
WHITMORE *(comes back)*: Mrs. Upjohn, I think I am better able to advise Miss—
MRS. UPJOHN: I don't want to hear any more about it! Oh, I— I can't stand this excitement! I know this will cause a relapse! Oh, my metabolism! Doctor! *(She throws her hands in the air and moves away from* JUDY *toward the door)*

Interior, Hallway

CAMERA *shoots at a low angle, revealing first* HACKENBUSH's *shadow and then his legs and two satchels as he slouches into the corridor.*
MRS. UPJOHN *(offscreen)*: Oh, Doctor!
The CAMERA PANS *him into the room as he passes* MRS. UPJOHN, *not noticing her.*
HACKENBUSH *(to* WHITMORE*)*: Here, boy. Here, boy . . .

Three Shot—Mrs. Upjohn, Hackenbush, and Whitmore

HACKENBUSH *(to* WHITMORE*)*: . . . take these bags and run up to my room. And here's a dime for yourself.
MRS. UPJOHN: Oh, no, no, no, no, no! This is Mr. Whitmore, our business manager.

HACKENBUSH: Oh, I'm terribly sorry. Here's a quarter.

MRS. UPJOHN: Oh! You mustn't take the doctor too seriously. He probably feels tired after his long trip.

HACKENBUSH: Why shouldn't I be tired? Did you ever ride four on a motorcycle? And me—top man!

Long Shot—Entire Room—the Four of Them and the Medical Staff

MRS. UPJOHN: Oh, this is Dr. Hugo Z. Hackenbush, your new chief of staff. *(Hackenbush bows to the* DOCTORS; *they bow to him)* And now, Doctor, I'd like you to meet Miss Standish. *(He bows again and the* MEDICAL STAFF *returns his bow)* Oh, Doctor— *(*HACKENBUSH *bows a third time; the* DOCTORS *do likewise)* uh, Doctor . . . *(*HACKENBUSH *bows yet another time; the* DOCTORS *bow back)*

HACKENBUSH: Just a moment, till I calm these paralytics. *(He bows again; they bow with him)*

MRS. UPJOHN: Oh, dear. Oh, Doctor . . .

Three Shot—Hackenbush, Mrs. Upjohn, and Whitmore

MRS. UPJOHN: Oh, Doctor, this is Miss Standish.

Medium Close-up—Judy

MRS. UPJOHN *(offscreen)*: Owner of the sanitarium.

Three Shot—Mrs. Upjohn, Hackenbush, and Whitmore

HACKENBUSH *oozes over to* JUDY *and shakes her hand.*

HACKENBUSH: Oh, how do you do, Miss Standish.

JUDY: How do you do. *(They shake hands)*

HACKENBUSH: You're the prettiest owner of a sanitarium I've ever seen.

JUDY: Thank you.

HACKENBUSH: You have a charming place here. *(He looks at a portrait of a distinguished-looking patriarch that is over the fireplace)* Ah, I knew your mother very well. I'll let you in on a little

137

secret. Many, many years ago in the dear dim past, I proposed to your mother.

JUDY: Oh, but that's my father.

HACKENBUSH: No wonder he turned me down.

MRS. UPJOHN: Now, Doctor, I'd like you to meet your new associates.

Long Shot—Everyone
The FIRST DOCTOR *steps forward.*

FIRST DOCTOR: Johnson, Bellevue Hospital, Nineteen-eighteen. *(He steps back)*

SECOND DOCTOR *(steps forward)*: Franko, Johns Hopkins, twenty-two. *(He steps back)*

THIRD DOCTOR *(steps forward)*: Wilmerding, Mayo Brothers, twenty-four. *(He steps back.* HACKENBUSH *steps forward, clicks his heels)*

HACKENBUSH: Dodge Brothers, late twenty-nine. *(He steps back)*

Three Shot—Mrs. Upjohn, Hackenbush, and Whitmore
JUDY *walks over to them.*

JUDY: Doctor, I'm happy to welcome you as chief of staff. I hope you'll be able to pull the sanitarium out of its difficulties.

MRS. UPJOHN: Oh, the sanitarium is having a little financial trouble.

HACKENBUSH: I get it. I'm not going to get paid, huh? *(He picks up his bag and starts to leave.* MRS. UPJOHN *grabs him by the coattails and pulls him back)*

MRS. UPJOHN: Oh, no—no—no, Doctor—please don't go. I'll take care of your salary.

HACKENBUSH: Oh, yeah? The last job I had, I had to take it out in trade and this is no butcher shop—not yet, anyhow.

Close-up—Whitmore
WHITMORE: Judy, it seems to me, if I may say so, we are making rather a hasty decision.

Medium Long Shot—Judy, Mrs. Upjohn,
Hackenbush, and Whitmore
MRS. UPJOHN: Surely, you don't question the doctor's ability.
WHITMORE: No, not exactly. But running a sanitarium calls for a
man with peculiar talents.

Three Shot—Mrs. Upjohn, Hackenbush, and Whitmore
HACKENBUSH: You don't have to look any further. I've got the
most peculiar talents of any doctor you ever met.

Two Shot—Judy and Mrs. Upjohn
JUDY: I'm satisfied with Mrs. Upjohn's recommendations. And,
if you'll excuse me, I'll go and bring in the rest of the staff. *(She
turns to leave)*

Three Shot—Hackenbush, Mrs. Upjohn, and Whitmore
HACKENBUSH *(to WHITMORE)*: Why don't you go out and bring in
something? Preferably your resignation?
WHITMORE: Tell me, Dr. Hackenbush, just what was your medical
background?
HACKENBUSH: Medically?
WHITMORE: Yes.

Two Shot—Hackenbush and Whitmore
HACKENBUSH: Well, uh, at the age of fifteen I got a job in a
drugstore, filling prescriptions.
WHITMORE: Don't you have to be twenty-one to fill prescriptions?
HACKENBUSH: Well, ah, that's for grownups. I just filled them
for children.
WHITMORE: No, no, Doctor. I mean where did you get your train-
ing as a physician.
HACKENBUSH: Oh, well, to begin with, I took four years at Vassar.
CAMERA PANS LEFT *to include* MRS. UPJOHN.
MRS. UPJOHN: Vassar! But that's a girls' college.
HACKENBUSH: I found that out the third year. I'd've been there
yet but I went out for the swimming team.

Close-up—Whitmore

WHITMORE: The doctor seems reluctant to discuss his medical experiences.

Three Shot—Upjohn, Hackenbush, and Whitmore

HACKENBUSH: Well, medically, my experiences have been most unexciting, except during the flu epidemic.

WHITMORE: Ah, and what happened?

HACKENBUSH: I got the flu.

MRS. UPJOHN: Oh, Doctor, I think it's time for my pill.

HACKENBUSH *(privately, to* MRS. UPJOHN*)*: Ixnay on the opeday.

MRS. UPJOHN: Now you told me to take them regularly.

HACKENBUSH *rummages through his bag, pulls out some pills and hands them secretively to* MRS. UPJOHN, *making sure* WHITMORE *can't see.*

WHITMORE: Just a minute, Mrs. Upjohn, that looks like a horse pill to me.

HACKENBUSH: Oh, you've taken them before?

MRS. UPJOHN: Are you sure, Doctor, you haven't made a mistake?

HACKENBUSH: You have nothing to worry about. The last patient I gave one of those to won the Kentucky Derby.

WHITMORE *(takes a pill from* MRS. UPJOHN*)*: Uh, may I examine this, please?

Two Shot—Hackenbush and Whitmore

WHITMORE *(holding up the pill)*: Do you actually give those to your patients? Isn't that awfully large for a pill?

HACKENBUSH: No. It was too small for a basketball and I didn't know what to do with it. Say, you're awfully large for a pill yourself.

WHITMORE *(walks over to the line of* DOCTORS*)*: Dr. Wilmerding, just what is your opinion?

WILMERDING: It must take a lot of water to swallow that.

Two Shot—Hackenbush and Mrs. Upjohn

HACKENBUSH: Nonsense, you can swallow that with five gallons.

140

WHITMORE: Isn't that a lot of water for a patient to take?
HACKENBUSH: Not if the patient has a bridge in her mouth. You see, the water flows under the bridge and the patient walks over the bridge and meets the pill on the other side.

Three Shot—the Three Doctors
They are appalled at HACKENBUSH's *remarks. In the distance, a* BUGLE *sounds the beginning of a horse race.*

Three Shot—Mrs. Upjohn, Hackenbush, and Whitmore
HACKENBUSH *(hearing the bugle)*: So it's war! I'm off to the battlefield! *(He starts to leave)*
MRS. UPJOHN *(she grabs him by the coattails again)*: No—no, Doctor, that's from the race track.
HACKENBUSH: Race track? Well, what am I doing here?
MRS. UPJOHN: Oh, Doctor—Doctor, please—!
HACKENBUSH *runs out between the* DOCTORS.

Dissolve to:
Exterior, Race Track

Long Shot—the Track—*shooting from the stands. The* HORSES *are off and running.*

Two Shot—Whitmore and Morgan
They are seated in the best seats in the grandstand, watching the race.

Medium Shot—the Track—Stuffy (Harpo) and another Jockey
STUFFY *is riding neck and neck with another* JOCKEY.
JOCKEY: Guess you won it, Stuffy.
STUFFY *puts his riding crop in his mouth.*

Two Shot—Whitmore and Morgan
They get up to leave.

141

Dissolve to:
Interior, Stable
Medium Shot—Stuffy and Grooms
> STUFFY *walks through a stable door, carrying a racing saddle which he hangs on a peg.*
> GROOM: Nice work, Stuffy.
> MORGAN *enters and kicks* STUFFY *in the behind.* STUFFY *flies up into the air.*

Medium Close-up—Stuffy
> *He flies face first into the wall.*

Medium Shot—Stuffy and Morgan
> MORGAN *pulls* STUFFY *down from the wall and punches him in the face.* STUFFY *falls to the ground.*
> MORGAN: I told you to lose that race!
> MORGAN *takes another swing at* STUFFY, *misses and drives his fist into the wall.*
> MORGAN *(in pain)*: Ohhh!!
> STUFFY *crawls out from underneath and runs out the stable door.*

Medium Shot—Stuffy
> *He closes the Dutch stable doors.* MORGAN *lunges at him, through the top half, but* STUFFY *gets away.* MORGAN *opens the bottom half and runs after him.*

Long Shot—Stables
> *A row of* HORSES *are in their stalls.* STUFFY *runs in past the* HORSES *and dives into a stall.*

Interior, Stall
Medium Shot—Stuffy and Gil
> STUFFY *burrows into a haystack and hides near* GIL *who is taping* HI-HAT's *foot.*

MORGAN (*offscreen*): Stuffy, where are you? Where's Stuffy?
MORGAN *comes to the stable door and startles* HI-HAT.
MORGAN (*offscreen*): Have you seen my jockey?

Close Shot—Gil
He tries to soothe HI-HAT.
GIL: Whoa, boy! Please, Mr. Morgan, don't stay here!

Close Shot—Morgan
He's at the entrance to the stall.
MORGAN: You ought to beat the head off that ornery devil!

Close Shot—Gil
He tries to calm HI-HAT *as he rears.*
GIL: He only acts this way when he sees or hears you!

Close Shot—Morgan
He's afraid of HI-HAT.
MORGAN: Aw!

Close Shot—Haystack
STUFFY *sticks his leg out of the hay and kicks* MORGAN.
MORGAN *thinks it's* HI-HAT.

Close Shot—Morgan
MORGAN: I should have plugged that nag when I owned him!
HI-HAT's *tail swats* MORGAN *in the face.*

Close Shot—Gil
He struggles with HI-HAT.
GIL: Please, Mr. Morgan, don't stay here!

Close Shot—Morgan
He leaves.

Medium Shot—Stuffy

He gets out of the haystack. (See film still 7.)

GIL *(offscreen)*: Calm down now—he's gone now—that's the boy.

Medium Shot—Gil and Hi-Hat

STUFFY *comes over to them, pats* GIL *on the back, and embraces* HI-HAT.

GIL: You better stay out of Morgan's way for a while.

TONY *(offscreen)*: Get your ice cream. Get your tootsie-frootsie ice cream.

STUFFY *runs off in the direction of the tootsie-frootsie ice cream.*

Exterior, Stable
Medium Long Shot—Stuffy and Tony

STUFFY WHISTLES *to* TONY. TONY *is pulling his ice-cream cart.*

TONY: Stuffy!

STUFFY *runs to embrace* TONY, *but at the last minute goes around him and heads for the ice cream.* TONY *slams the ice-cream-wagon lid down.*

TONY: Hey, hey, get out of there! Yeah, that was some ride you put up. I had five bucks right on the nose. I won sixty cents.

Two Shot—Stuffy and Tony

TONY: Who you ridin' tomorrow? What's the matter? *(*STUFFY *strikes a match)* What happened? You fired? *(*STUFFY *blows out the match and nods his head "yes")* Oh, Morgan fired you, eh? *(*STUFFY *nods "yes")* He wanted you to throw the race? *(He nods "yes" again)*

GIL *comes out of the stable behind them.*

GIL: He wanted Stuffy to be crooked, eh?

Three Shot—Stuffy, Tony, and Gil

TONY: Yeah. You know he's honest. *(*STUFFY *reaches into the ice cream wagon and* TONY *slams the lid on his hand)* He's honest but you gotta watch him a little. Hey, Gil, why don't you give Stuffy a job? Let him ride Hi-Hat.

GIL: Why Tony, you know we can't afford a jockey. We haven't enough money to eat on ourselves.

TONY: Eat—eat—eat, all the time eat! We don't have to eat. I'll eat!

SHERIFF *(offscreen)*: Hey, you!

GIL: Why hello, Sheriff.

SHERIFF *(enters)*: Well, have you got the money for the feed bill?

GIL: You see, Sheriff, it's this way—

SHERIFF: Say, listen . . .

Three Shot—Sheriff between Stuffy and Tony

Standing behind the SHERIFF, STUFFY *mimics his anger.*

SHERIFF: . . . you guys have been stallin' me for weeks. Either I get some money on account right now or I'm taking Hi-Hat.

TONY: Hey wait—wait, I give you some money. *(He reaches into his pocket and hands the* SHERIFF *a bill)* There you are.

SHERIFF: Five dollars! *(He pockets it)* That's not enough. *(STUFFY picks the* SHERIFF'*s pocket and hands the five-dollar bill back to* TONY, *behind the* SHERIFF'*s back)* Come on, well!

TONY: All right, all right, I got it some more. There you are. *(He hands him the same five-dollar bill)*

SHERIFF: That makes ten. *(He pockets it, but this time keeps his hand in his pocket.* STUFFY *tickles his neck with a piece of straw)* Chicken feed. Come on, you got some more!

TONY *(stalling)*: Yeah, I got some more but it's hard to get at, you know.

The SHERIFF *scratches his neck.*

SHERIFF: Come on, come on!

TONY: All right, don't hurry. I got it some place. I know it's some place. *(While the* SHERIFF *is scratching,* STUFFY *takes the five-dollar bill from the* SHERIFF'*s pants pocket and hands it back to* TONY*)* There, I knew it was some place. *(He hands the five back to the* SHERIFF*)*

SHERIFF: Well, that's fifteen. *(He puts the bill in his vest pocket)* Have you got any more?

    STUFFY *reaches into the* SHERIFF's *pants pocket, but the bill is not there. He digs deeper and deeper, surprised there's no money. (See film still 8.)*

TONY: Ah—I let you know in a minute.

SHERIFF: Quit stallin'—come on, hurry!

TONY: All right, I got some more but I can't hurry.

SHERIFF *(to* STUFFY*)*: Hey, what're you doing there! *(*STUFFY *goes limp, his hand is in the* SHERIFF's *pants pocket so deeply that he pulls out a sock. The* SHERIFF *lifts his pants leg, looks at his bare ankle, and chases* STUFFY*)* Hey, come back here!

Two Shot—Tony and Gil

TONY: Well, thatsa fine. Now we owe the sheriff a hundred and twenty dollars and a sock.

GIL: Well it's a good thing Judy doesn't have to depend on me. I can't even hold on to the horse.

TONY: No? Well, we hold on to the horse. *(He closes the stable door)*

GIL: Say, if we only had some dough. I got a tip on Sun-Up!

TONY: Sun-Up?

GIL: Yeah.

TONY: He's in the next race. We no gotta much time!

GIL: Hey, wait a minute! What're we going to use for money?

Long Shot—Front of the Stable—Tony and Gil

    TONY *hurriedly pushes his ice-cream wagon underneath the* HORSE. GIL *runs after him.*

Dissolve to:
Exterior, Betting Windows
Medium Shot—Tony and Gil

    They look at the odds board for the next race. TONY *is still pushing the ice-cream wagon.*

TONY: Hey, boy, look—look! Sun-Up, he's ten to one!

146

Medium Shot—the Odds Board
Among the other names, it reads:
SUN-UP 10–1

Two Shot—Tony and Gil
TONY: Boy, are we going to clean up! Ten to one.
GIL: We haven't any money to bet.
TONY: Don't worry, I getta some money. I find a sucker some place. Scram, I think I see a sucker coming now. Get out of here.

Long Shot—Hackenbush
He enters, wearing a white linen jacket and a Panama hat. He looks at the betting windows and steps up to the two-dollar window.
TONY *(offscreen)*: Get your ice cream!
HACKENBUSH *(at the two-dollar window)*: Two dollars on Sun-Up.
TONY: Hey! Hey, boss! Boss! *(Yanking HACKENBUSH by the coattails)* Come here. You wanna something hot? *(See film still 9.)*
HACKENBUSH: Not now, I just had lunch. Anyhow, I don't like hot ice cream.
TONY: Hey! *(HACHENBUSH goes back to the betting window. TONY pulls him by the coattails again)* Come here! I no sella ice cream. That's a fake to foola the police.

Two Shot—Tony and Hackenbush
TONY: I sella tips on the horses. I gotta something today can't lose. One dollar. *(See film still 9.)*
HACKENBUSH: No, some other time. I'm sorry, I'm betting on Sun-Up. Some other time, eh? *(He goes to the window)* Two dollars on Sun-Up. *(TONY pulls him back by the coat)*
TONY: Hey, come here.

Closer Two Shot—Tony and Hackenbush
TONY: Sun-Up is the worse horse on the track.
HACKENBUSH: I notice he wins all the time.
TONY: Aw, thatsa just because he comes in first.

HACKENBUSH: Well, I don't want him any better than first. *(He goes back to the window)* Two dollars on Sun-Up. *(TONY pulls him back by his coattails)*
TONY: Hey, boss, come here. Come here. Suppose you bet on Sun-Up. What are you gonna get for your money? Two to one.

Medium Shot—Tony and Hackenbush
TONY: One dollar and you remember me all your life.
HACKENBUSH: That's the most nauseating proposition I've ever had.
TONY: Come on, come on, you look like a sport. Come on, boss— don't be a crunger for one buck. *(HACKENBUSH thinks about it, hands him the dollar, and takes the envelope)* Thank you.
HACKENBUSH: What's this?
TONY: Thatsa the horse.
HACKENBUSH: How'd he get in here?

Medium Shot—Tony and Hackenbush
TONY: Get your ice cream. Tootsie-frootsie ice cream. *(He walks away from HACKENBUSH)*

Close Shot—Hackenbush
HACKENBUSH *(reading from the paper that TONY gave him)*: Z . . .

Close-up—Insert—ZVBXRPL Lettered on the Paper
HACKENBUSH *(offscreen)*: V–B–X–R–P–L–

Close Shot—Hackenbush
HACKENBUSH: I had that same horse when I had my eyes examined. Hey, Ice Cream.

Two Shot—Hackenbush and Tony
HACKENBUSH: What about this optical illusion you just slipped me? I don't understand it.

148

TONY: Oh, that's not the real name of the horse, that's the name of the horse's code. Look in your code book.

HACKENBUSH: What do you mean, code?

TONY: Yeah, look in the code book. That'll tell you what horse you got.

HACKENBUSH: Well, I haven't got any code book.

TONY: You no gotta code book?

HACKENBUSH: You know where I can get one?

TONY *(opens ice-cream wagon)*: Well, just by accident, I think I got one here. Here you are. *(He holds up the book)*

HACKENBUSH: How much is it?

Closer Two Shot—Tony and Hackenbush

TONY: That's free.

HACKENBUSH: Oh, thanks. *(He takes the book from TONY)*

TONY: Justa one-dollar printing charge.

HACKENBUSH: Well give me one without printing. I'm sick of printing. *(He tosses the book back to TONY)*

TONY: Aw come on, you want to win.

HACKENBUSH: Yeah, sure, of course I want to win.

TONY: Well then, you gotta have this. *(He gives the book back)*

HACKENBUSH: I want to win but I don't want the savings of a lifetime wiped out in a twinkling of an eye. *(He takes his money out secretly and gives it to TONY)* Here.

TONY: Thank you very much. *(Tony goes back to his ice-cream wagon)* Ice cream! *(He exits, singing "Tootsie-Frootsie Ice Cream")*

Medium Close-up—Hackenbush

He begins leafing through the book.

HACKENBUSH *(reading)*: Z–V–B–X–R–P–L. Page thirty-four. *(Calling offscreen)* Hey, Ice Cream, I can't make head or tail out of this.

Medium Shot—Tony and Hackenbush

TONY *is rolling his ice-cream wagon along.*

TONY: Oh, that's all right, look in the master code book . . . that'll tell you where to look.

149

HACKENBUSH: Master code? I haven't got any master code book.

TONY: You no gotta master code book?

HACKENBUSH: No, do you know where I can get one?

TONY: Well, just by accident, I think I got one right here. *(He takes another book from the ice-cream wagon)* Huh—here you are.

HACKENBUSH: Lots of quick accidents around here for a quiet neighborhood.

Two Shot—Tony and Hackenbush

HACKENBUSH: Just a minute, ah, is there a printing charge on this?

TONY: No.

HACKENBUSH: Oh, thanks. *(He takes the book)*

TONY: Just a two-dollar delivery charge.

HACKENBUSH: What do you mean, delivery charge? I'm standing right next to you.

TONY: Well, for such a short distance, I make it a dollar.

HACKENBUSH: Couldn't I move over here *(He steps closer to* TONY*)* and make it—uh—fifty cents?

TONY *(stepping away)*: Yes, but I'd move over here and make it a dollar just the same.

HACKENBUSH: Say, maybe I better open a charge account, huh?

TONY: You gotta some references?

HACKENBUSH: Well, the only one I know around here is you.

TONY: Thatsa no good. You'll have to pay cash.

HACKENBUSH *(turning to the side to hide his money)*: You know, a little while ago I could have put two dollars on—on Sun-Up and have avoided all this.

TONY: Yeah, I know—throw your money away. *(He takes the money)* Thank you very much.

HACKENBUSH: Now I'm all set, huh?

TONY: Yes, sir.

Medium Shot—Tony and Hackenbush

As TONY *turns back to his ice-cream wagon,* HACKENBUSH *looks over his books.*

TONY: Get your tootsie-frootsie ice cream.

150

Medium Close-up—Hackenbush

TONY *(offscreen)*: Get your ice cream . . . tootsie-frootsie . . .

HACKENBUSH *(reading)* Master code . . . plain code . . . X–V–B–X–I–P–L. The letter Z stands for J unless the horse is a filly.

TONY *(offscreen)*: Get your tootsie-frootsie ice cream.

HACKENBUSH: Hey, Tootsie-Frootsie . . .

Medium Close-up—Tony

HACKENBUSH *(offscreen)*: Is the horse a filly?

TONY: I don't know. Look in your breeder's guide.

Medium Close-up—Hackenbush

TONY *(offscreen)*: Get your ice cream. Tootsie . . .

HACKENBUSH: What do you mean, breeder's guide? I haven't got a breeder's guide.

Medium Shot—Tony and Hackenbush

TONY: You haven't got a breeder's guide?

HACKENBUSH *(embarrassed)*: Not so loud. I don't want it to get around that I haven't got a breeder's guide. Even my best friends don't know I haven't got a breeder's guide.

TONY: Well, boss, I feel pretty sorry for you walking around without a breeder's guide. Why you're just throwing your money away buying those other books without a breeder's guide. *(A long wait while HACKENBUSH thinks about it)*

Medium Close-up—Hackenbush

He is still thinking about it.

HACKENBUSH *(finally)*: Where can I get one, as though I didn't know.

Medium Close-up—Tony

TONY: One is no good. You got to have the whole set.

Close-up—Hackenbush

TONY *(offscreen)*: Get your tootsie-frootsie . . .

HACKENBUSH: Hey, you know, all I wanted was a horse, not a public library. What d'you mean?

Two Shot—Hackenbush and Tony
HACKENBUSH: How much is the set?
TONY: One dollar.
HACKENBUSH: One dollar?
TONY: Yeah, four for five. *(He goes back into his wagon and pulls out a stack of books)*
HACKENBUSH: Well, all right, I'll . . . I'll . . . Give me the four of them. There's no use throwing away money, eh.
TONY: Oh, yeah, here you are. *(See film still 10.)*
HACKENBUSH: This is all I'm buying, too. I didn't want so many. *(TONY hands the stack to HACKENBUSH)* I thought you could do this quickly.
TONY: Here you are. *(He crosses to the betting window behind HACKENBUSH)*

Medium Close-up—Tony at the Betting Window
TONY: Six dollars on Sun-Up.

Medium Shot—Hackenbush and Tony
HACKENBUSH *is in the foreground leafing through his guides;* TONY *leaves the betting window and heads for his ice-cream wagon.*
TONY: Hurry up—tootsie frootsie ice cream!

Medium Close-up—Hackenbush
His arms are filled with guidebooks and codes.
HACKENBUSH: Z–V–B–X–R–P–L is Burns.
TONY *(offscreen)*: Yeah, thatsa right.
HACKENBUSH: Heh, Burns? *(TONY joins him)*
TONY: Yeah, yeah. Someday the code gives you the name of the jockey instead of the horse. Now you find out who jockey Burns

152

1

2

3

4

5

6

7

8

9

10

11

12

13

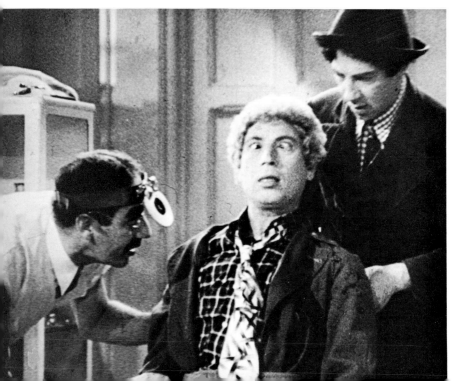

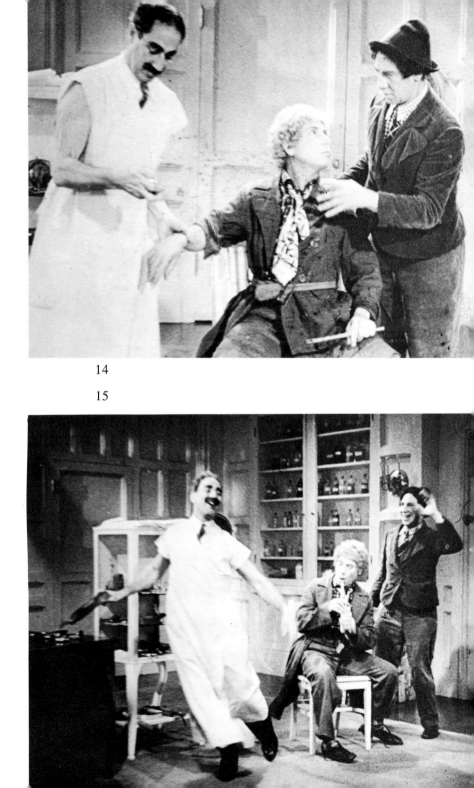

14

15

16

17

18

19

20

21

22

23

24

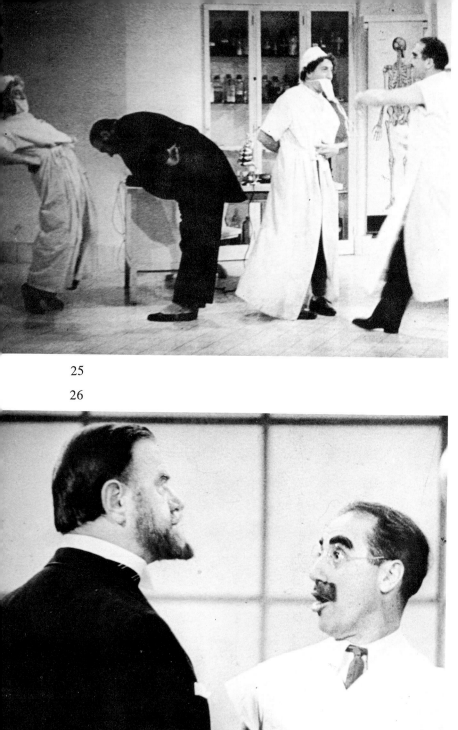

25

26

27

28

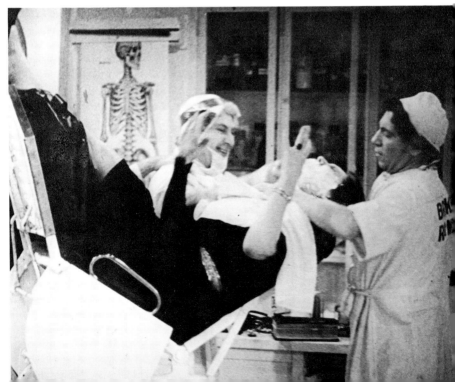

29

30

31

32

33

35

36

is riding and that's the horse you bet on. It's easy. Get your ice cream, tootsie-frootsie . . .

HACKENBUSH: Oh, I'm . . . I'm gettin' the idea of it . . .

Medium Shot—Tony and Hackenbush
   HACKENBUSH *looks through his load of books, two of which are between his legs.*
HACKENBUSH: I didn't get it for a long time you know. It's pretty tricky when you don't know it, isn't it, huh? *(He leafs through one of the books)*
TONY: It's not that book.
HACKENBUSH: Huh?
TONY: It's not that book.
HACKENBUSH: It's not—it's not that book . . . ?
TONY: No.
HACKENBUSH: Oh, I see. *(He leafs through another)*
TONY: No, it's not that book.
HACKENBUSH: Huh? *(He checks the books that are between his legs)*

Medium Close-up—Hackenbush
   He is leafing through all his books.
HACKENBUSH: You've got it, huh?

Medium Shot—Tony and Hackenbush
   TONY *nods "yes."* HACKENBUSH *nods "yes" with him.*
HACKENBUSH: I'll get it in a minute, though, won't I?
TONY: Get your tootsie-frootsie . . .

Medium Close-up—Hackenbush
HACKENBUSH: I'm getting a fine tootsie-frootsing right here.

Medium Shot—Tony and Hackenbush
TONY: Get your ice cream . . .
HACKENBUSH: How much is it?
TONY: One dollar. *(He reaches back into the wagon)*
HACKENBUSH: And it's the last book I'm buying.

153

TONY: Sure, you don't need no more. Here . . . *(He hands* HACKENBUSH *the book)*

We hear the BUGLE *calling the* HORSES *to post.*

HACKENBUSH: Here's . . . ah . . . here's ah . . . ten-dollar bill *(He hands him the money)* and shoot the change, will you. They're going to the polls.

TONY: I gotta no change. I'll have to give you nine more books. You don't mind, huh, boss? You take the nine more books. *(He pulls lots of books out)*

HACKENBUSH: Nine more . . .

TONY: Yeah.

HACKENBUSH: Say, you don't handle any bookcases there, do you?

TONY: Well, you come tomorrow, anyhow. *(He piles the additional books onto* HACKENBUSH's *arms)*

HACKENBUSH: I didn't know that you needed so many.

TONY: That's all right, you're going to win on the horses today.

HACKENBUSH *(mumbling to himself)*: Just walk up and bet on a horse.

TONY: Yeah. Open . . .

HACKENBUSH: Huh?

TONY: Open . . . open . . . *(HACKENBUSH opens his legs;* TONY *stuffs the books between his knees)*

HACKENBUSH: Say, am I shedding books down there?

TONY: Close.

HACKENBUSH: Huh?

TONY: Close . . . *(HACKENBUSH closes his legs, locks the books in place)* thatsa it. Now . . .

HACKENBUSH: Good thing I brought my legs with me, huh?

TONY: Yeah, yeah.

HACKENBUSH: Tell me what horse have I got? Hurry up, will you.

TONY: I'll find it, *(He looks through one of the books)* here it is, here it is . . . right here . . .

HACKENBUSH: I just heard the fellow blowing his horn.

TONY: Here it is, here . . . Jockey Burns—hundred and fifty two . . . thatsa Rosie . . .

HACKENBUSH: Rosie, huh?

154

TONY: Sure . . . oh, boy, look—forty to one.

HACKENBUSH: Forty to one.

TONY: Oh, what a horse, Rosie. Look *(He points to the odds board)*

HACKENBUSH: Am I going to give that bookie a whipping.

TONY: Oh, boy . . .

HACKENBUSH: I was going to bet on Sun-Up at ten to one. *(He hobbles over to the betting window)*

TONY: Look—forty to one. Thatsa it.

HACKENBUSH: I'll show them a thing or two. Say, there . . .

Two Shot—Hackenbush and Tony
At the betting window.

HACKENBUSH: Big boy, two dollars on Rosie, huh?

BOOKIE: Sorry, that race is over.

HACKENBUSH: Huh?

BOOKIE: I say, that race is over.

HACKENBUSH: Over? Who won?

BOOKIE: Sun-Up.

TONY: Sun-Up! Thatsa my horse. *(He runs off)*

Medium Shot—Tony and Hackenbush
TONY *runs to the window to collect.* HACKENBUSH, *stunned, watches him.*

TONY: Sun-Up! Sun-Up! Hurry . . . Good-ah-by boss. *(Counting his money)* ten . . . twenty . . . thirty . . . *(He walks off)*

HACKENBUSH *dumps all his books back into the ice-cream wagon and pushes it off, trailing books as he goes.*

HACKENBUSH: Get your tootsie-frootsie nice ice cream . . . nice tootsie-frootsie ice cream . . .

Fade out

Fade in:
Interior, Sanitarium
Close Shot—Telephone Switchboard
We see part of the OPERATOR.

OPERATOR *(offscreen)*: Oh, Miss Standish.

JUDY *(offscreen)*: Yes.

OPERATOR *(offscreen)*: These calls came for you while you were out.

JUDY *(offscreen)*: Oh, thank you.

The OPERATOR *hands a stack of phone messages to* JUDY. *We see the messages and the* OPERATOR'*s and* JUDY'*s hands.* JUDY *leafs through the stack of messages.* CAMERA PANS UP *to* JUDY'*s face as she tears the messages in half and dumps them in the* OPERATOR'*s wastebasket.*

OPERATOR *(into telephone mouthpiece)*: Hello . . . Mr. Stewart?

JUDY *(to the* OPERATOR*)*: I'm still out.

Close Shot—Operator

OPERATOR: I'm sorry but Miss Standish is still out. . . . *(She plugs in another call)* Yes, Mr. Whitmore.

Interior, Whitmore's Office
Medium Shot—Whitmore and Morgan

WHITMORE *is on the phone.* MORGAN *listens.*

WHITMORE *(into phone)*: What about that call to the Florida Medical Board? What? Well, keep on trying. Call me the moment you get it. *(He hangs up and sits on the desk)*

MORGAN: That's great. You can't even get any action from your own telephone operator.

WHITMORE: Don't worry, I'll get the dope on that Florida quack.

MORGAN: Now listen, Whitmore. I want to turn this place into a gambling casino before the season ends. With my race track and my night club and this, I'll have every sucker in America flocking here. But every day counts.

WHITMORE: I'll let you know the moment I get the call.

MORGAN: I'll be waiting. *(He turns to leave)*

Interior, Lobby
Two Shot—Judy and Hackenbush

He is wearing a white doctor's coat. PATIENTS *lounge about in the background.*

156

JUDY: Doctor, may I have one of your photographs?

HACKENBUSH: Why, I haven't one. I can let you have my foot-prints, but they're upstairs in my socks.

JUDY: No. I want to announce your association with the sanitarium. We'll send your picture to all the papers. *(They move across the room;* JUDY *sits down)*

HACKENBUSH: The Florida papers?

JUDY: Yes, it'll be wonderful publicity.

HACKENBUSH: Publicity? Oh, we mustn't have any of that, Miss Standish. You know, the ethics of my profession. *(He sits next to her)*

JUDY: But—we have to get new patients.

HACKENBUSH: Well after all, the old patients were good enough for your father. Besides, who wants to see my picture—I'm not a famous man. I'm just a simple country doctor with horse sense.

JUDY: Oh, you're too modest. Never mind, we'll forget about the pictures. And Doctor, remember—I'm counting on you. The success of the sanitarium is in your hands.

HACKENBUSH: Ummm . . . Look, Miss Standish . . . Suppose, suppose that I were to tell you that . . . that I'm not the doctor you think I am.

JUDY: Well, you're the only one that can help me. *(She stands)* And do be nice to Mrs. Upjohn, won't you?

Medium Close Shot—Hackenbush
Shooting over JUDY'*s shoulder.*

HACKENBUSH: Well she's not exactly my type, but for you, I'd make love to a crocodile.

JUDY: Silly. *(She giggles and leaves)*

Medium Shot—Hackenbush and Operator
He moves quickly over to the telephone OPERATOR.

HACKENBUSH: Have the florist send some roses to Mrs. Upjohn, and write "Emily, I love you" on the back of the bill.

OPERATOR: Oh, just a moment, Dr. Hackenbush.

157

Medium Close Shot—Operator

OPERATOR: Yes, Mr. Whitmore. No, I haven't been able to get that call through to the Florida Medical Board.

Medium Shot—Operator and Hackenbush

He reacts to her saying "call through to the Florida Medical Board."

OPERATOR: Well, I'm doing the best I can! It ought to be here any minute.

HACKENBUSH: If that call's what I think it is, she can cancel those roses and make it lilies for me!

CAMERA PANS HACKENBUSH *as he hurries away from the* OPERATOR.

Interior, Office
Medium Shot—Hackenbush

He hurries in, sits at the desk and grabs the telephone.

HACKENBUSH *(into the phone)*: Get me Mr. Whitmore.

Medium Long Shot—Hackenbush

The screen splits diagonally: HACKENBUSH *on the phone in his office on the left, and* WHITMORE *in his office picking up the* RINGING *phone on the right. (See film still 11.)* HACKENBUSH *holds his nose and talks like an operator.*

WHITMORE: Hello.

HACKENBUSH *(Operator's voice)*: Here's your Florida call, Mr. Whitmore.

WHITMORE: All right. Hello.

HACKENBUSH *(he changes to a Southern woman's voice)*: Florida Medical Board. Good morning.

WHITMORE: I'd like to talk to the man in charge of the records, please.

Medium Close-up—Hackenbush

HACKENBUSH *(Southern woman's voice)*: Record department? Just a moment, sugar.

Medium Close-up—Whitmore
Medium Close-up—Hackenbush
HACKENBUSH *(putting on his Southern-colonel voice)*: Record
department. Colonel Hawkins talking.

Medium Close-up—Whitmore
WHITMORE *(into phone)*: Colonel Hawkins, did you get a wire
from me regarding Dr. Hackenbush?

Medium Close-up—Hackenbush
He turns on a small table fan next to the telephone.
HACKENBUSH: I'm sorry, sir, but there's a hurricane blowing down
here *(He puts paper into it to make more* NOISE*)* and you'll have
to talk a little louder. Whew—it certainly is the windiest day we
ever did have!

Medium Close-up—Whitmore
*He looks at his phone receiver, trying to figure out what's
going on.*
HACKENBUSH *(offscreen)*: Whew! It certainly is windy!
WHITMORE: I want to know about Doctor . . .

Medium Close-up—Hackenbush
He leans back in his chair and lifts his leg.
WHITMORE *(offscreen)*: . . . Hackenbush.

Close-up—Hackenbush's Foot
He BUZZES WHITMORE*'s intercom, pushing the button with his
foot.*

Medium Close-up—Whitmore
He hears the intercom, gets up, walks over to it.
WHITMORE *(into the intercom)*: Yes.

Medium Close-up—Hackenbush
HACKENBUSH *(in his own voice)*: Whitmore, you'll have to cut out
that squawkin'. The patients are all complaining.

159

Medium Close-up—Whitmore

He turns off the intercom and hurries back to the telephone.

HACKENBUSH *(offscreen, back to his Colonel Hawkins' voice)*: And I hope sir, that is the information that you require.

WHITMORE *(seated)*: I'm sorry, Colonel, I didn't hear it. I was called to the Dictograph.

Medium Close-up—Hackenbush

HACKENBUSH *(as Colonel Hawkins)*: What was that you said, sir?

Close Shot—Whitmore

WHITMORE: I was called to the Dictograph.

Close Shot—Hackenbush

He moves his foot to the intercom and BUZZES.

Medium Close-up—Whitmore

He moves to the intercom and CLICKS *it on.*

Medium Close-up—Hackenbush

HACKENBUSH *(into the intercom in his own voice)*: Whitmore, one more yelp out of you and I'll have you bounced out of here.

Close Shot—Whitmore

He goes back to his desk and the phone.

HACKENBUSH *(offscreen, Colonel Hawkins' voice)*: And I trust, suh, that that answers your question.

WHITMORE: I'm terribly sorry, Colonel, I didn't hear you.

Close Shot—Hackenbush

HACKENBUSH *(Colonel Hawkins' voice)*: I can't hear you. You'll have to talk a little louder.

Medium Close Shot—Whitmore

WHITMORE: I want to find out something about Hackenbush!

(The intercom BUZZES*)* Well, what is it now? *(Furious, he rushes to the intercom)*

Medium Close-up—Hackenbush
HACKENBUSH *(leans back in his chair with his foot on the intercom button; in his own voice)*: Whitmore, that's the last time I'm going to warn you about that yowling!

Medium Close-up—Whitmore
He goes back to his desk.
HACKENBUSH *(offscreen, Colonel Hawkins' voice)*: And in conclusion, let me say—
WHITMORE: I'm sorry, Colonel. What was that you said about Hackenbush?

Close Shot—Hackenbush
HACKENBUSH *(into the phone, Colonel Hawkins' voice)*: Hacken— You mean Dr. Hackenbush? Oh, no . . .

Close Shot—Whitmore
HACKENBUSH *(offscreen)*: . . . he's not here.
WHITMORE *(into phone)*: I know he's not there. He's here.

Close Shot—Hackenbush
HACKENBUSH *(Colonel Hawkins' voice)*: Then what are you bothering me for, Yankee?

Close Shot—Whitmore
WHITMORE: But I want to know something about his Florida record!

Close Shot—Hackenbush *(holds his nose; the operator's voice again)*: Here's your Florida call, Mr. Whitmore.

Close Shot—Whitmore
WHITMORE: Operator, will you get off the line! Hello. Hello, Colonel.

161

HACKENBUSH (offscreen, Colonel Hawkins' voice): Yes?

WHITMORE: Are you sure you're speaking of Doctor . . .

Close Shot—Hackenbush

WHITMORE (offscreen): Hugo Z. Hackenbush?

HACKENBUSH (Colonel Hawkins' voice): Who?

Close Shot—Whitmore

WHITMORE: Hugo Z. Hackenbush.

Close Shot—Hackenbush

HACKENBUSH (Colonel Hawkins' voice): Who's calling him?

Close Shot—Whitmore

WHITMORE: The Standish Sanitarium.

Close Shot—Hackenbush

HACKENBUSH (Colonel Hawkins' voice): Yes, that's where he works. Say I understand he's doing a mighty fine job up there.

Close Shot—Whitmore

WHITMORE: I . . . I want some information regarding his qualifications for the job.

Close Shot—Hackenbush

HACKENBUSH (Colonel Hawkins' voice): What job?

Close Shot—Whitmore

WHITMORE: As head of the sanitarium.

Close Shot—Hackenbush

HACKENBUSH (Colonel Hawkins' voice): Who?

Close Shot—Whitmore

WHITMORE: Hackenbush.

162

Medium Close-up—Hackenbush

He BUZZES *the intercom.*

Medium Close-up—Whitmore

He turns to the BUZZING *intercom.*

Close Shot—Hackenbush

HACKENBUSH *(in his own voice)*: Whitmore, you calling me?

Medium Shot—Whitmore

WHITMORE *(into intercom)*: No, you sap! *(Into phone)* Hello . . .

Close Shot—Hackenbush

HACKENBUSH *(Colonel Hawkins' voice)*: Yes, now . . . now what was that name?

Medium Close-up—Whitmore

WHITMORE: Hackenbush! Hackenbush!

Close Shot—Hackenbush

HACKENBUSH *(Colonel Hawkins' voice)*: Uh, huh, well as soon as he comes in I'll have him get in touch with you.

Medium Close-up—Whitmore

WHITMORE: Bah! *(He slams the receiver down)*

Medium Shot—Whitmore

The windows behind him open slightly and someone peers in as WHITMORE *storms out of the room.*

Medium Shot—Stuffy and Tony

TONY *(through the open window)*: You see that sourpuss? Thatsa Whitmore, the man you gotta watch. Hesa no good. He's ina with Morgan and I think they're trying to get the sanitarium away from Miss Judy.

163

That angers STUFFY *and he jumps into the room head first.*
TONY *follows him.* STUFFY *moves toward the door as though
he's going to find* WHITMORE *and kill him.*
TONY *(stopping him)*: Hey, hey, hey! No! No! You no wanna fight
him. You're gonna watch 'im. You gotta watch him like a hawk.
*(*STUFFY *nods "yes" and tries to run to the door anyway.* TONY
stops him) Not so fast. No! Not so fast. Now look, first I gotta get
you in here as a patient or elsa Whitmore is gonna get wise to you.
Come on, I take you to the doctor. *(*STUFFY *doesn't like that and
makes a dash for the window)*

Wider Shot—Stuffy and Tony
STUFFY *goes out the window head first.* TONY *grabs him and
pulls him back into the room.*
TONY: Hey Stuffy, Stuffy, hey, come here! Hey, he won't hurt you.
*(*STUFFY *mimes his arm being cut off)* No, no, come here. This
fellow's a nice doc. You're hungry, eh? *(*STUFFY *nods his head
"yes")* You wanna some ice cream? *(*STUFFY *again nods "yes")*
You wanna a nice big steak? *(*STUFFY *nods "yes")* With spinach?
(See film still 12.) *(*STUFFY *turns to dive out the window;* TONY
pulls him back) All righta, all right, no spinach, no spinach. Apple
pie? Anda beautiful nurses? *(*TONY *shows how curvy the nurses are
and* STUFFY *begins to grin)* Oh, baby, come on, you're gonna get
a nurse. *(*TONY *leads* STUFFY *to the door)*

Interior, Sanitarium Examination Room
Long Shot—Wilmerding and Intern
WILMERDING: Have you seen Doctor Hackenbush?
INTERN: No, I haven't, Doctor.
WILMERDING: Well, go and find him right away. Mrs. Upjohn
wants him.
The door opens and a SECRETARY *followed by a* NURSE *enters.
Another* NURSE *moves quickly across the room in the back-
ground.*
INTERN: What's the matter with Mrs. Upjohn?
WILMERDING: Nothing. In its most violent form.

Medium Shot—the Doorway

The door opens and DR. HACKENBUSH, *in a wheelchair pushed by an* ORDERLY, *is rolled to the center of the room. He rises, puffs on his cigar.*

HACKENBUSH *(to the* ORDERLY*)*: Ah, pick me up at five.

ORDERLY: Yes, sir.

HACKENBUSH *goes to his desk, hangs his head reflector on a clothes tree and sits.*

Two Shot—Secretary and Hackenbush

SECRETARY *(she hands him a note)*: Doctor, may I have an okay on this, please?

HACKENBUSH: Ummm, I'm too busy right now. I'll tell you what. I'll put the "O" on now and come back later for the "K."

Medium Long Shot—All of Them

WILMERDING *steps forward.*

WILMERDING: Doctor Hackenbush . . .

HACKENBUSH: Ummm—a little later. Get me the Turkish bath.

A NURSE *picks up the phone.*

WILMERDING: Doctor Hackenbush . . .

Close-up—Wilmerding

WILMERDING: Mrs. Upjohn is complaining again—and these X-rays show absolutely nothing wrong with her.

Medium Shot—Hackenbush and Nurse

She's on the phone, trying to reach the Turkish bath.

HACKENBUSH: Is that so? Who are you going to believe—me or those crooked X-rays?

NURSE: Doctor—the Turkish bath. *(She hands him the phone)*

HACKENBUSH *(into phone)*: Oh, hello.

Medium Close-up—Hackenbush

HACKENBUSH *(into the phone)*: Gus, will you look in the steam room and see if my frankfurters are done?

Medium Long Shot—All of Them

HACKENBUSH *hangs up the phone and stands.*

HACKENBUSH: That will be all. I have some important research.

Everyone leaves.

Close-up—Desk Drawer

He opens the drawer and pulls out the racing chart. CAMERA PULLS BACK *as he puts his feet up on the desk and reads.* TONY *enters.*

Close-up—Racing Chart

HACKENBUSH *is behind it, reading.*

Medium Shot—Hackenbush and Tony

TONY *walks to* HACKENBUSH *and leans over the racing chart.*

TONY: Excuse me.

HACKENBUSH *puts the racing chart away and sits up.* TONY *recognizes him from the race track and backs away.*

TONY: Oh, so you're the doctor?

HACKENBUSH: Yeah, remember me? I used to be in the book business.

Two Shot—Tony and Hackenbush

TONY *backs away as* HACKENBUSH *follows him around the room.*

TONY: Hey, forgetta about that, Doc. I gotta some good news for you.

HACKENBUSH: Yeah, what are the odds?

TONY: No, no, it's no horse. I gotta patient for you.

HACKENBUSH: Oh, a patient. Oh, fine. *(Wiggling his foot in the air)* What size?

Medium Shot—Stuffy

He comes through the door dancing and PLAYING *his flute.* CAMERA PANS *him into the room with* TONY *and* HACKENBUSH.

166

HACKENBUSH: Well, you didn't get him here any too soon.

TONY: Hey, Stuffy!

HACKENBUSH *grabs* STUFFY *as he goes by and puts him in a chair.*

HACKENBUSH: Sit down here till I snatch you from the jaws of death. Just sit quiet there. Now, that's it. *(See film still 13.)*

TONY: Thatsa doctor.

Three Shot—Hackenbush, Stuffy, and Tony

HACKENBUSH *is taking* STUFFY'*s pulse. (See film still 14.)* STUFFY *looks very nervous as* HACKENBUSH *stares at his watch.*

HACKENBUSH: Either he's dead or my watch has stopped. *(He goes to a cabinet and takes a thermometer)*

TONY: He's a good doctor. He knows his business.

HACKENBUSH *shakes the thermometer down and* SINGS. STUFFY *watches him and* PLAYS *his flute.*

HACKENBUSH: Good-by forever, good-by forever. Here you are. *(*STUFFY *shuts his mouth tight, he doesn't want any part of the thermometer)* Oh, come on, this isn't going to hurt.

TONY: Oh, come on—everybody gets this.

HACKENBUSH: Come on, open up those pearly gates. Just flip this under your flapper. *(He slips the thermometer into* STUFFY'*s mouth)* Atta boy. It didn't hurt, did it, huh? *(*STUFFY *shakes his head—"yes," it did)*

TONY: He's pretty sick, eh, Doc?

Medium Close-up—Stuffy

He starts to chew up the thermometer.

Three Shot—Stuffy, Tony, and Hackenbush

STUFFY *chews.* HACKENBUSH *looks at his watch.*

HACKENBUSH *(when the thermometer is gone)*: Well, that temperature certainly went down fast.

STUFFY *gets up and goes to the cabinet.*

167

Close-up—a Bottle in Cabinet

STUFFY'S *hand takes the bottle with a skull and crossbones, marked: Poison.*

Three Shot—Hackenbush, Stuffy, and Tony

STUFFY *starts to drink the poison.* HACKENBUSH *grabs the bottle away from him.*

HACKENBUSH: Hey, don't drink that poison. That's four dollars an ounce.

HACKENBUSH *kneels in front of* STUFFY. *He looks through the mirror at* STUFFY *who jumps up, frightened.* TONY *grabs him.* HACKENBUSH *pushes up* STUFFY'S *pants leg and begins tapping on his knee and then his foot and then his other foot.*

TONY: I think we better put him to bed, Doc. He looks awfully sick today. Better get him a nurse too.

HACKENBUSH *(muttering)*: If he knows that, he'll go to bed.

TONY: Come on.

HACKENBUSH *puts on his head mirror and goes back to* STUFFY *to continue the examination.*

HACKENBUSH: There now, take it easy, will ya, take it easy.

TONY: He's been a doctor for years, this fella.

HACKENBUSH: I've been a doctor longer than you've been a patient, I'll tell you that.

STUFFY *climbs on* HACKENBUSH'S *back as if he were a horse.*

HACKENBUSH *immediately dumps him back in the chair.*

TONY: Come here! What makes you do like that? What do you think he's gonna play with you?

HACKENBUSH *tries to look through his head mirror at* STUFFY'S *eyes.* STUFFY *peers back at* HACKENBUSH *through the head mirror; they stare into each others eyes.*

HACKENBUSH: No, don't look at me—let me look at you, huh? No, don't look at me—what do you think I am—a peep show? *(*STUFFY *pulls his head away, shakes it, and looks back into the head mirror)* Get away there, will you? Hmmm. Rather a strange-looking sight.

168

TONY: It's serious, eh, Doc?

HACKENBUSH: I haven't seen anything like this in years. The last time I saw a head like that was in a bottle of formaldehyde.

TONY: I told you he was sick.

HACKENBUSH *(he touches* STUFFY's *neck)*: That's all pure desiccation along there.

Medium Close-up—Stuffy; Tony in Background

HACKENBUSH's *hands inspect the side of his neck.*

HACKENBUSH: He's got about a fifteen per cent metabolism with an overactive thyroid and a glandular affectation of about three per cent.

TONY: That's bad, huh?

HACKENBUSH: With a one per cent mentality. *(*STUFFY *grins and leans back)* He's what we designate as the Crummy Moronic type. Mmmm.

Three Shot—Hackenbush, Stuffy, and Tony

HACKENBUSH *(continues his examination)*: All in all, this is the most gruesome looking piece of blubber I've ever peered at . . .

TONY: Hey, Doc! Hey, Doc!

HACKENBUSH: Huh?

TONY: You gotta da looking glass turned around—you're looking at yourself!

Medium Long Shot—Hackenbush, Stuffy, and Tony

HACKENBUSH: I knew it all the time. *(He skips and dances across the room, laughing and singing. See film still 15)* That was a good joke on all of us, wasn't it? Let's do it again sometime, huh?

Three Shot—Hackenbush, Stuffy, and Tony

HACKENBUSH *leans over next to* STUFFY. STUFFY *opens his mouth but of course nothing comes out.*

HACKENBUSH: Say "Ah." Louder! *(Still nothing)* Louder! *(He opens* STUFFY's *mouth wider still—nothing)*

169

Medium Close-up—Hackenbush

He runs across the room to the door.

TONY *(offscreen)*: Hey, Doc, where you doing?

HACKENBUSH: I'm going to the ear doctor. I'm deaf.

TONY *(offscreen)*: Aw, come on back. It's notta you—it's him.

HACKENBUSH: Well, sometimes I'm not sure who's getting the examination here. *(He crosses back to* STUFFY*)*

Three Shot—Hackenbush, Stuffy, and Tony

HACKENBUSH *puts his hand on* STUFFY*'s heart.*

HACKENBUSH: Now take it easy, huh? *(He then pushes on his chest; as he does* STUFFY *begins to blow a bubble. When* HACKENBUSH *lets up the pressure the bubble disappears)* Say, am I stewed or did a grapefruit just fly past? *(He means the bubble)*

TONY: I don't see nothing.

Closer Three Shot—Hackenbush, Stuffy, and Tony

HACKENBUSH *pushes lightly on* STUFFY*'s chest, then on the mid-chest, then on his stomach and the bubble comes out again. He lets up his pressure and looks up at* STUFFY*'s face but the bubble disappears before he can see it.*

HACKENBUSH: If that's his Adam's apple—he's got yellow fever.

TONY: He's got ingrown balloons.

HACKENBUSH: He has, huh? Well, we'll soon find out. *(He presses on* STUFFY*'s chest, mid-chest and stomach. On the third press the bubble comes out again. This time* HACKENBUSH *sees it, grabs* STUFFY *by the throat so the bubble will last)*

TONY: Look—look—he's got a blister on his tongue.

HACKENBUSH: Is that what it is?

TONY: Yeah—I think it's a Ubangi.

HACKENBUSH: Well, I'll get a hammer and Ubangi that right off. *(He leans over and picks up a mallet)* I had a case like that once in Dusseldorf, many years ago. And a—*(*STUFFY *is leaning over and* HACKENBUSH *sees the top of his head and thinks it's the bubble)*— Say, it's grown considerably, hasn't it, huh? What's that hairy fungus all over it?

TONY: Some fungus, hey, Doc?

HACKENBUSH: Not a great deal, no. I don't know . . .

TONY: Hey, you're making a mistake—that's his head.

HACKENBUSH: Well, if that's his head, he's making a mistake, not me.

Medium Close-up—Hackenbush

HACKENBUSH *(puts the hammer down)*: I can't do anything for him. That's a case for Frank Buck.

Two Shot—Tony and Stuffy

STUFFY *has a stethoscope stuck to his forehead.*

TONY: All right, put him in the room until Frank Buck gets here.

HACKENBUSH: Oh, fine, shall we say a fifty-buck room—or would you prefer something better?

TONY: We'll take something better.

HACKENBUSH: Oh, that will be nice.

TONY: Yeah, but we'll talk about the money tomorrow.

HACKENBUSH: Oh, no, money on the line or out you go.

Medium Close-up—Stuffy

He's playing with the stethoscope.

Close Shot—Tony and Hackenbush

TONY *picks up* HACKENBUSH's *watch from the desk and reads the inscription.*

TONY: "To Dr. Hugo Z. Hackenbush for saving my horse."

HACKENBUSH: Here, gimme that. Come here with that watch.

TONY: You—a horse doctor!

HACKENBUSH: Shhh! A little easy with that talk.

TONY: A horse doctor.

HACKENBUSH: Don't mention that word around here.

TONY: Hey, that's terrible. I'm gonna tell Miss Judy, quick. *(He walks to the door, followed by* HACKENBUSH*)* No, that's no good. *(He turns and follows* HACKENBUSH *back into the center of the room)* Miss Judy, shesa-depending on you. A horse doctor.

HACKENBUSH: Now listen, boys, I admit it. You've caught me with my coat down. Well, it's been nice knowing you. *(He starts running away;* TONY *stops him)*
TONY: Oh, no you don't. Oh, no.
HACKENBUSH: Now let's get together on this. I'm open to any kind of a proposition.
TONY: All right. You stick on to this job. You make Mrs. Upjohn happy or we're gonna have you thrown in jail.
HACKENBUSH: Well, that—that doesn't leave me much choice, does it.

Medium Close-up—Stuffy
He picks up a hypodermic syringe and starts to fill it from a pan under the cabinet.
TONY *(offscreen)*: Listen, Hackenapuss, nobody must know you're a horse doctor.

Close-up—Hypodermic Syringe and Bottle
The label on the bottle reads: "Novocaine—for hypodermic use only."
TONY *(offscreen)*: You understand, you make one false move and we fix you . . .

Medium Close-up—Stuffy
He jabs the needle into HACKENBUSH's *leg.*
TONY *(offscreen)*: . . . good.

Medium Long Shot—Hackenbush, Stuffy, and Tony
HACKENBUSH: I hate to admit it, but—I haven't got a leg to stand on. Now let's *(He stands on his Novocained leg and collapses)* . . . hey, wait a minute. Hey, bring that over here, will ya.
TONY: Hey Stuff . . . *(*HACKENBUSH's *numb leg spins and turns freely)* There it goes.
HACKENBUSH: Now . . .
    TONY *and* STUFFY *try to help him to his feet.*

TONY: Get it around, Stuffy.

STUFFY *grabs the numb leg.*

HACKENBUSH: No, whip it around the other way.

TONY: You keep quiet—we know . . .

HACKENBUSH: You're goin' the wrong way.

TONY: We know what we're doin'.

HACKENBUSH: Okay. *(He walks around the room with his legs crossed)* There. For a while I thought I wasn't going to be able to walk again.

TONY: Hey, look, I got it too. *(He walks with his legs crossed)*

HACKENBUSH: It worked out fine. It's fine now. Yes, it's . . .

TONY: Hey, Stuffy, I got it. Come on.

HACKENBUSH: . . . better than it ever was . . .

TONY *and* STUFFY *follow* HACKENBUSH *out, walking with their legs crossed, imitating him.*

Fade out

Fade in:
Exterior, Race Track
Medium Shot—Track

GIL *is timing* HI-HAT *with* STUFFY *riding him. As* HI-HAT *whizzes by,* TONY *comes over to* GIL.

GIL: One forty-four. That's bad.

TONY: You thinka that's bad. I know something worse than that. Did Stuffy tell you?

GIL: Tell me what?

TONY: Hackenapuss—he's a horse doctor.

GIL: What!

TONY: Sure. Here, ask Stuffy.

STUFFY *comes in leading* HI-HAT.

GIL: A horse doctor!

Two Shot—Tony and Gil

GIL: Does anyone else know about this?

TONY: Only Hackenapuss and he won't talk.

173

GIL: Ah, it's bound to get out sooner or later. There must be something we can do to help Judy.

TONY: Yes! Hi-Hat.

Three Shot—Tony, Gil, Stuffy, and a Hi-Hat Horse

TONY *strokes* HI-HAT'*s nose and talks to him.*

TONY: You gotta wina race and maka us plenty a money. *(*STUFFY *rubs his stomach and points to his mouth)* Stuffy's right. Hi-Hat's too hungry to run.

GIL: Oh, I can take care of that. I'm going to get paid extra for singing at the water carnival tonight.

TONY: Ah, thatsa fine. You sing—I sella some more books and Stuffy, he's goin' to put Hi-Hat to bed.

GIL: Okay, boys, I've got to go to rehearsal. See you later.

TONY: All right, good luck.

GIL *leaves.*

Medium Shot—Tony and Stuffy with Hi-Hat

SHERIFF *(offscreen)*: Hey, you!

TONY: Hello, Sheriff.

SHERIFF *(walking to them)*: I thought I told you guys not to take this horse out of the stable until I got the rest of my dough.

TONY: Hey, we didn't take him out. He walked out and we followed him.

SHERIFF: Well, I warned you. Now I'm taking the nag.

TONY: Hey, Sheriff, you can't take that horse. We're just getting him into condition. How we gonna win the money to pay the feed bill?

SHERIFF: That don't mean a thing to me. I'm gonna put him where nobody'll take him out. *(He leads* HI-HAT *off)*

Extreme Long Shot—Sheriff with Hi-Hat; Tony and Stuffy Follow

He leads HI-HAT.

Medium Shot—Tony and Stuffy Next to Hi-Hat

The SHERIFF *doesn't see them. They untie his bridle.*

174

Medium Shot—Sheriff

As he walks across the field, we see that the bridle is now attached to STUFFY, who lopes along behind him. STUFFY stops for a moment and the SHERIFF turns and sees that HI-HAT is gone. STUFFY runs away and the SHERIFF chases him.

Medium Long Shot—Tony and Hi-Hat

TONY climbs on HI-HAT, and starts to ride away. STUFFY runs up to them and jumps on the back of the HORSE. They ride off across the track, the SHERIFF shaking his fist after them.

Fade out

Fade in:

Close-up—Insert of Program

TONIGHT

GALA

WATER CARNIVAL

Sparkling Springs Lake

Dining Dancing Entertainment

A hand turns the page to:

Picture	Picture
of	of
VIVIEN FAY	GIL
Captioned:	Captioned:
VIVIEN FAY	GIL STEWART
and her ballet	Tenor

Dissolve to:

Exterior, Lake

Long Shot—Lake and Fountain

Elegant PEOPLE walk in front of the spray.

Medium Long Shot—Waiter

He comes up to PEOPLE at a table in a boat.

Long Shot—Fountain

PEOPLE *sit at tables in front of the fountain.*

Medium Long Shot—Gil and Girls

As the fountain stops and the spray dies, it reveals GIL *in a white dinner jacket standing in a boat surrounded by beautiful* GIRLS STRUMMING *mandolins.*

GIL *(sings):*

> Tonight, we will be gay
> Turning away from all regret.

Medium Close Shot—Gil

GIL *(sings):*

> Tonight, saying good-by to every sigh, we will . . .

Two Shot—Hackenbush and Judy

They are in MRS. UPJOHN'S *boat.*

HACKENBUSH: He couldn't get you, so he took six other girls.

GIL *(offscreen, sings):*

> . . . forget. And in . . .

Medium Close Shot—Gil

GIL *(sings):*

> . . . fancy 'neath a distant moon.

Close-up—Judy

She pouts.

GIL *(offscreen, sings):*

. . . blue lagoon. On blue Venetian waters, together we'll dream.

Long Shot—Gil and Girls in Boat

The fountain cascades behind him.

GIL *(sings):*

> On blue Venetian waters, how lovely 'twill seem.

Medium Close Shot—Gil and Girls

GIL *(sings)*:

> Starlight tumbling down.

Close-up—Gil

GIL *(singing to* JUDY, *across the water)*:

> You shall wear, as a silver crown for your hair.

Close-up—Judy

She looks at him but pretends not to notice.

GIL *(offscreen, sings)*:

> The blue Venetian moonlight will soon light our way.

Close-up—Gil

GIL *(sings)*:

> Your eyes will tell me secrets your lips dare not say.

Long Shot—Gil and Girls

GIL's *boat turns and moves across the lake.*

GIL *(sings)*:

While I'm singing a love song of love dreams come true, of blue Venetian waters and you.

> *His boat disappears at the bottom of the screen and only the water curtain is left. As the water curtain falls away it reveals the* CORPS DE BALLET: *beautiful* GIRLS *in diaphanous gowns dance out onto the platform and begin their Busby-Berkeley-style ballet.*

Long Shot—Corps de Ballet

They are reflected in the water as they dance.

Medium Shot—the Dancers

Low Angle—Corps de Ballet

As they twirl, a lot of attractive legs are shown.

Long Shot—Dancers
Shooting past PEOPLE *seated at tables.*

Medium Long Shot—Dancers
The lighting changes: dark, and shadowy.

Medium Long Shot—Another Angle—Dancers
The lighting changes back to bright.

Four Shot—Four Girls Dancing
The MUSIC *becomes Spanish.*

Medium Shot—Dancers
Shooting past the SPANISH ORCHESTRA PLAYING *in the foreground.*

Medium Shot—Dancers
The GIRLS *bow and dip as they cross the stage. (See film still 16.)*

Close Shot—Dancers
Their skirts fly as they twirl.

Close Shot—Vivien Fay
Leaves from the trees fall on her. She starts across bridge.

Medium Shot—Vivien Fay
She starts to toe-dance down the bridge. GIRLS *pose on either side of her.*

Medium Long Shot—Vivien Fay
She dances her heart out in front of the GIRLS.

Two Shot—Stuffy and Tony
They're sitting on a diving board, watching the ballet.

178

Medium Long Shot—Vivien Fay

The DANCERS *break their pose and join her.*

Medium Close Shot—Spanish Orchestra

We can see the ballet in the background through the MARIMBA
PLAYERS.

Medium Long Shot—Corps de Ballet

*They are arranged as a bouquet of flowers and are reflected in
the water.*

GIRLS *(sing)*:

When you're singing a love song, your love dreams come true.
A ripple across the lake washes away the reflection.

Close Shot—Violinist

Close Shot—Vivien Fay

She dances away.

Long Shot—Vivien Fay and Girls

They dance past the MUSICIANS.

Extreme Long Shot—Vivien Fay and Girls

She dances and the GIRLS *pose behind her.*

Extreme Long Shot—Vivien Fay and Girls—Another Angle

She begins to toe-dance again.

Medium Long Shot—Vivien Fay

She twirls across the stage.

Medium Long Shot—Another Angle—Vivien and Girls

She twirls around the platform.

Close Shot—Vivien Fay

She crosses past CAMERA, *still twirling.*

Long Shot—Vivien and Girls

Still more twirling.

Medium Close Shot—Vivien

She dances toward the CAMERA, *still twirling.*

Medium Shot—Vivien Fay and Girls

She twirls into the foreground and poses victoriously at the height of the crescendo.

Long Shot—Dancers and Audience

Shooting past the PEOPLE *at tables,* VIVIEN *takes bows and they* APPLAUD.

Medium Long Shot—Hackenbush and Mrs. Upjohn

They are in MRS. UPJOHN's *canopied boat applauding.* JUDY *is between them.*

Medium Close-up—Flo

She is an attractive blonde. She flirts with HACKENBUSH *as she walks by him.*

Medium Shot—Hackenbush and Mrs. Upjohn

She is APPLAUDING *enthusiastically while he is flirting with* FLO.
MRS. UPJOHN: Isn't it beautiful?
HACKENBUSH *(meaning* FLO*)*: The prettiest number I've ever seen. *(He climbs out of the boat)*

Long Shot—Hackenbush and Mrs. Upjohn

He is climbing on all fours off to the left. MRS. UPJOHN *is still* APPLAUDING.
MRS. UPJOHN: Oh, Hugo, it's so impressive . . . *(She sees* HACKENBUSH *is gone; she rises)* Now what? *(She stalks off the boat)* The idea! *(As she leaves,* GIL *climbs into the boat.* JUDY *rises)*

Medium Shot—Gil and Judy

He pushes her back into her seat.

GIL: Oh now Judy, wait a minute, wait a minute. Look, I want to talk to you.

Close-up—Gil and Judy

GIL: It's about Hackenbush. You can't depend on him.

JUDY *(formally)*: Mrs. Upjohn is perfectly happy with Doctor Hackenbush and that's all that matters. As a matter of fact, she may take over the notes tomorrow.

Medium Shot—Gil and Judy

GIL *(discouraged)*: Well, I guess everything's all right.

JUDY *(avoiding him)*: Yes.

GIL: Well, there's nothing to worry about, is there.

JUDY *(still cool, but obviously wanting something else)*: No, not a thing. *(GIL rises)* Except that horse of yours.

GIL: Now wait a minute. That horse is all right. He's in the pink. Why today he ran the mile in one thirty-six.

Close-up—Judy

She's cynical but impressed.

GIL *(offscreen)*: The horse is going places.

JUDY: Oh, that's wonderful. I wish you luck.

Medium Shot—Judy and Gil

GIL: Thanks. I'm sorry I bothered you.

JUDY: That's all right.

GIL: Aw, now, Judy . . .

Two Shot—Judy and Gil

He sits down beside her.

GIL: . . . I'm the biggest liar in seven states. He isn't all right—and he isn't in the pink. It was one forty-four instead of one thirty-six. And the only place he'll ever go is where the Sheriff takes him.

Medium Close-up—Judy

Shooting over GIL's *shoulder.*

JUDY: Oh, you can't possibly mean Hi-Hat.

Medium Close-up—Gil

Shooting over JUDY's *shoulder.*

GIL: Well, there's only one horse in my stable. Come on, let me have the rest of it.

Two Shot—Judy and Gil

JUDY: The only thing I'm going to say is this, Gil. Don't ever let a horse come between us again!

Two Shot—Stuffy and Tony

They are still on the diving board, they're watching GIL *and* JUDY.

TONY: She loves him. Everything is going to be all right now.

Medium Shot—Dance Floor

As HACKENBUSH *dances with* MRS. UPJOHN, *he ogles* FLO, *offscreen. (See film still 17.)*

Medium Shot—Stairs

FLO *is there. She smiles at* HACKENBUSH.

Medium Close Shot—Hackenbush and Mrs. Upjohn

He glances at FLO *as he dances with* MRS. UPJOHN.

Medium Shot—Flo

She smiles back and starts down the steps.

Medium Shot—Hackenbush and Mrs. Upjohn

He dances her around the floor with one eye on FLO.

HACKENBUSH *(like a square-dance caller)*: Change your partners!

He twirls MRS. UPJOHN *around and away from him and while she's spinning, he dances away toward* FLO.

182

Medium Long Shot—Dance Floor
HACKENBUSH *spins up toward* FLO, *doing an elaborate improvised dance step. He and* FLO *begin to tango.*

Medium Long Shot—Another Angle—Dance Floor
FLO *is tangoing sexily around* HACKENBUSH. *He takes a silk handkerchief and rolls it around his rear end which he thinks is sexy.* FLO *continues to dance.*

Medium Close-up—Mrs. Upjohn
She looks through her lorgnette, shocked.

Medium Long Shot—Dance Floor
HACKENBUSH *leaves* FLO *and dances with* MRS. UPJOHN.
MRS. UPJOHN: Hugo, I'm surprised at you! *(He begins to rumba with her)*
HACKENBUSH: Oh, you didn't know I could rumba?

Medium Close-up—Flo
Her back is toward them. She turns and smiles at HACKENBUSH.

Medium Close-up—Hackenbush and Mrs. Upjohn
They're dancing. He glances at FLO *over* MRS. UPJOHN'S *shoulder.*

Medium Close-up—Flo
She smiles at HACKENBUSH *as he dances.*

Close Shot—Mrs. Upjohn and Hackenbush
They are dancing.
HACKENBUSH *(like a square-dance caller)*: Change your partners!
He twirls MRS. UPJOHN *away.*

Medium Long Shot—the Dance Floor
HACKENBUSH *slouches through the crowd toward* FLO, *takes her in his arms and they begin to dance.*

183

Medium Long Shot—Another Angle—Hackenbush and Flo
He twirls her toward the CAMERA *and slides along the floor next to her.*

Medium Close-up—Mrs. Upjohn
She watches them disapprovingly.

Medium Shot—Hackenbush and Flo
They are tangoing wildly. The MUSIC *changes.* HACKENBUSH *dances away from Flo.*

Medium Shot—Mrs. Upjohn
HACKENBUSH *dances back into* MRS. UPJOHN's *arms.*
MRS. UPJOHN: How would you like me to dance away from you?
HACKENBUSH: I'd be satisfied if you danced off my feet.

Medium Close Shot—Flo
She watches HACKENBUSH *and* MRS. UPJOHN *dance. She winks at him.*

Two Shot—Mrs. Upjohn and Hackenbush
His eye is on FLO. *He grins at her through* MRS. UPJOHN's *feathered hat.*

Medium Close Shot—Flo
She sees HACKENBUSH *looking at her and moves toward him.*

Medium Long Shot—Dance Floor
HACKENBUSH *stoops down, dances in a circle around* MRS. UPJOHN *and then dances away from her into the crowded dance floor.*

Medium Close Shot—Dance Floor
The MUSIC *changes again and* HACKENBUSH *dances over to* FLO *and they begin to Charleston wildly.* HACKENBUSH *spins away from* FLO *and back to* MRS. UPJOHN.

Two Shot—Mrs. Upjohn and Hackenbush
MRS. UPJOHN: Hugo, I'm disappointed in you. To think of your dancing with that strange woman.
HACKENBUSH: Well, don't think of it. Think of me dancing with you! *(He glances over* MRS. UPJOHN *to* FLO*)*

Medium Close Shot—Flo
She smiles back at HACKENBUSH.

Two Shot—Hackenbush and Mrs. Upjohn
HACKENBUSH: I'm crazy about you.

Medium Close Shot—Dance Floor
HACKENBUSH *dances with* MRS. UPJOHN *but* SPEAKS *to* FLO. MRS. UPJOHN *hears him and she's in heaven.*
HACKENBUSH: Nothing will ever come between us again. You don't know how lonely I get, night after night, in my little room at the sanitarium. Room Four-twelve.
MRS. UPJOHN: Perhaps I could come in and say good night to you.

Two Shot—Mrs. Upjohn and Hackenbush
They are dancing. HACKENBUSH *continues to* SPEAK *to* FLO. MRS. UPJOHN *hasn't a clue to what's going on.*
HACKENBUSH: Yes! We could have a midnight snack.

Medium Close Shot—Flo
She is listening to HACKENBUSH.
HACKENBUSH *(offscreen)*: A nice little steak between us.

Two Shot—Mrs. Upjohn and Hackenbush
MRS. UPJOHN: Oh, Hugo!
HACKENBUSH *(to* MRS. UPJOHN*)*: Oh, you would stay up until midnight! That's the way you follow doctor's orders!

Medium Long Shot—Dance Floor
HACKENBUSH *hustles* MRS. UPJOHN *off the floor, past* FLO.

185

HACKENBUSH: You're supposed to be in bed by ten o'clock! *(To FLO)* Twelve o'clock. *(To MRS. UPJOHN)* Ten o'clock!

Two Shot—Stuffy and Tony on Diving Board
STUFFY *looks up, frightened.*

Medium Close Shot—Sheriff
He's creeping up on the diving board toward STUFFY *and* TONY.

Medium Long Shot—Lake
The SHERIFF *walks on the diving board toward* TONY *and* STUFFY. *They swing down to a lower diving board to avoid him and the* SHERIFF *lunges at them and tumbles off the diving board.*

Medium Shot—Lake
The SHERIFF *splashes into the water.*

Medium Close Shot—Sheriff
He thrashes about in the water.

Medium Shot—Tony and Stuffy
They run away toward the ORCHESTRA.

Two Shot—Manager and Sheriff
The SHERIFF *is dripping wet.*
MANAGER: Sheriff, listen! We mustn't have any disturbance here tonight.

Medium Shot—Orchestra
TONY *is at the piano and* STUFFY *has the conductor's baton.*

Two Shot—Manager and Sheriff
The SHERIFF *is wringing out his coat.*
SHERIFF: All right—I can wait!

186

Medium Shot—Orchestra
They are TUNING UP. STUFFY *begins to conduct.* TONY *begins to* PLAY *a Rachmaninoff prelude.*

Medium Close Shot—Tony
He continues to PLAY *the piano but changes the music to "On the Beach at Bali Bali." (See film still 18.)*

Close Shot—Tony
He continues to PLAY.

Medium Close Shot—Tony
PLAYING *the piano.*

Close Shot—Tony
PLAYING *the piano.*

Medium Close Shot—Tony
Still PLAYING *the piano.*

Medium Shot—Orchestra
STUFFY *continues to conduct as* TONY *finishes* PLAYING.

Medium Close Shot—Sheriff
He watches, mayhem in his eyes.

Medium Shot—Orchestra
TONY *sees the* SHERIFF *and runs off.*

Medium Long Shot—Dance Floor—Tony and Sheriff
TONY *jumps over a low wall, and over the* SHERIFF, *and runs away. The* SHERIFF *chases him.*

Medium Shot—Orchestra
STUFFY *watches* TONY *run away and runs after him.*

187

Medium Shot—Sheriff, Manager, and Two Assistants
The SHERIFF *sees* STUFFY *and runs toward him.*

Medium Close Shot—Stuffy
He sees the SHERIFF *coming after him and quickly sits down at the piano.*

Medium Shot—Sheriff, Manager, and the Assistants
The SHERIFF *is stymied. He can't arrest* STUFFY *while he's* PLAYING.

Medium Close Shot—Stuffy
He's at the piano and begins to PLAY *the Rachmaninoff prelude.*

Medium Long Shot—Stuffy
He PLAYS *the piano.*

Medium Close Shot—Stuffy
He is baffled by the music he's PLAYING.

Medium Long Shot—Stuffy
He PLAYS *the piano.*

Medium Long Shot—Another Angle—Stuffy
He begins to attack the piano and PLAYS *wildly.*

Medium Close Shot—Stuffy
He POUNDS *on the keys.*

Long Shot—Stuffy
The piano begins to fall apart. STUFFY *continues to* PLAY.

Medium Close Shot—Stuffy
He grins and cleans his ear out with his finger. The keys begin to fly off the piano.

188

Long Shot—Stuffy

He tries to keep PLAYING. *More of the piano falls apart.*

Medium Close Shot—Stuffy

He PLAYS *as the piano disintegrates around him.*

Medium Long Shot—Stuffy

He dives into what's left of the piano and he pulls the string block out of the mess and decides it's a harp. He pulls the harp out of the rubble.

Medium Close Shot—Sheriff, Manager, and an Assistant

They're all furious.

Medium Long Shot—Orchestra

STUFFY *sits down at the harp and begins to* PLAY.

Medium Close Shot—Stuffy *(See film still 19.)*

He's at the harp.

Medium Close Shot—Another Angle—Stuffy

Shooting through the harp strings, he PLAYS.

Medium Close Shot—Another Angle—Stuffy

He continues to PLAY.

Close Shot—Harp Strings and Stuffy's Fingers
Medium Close Shot—Stuffy

He continues to PLAY.

Close Shot—Harp Strings and Stuffy's Fingers
Medium Close Shot—Stuffy

He continues to PLAY *and finishes. The* ORCHESTRA APPLAUDS *him and he raises his clasped hands above his head like a boxer who has just won his fight.*

Medium Shot—Sheriff, Manager, and Assistant
They are watching STUFFY, *waiting for their opportunity.*

Medium Shot—Stuffy
He is standing by the harp. He sees the SHERIFF *and twirls the seat of the piano stool up as high as it will go, sits down on it, and it catapults him up above the harp and into the air.*

Medium Shot—Sheriff, Manager, and Assistant
They watch STUFFY *fly over their heads.*

Medium Shot—Lake
STUFFY *splashes into the water.*

Medium Shot—Another Angle—Lake
STUFFY *splashes about.*

Medium Long Shot—Lake
STUFFY *swims away. The* SHERIFF *runs to the edge of the water and then runs along the side of the lake.*

Medium Shot—Whitmore
He is pacing next to a tall hedge near the lake. FLO *joins him.*
WHITMORE: And . . . ?
FLO: Well, it's in the bag.

Two Shot—Flo and Whitmore
FLO: I have a date with him in his room at twelve.
WHITMORE: Nice going. And see that you stay there till I break in with Mrs. Upjohn. I want Hackenbush fired out of the sanitarium tonight!
FLO: Don't worry, toots. When you knock on the door, I'll have that moth-eaten Romeo playing the balcony scene.

Medium Close Shot—the Bottom of the Hedge
STUFFY, *carrying his wet clothes, bursts through. He's heard* WHITMORE *and* FLO *plotting. He shakes his fist after them.*

Medium Shot—Stuffy
He tosses his wet clothes over the hedge and runs off.

Medium Shot—Stuffy
He runs down a small stairway. CAMERA PANS *to a group of* GIRLS *in frilly dresses playing "blindman's buff." The "blind man" in the center is* TONY. *The* GIRLS *run off.* STUFFY *runs to* TONY. TONY, *still blindfolded, thinks* STUFFY *is one of the* GIRLS *and embraces him.*
TONY: I gotcha!

Two Shot—Stuffy and Tony
TONY: I gotcha!
He pulls his blindfold off, sees it's STUFFY *he's holding in his arms.*
TONY: Oh, you spoila my game. Whatsa matter? Whatsa matter?
*(*STUFFY WHISTLES *through his teeth, holds his fingers under his nose like a mustache)* Buffalo Bill?

Medium Long Shot—Stuffy and Tony
STUFFY *slouches in a circle.*
TONY: Buffalo Bill goes ice-skating. *(*STUFFY *begins hacking at a bush)* Oh, Hackenabush? *(*STUFFY *turns and shakes* TONY'*s hand wildly, congratulating him for getting it)*

Two Shot—Stuffy and Tony
TONY: Oh—whatsa matter with him? Dr. Hackenabush—*(*STUFFY *makes the outlines of a curvy girl with his hand)* He's gotta snake? *(*STUFFY *makes the curve again and adds a* WOLF WHISTLE*)* No? He's got apple dumpling? *(*STUFFY *shakes his head "no," makes the mustache sign)* Dr. Hackenabush—he's got apple dumplings— *(*STUFFY *makes an even curvier girl and adds a longer* WOLF WHISTLE*) (See film still 20.)* No, 'atsa no apple dumpling, no.

Medium Shot—Stuffy and Tony
STUFFY *pulls up his pants leg, turns his ankle and demurely shows his calf to* TONY.

191

TONY: No, no. Oh, it's a woman! (STUFFY *shakes his hand, congratulating him*) Oh, I get it. Oh, there's a woman . . . yes, smart, eh? (STUFFY *makes the mustache sign*) Dr. Hackenabush—there's a woman—(STUFFY *stomps his foot*) She got a wooden leg— (STUFFY *shakes his head*) No?— (STUFFY *stomps his foot again*) She's got a woodpecker? (STUFFY *slaps his forehead at* TONY's *obtuseness*) She got a headache? (STUFFY *shakes his head "no" and makes the mustache sign;* TONY *makes the mustache sign with* STUFFY *as if that will help him understand*) Dr. Hackenabush— (STUFFY *makes the curvy woman sign too*)—there's a woman— (STUFFY *stomps his foot again*) She knock on the door—(STUFFY *clasps his hand to congratulate him for getting it and jumps up and down,* WHISTLING) Ah, she knock on the door! All right, all right— (STUFFY *makes the mustache sign*)—Dr. Hackenabush—(STUFFY *makes the curvy sign*)—there's a woman—(STUFFY *stomps his foot*)—she knock on the door. (STUFFY *points over* TONY's *shoulder, does all the gestures at once rapidly, hopelessly confusing* TONY)—Ah, you're crazy, you maka me sick.

Two Shot—Stuffy and Tony

STUFFY *grabs a "House Rules Card" which is conveniently tacked to a nearby tree.*

TONY: Whatsa matter now? (STUFFY *hits it with his foot, knocks it out of the frame and holds the empty frame in front of his face*) Oh, she's gonna frame him.

Medium Shot—Stuffy and Tony

STUFFY, *overjoyed that* TONY *finally gets it, collapses into his arms.* TONY *drags him away.*

TONY: Oh, come on—hurry up—hurry up!

Fade out

Fade in:
Interior, Hackenbush's Room
Medium Long Shot—Hackenbush

The table is set for two. He's wearing a silk robe. He pirouettes

192

and waltzes around the room as he brushes his hair and fixes his tie. There's a KNOCK *at the door.*

Medium Close Shot—Hackenbush
HACKENBUSH: Who is it?
FLO *(offscreen, musically)*: It's Miss Marlowe.
HACKENBUSH: Just a moment, fruitcake.

Medium Long Shot—Hackenbush
He sprays perfume into the air: on the table, on the couch, on his shoes.
HACKENBUSH *(at the door)*: Yes?
FLO: Oh, Doctor. (HACKENBUSH *opens the door and* FLO, *carrying a fur stole, oozes her way into the room)* Thank-kew.
HACKENBUSH: Thank-yo. *(He picks up a box of flowers)* Do you like gardenias?
FLO: I adore them. How did you know?
HACKENBUSH: I didn't—so I got you a forget-me-not.

Two Shot—Hackenbush and Flo
HACKENBUSH *(he hands her a sunflower)*: One whiff of this and you'll forget everything. Won't you sit down?

Medium Shot—Hackenbush and Flo
They walk to the table. He pulls out the chair. She sits.
FLO: Thank-kew.
HACKENBUSH: Thank-yo.
FLO *(she hands him her fur)* Oh, ah—do you mind?
HACKENBUSH: Not at all. I always take the wrap. *(He tosses the fur on the floor behind him)*
FLO: You're such a charming host.
HACKENBUSH: The Hackenbushes were all like that. How about a short beer?
FLO: Nothing, thank-kew.
HACKENBUSH *(mimics her)*: Thank-yo. *(He sits across the table from her. Between them, in the center of the table, is an enormous*

floral arrangement) Ah, Miss Marlowe, I've dreamed of this moment ever since I met you. *(They both lean to the left to see each other around the flowers) (See film still 21.)* For days I've been trying to see you. And I still don't seem to be able to make the grade. Ah, a quiet evening alone with you. What more could anyone ask. *(He leans to the right; she leans to the left)*

Closer Two Shot—Flo and Hackenbush
They both look around opposite sides of the flowers trying to see each other. He looks under the table for her.
HACKENBUSH: Say, have you sneaked out of here?
FLO: Yoo-hoo! *(She waves)*
HACKENBUSH: Oh, there you are. *(He climbs on to the chair)* Yoo-hoo! Isn't this too, too devastating? *(He sits on the back of the chair; FLO is doing her best to look enraptured)* Would you mind carving? I can't reach the steak from here.
FLO: Me?

Medium Long Shot—Hackenbush and Flo
There's heavy KNOCKING at the door.
HACKENBUSH: Yes?
The door opens and STUFFY and TONY enter.
TONY: Hey, Doc!

Two Shot—Tony and Stuffy
TONY: Hey, Doc! Can you see us?

Medium Close Shot—Hackenbush
HACKENBUSH: If I can't, there's something wrong with my glasses.

Two Shot—Tony and Stuffy
STUFFY *begins making the curvy-girl sign and points to* FLO.
TONY: You mean her? She's the one? *(STUFFY nods "yes")* We fix her.

Medium Long Shot—the Room
TONY *(to FLO)*: Ah, signorina, gentile e bella. (Ah, lady, kind and

194

beautiful) Oh, baby, you looka good to me. *(He jumps on her lap and* STUFFY *clasps his hands and pats him on the back approvingly)*
FLO: Oh, oh—oh, stop it!

Medium Close Shot—Hackenbush
HACKENBUSH: Hey, wait a minute, wait a minute. I thought you came here to see me?

Medium Shot—Tony on Flo's Lap; Stuffy Behind Them
TONY: Well, I can see you from here.
STUFFY *jumps on* TONY'S *lap.*
FLO: Oh, oh, get up you . . . oh—oh . . .
   STUFFY *pulls up his pants leg,* WHISTLES *to* HACKENBUSH *and signals to him to come sit on his lap.*
TONY: You know my friend.

Medium Close Shot—Hackenbush
He shakes his head "no," indignantly.

Medium Shot—Tony, Stuffy, and Flo
   STUFFY *continues to urge* HACKENBUSH *to sit on his lap.*

Medium Close Shot—Hackenbush
HACKENBUSH *(shaking his head "no")*: No, no. Not for me—three men on a horse.

Medium Long Shot—Tony, Stuffy, Flo, and Hackenbush
FLO: Oh, what is the meaning of this? *(She pushes* STUFFY *and* TONY *off her lap)* Oh! *(*STUFFY *flops right back down)* Why you little pest! *(She gets up indignantly and turns to* HACKENBUSH*)* Well!
HACKENBUSH *(gets down from his chair)*: Say, what's the matter with you mugs? Haven't you got any gallantry at all?

He walks to TONY *and* STUFFY, *and* FLO *turns her back on them.*

TONY *(privately)*: She's in with Whitmore. She's trying to frame you.

HACKENBUSH: I wouldn't mind framing her. A prettier picture I've never seen.

FLO: Thank-kew. *(She turns;* HACKENBUSH *bows to her quickly)*

HACKENBUSH: Thank-yo.

He turns back to TONY *and* STUFFY.

TONY *(screaming)*: Hey, Doc! Doc, I'ma tell you a secret—she's out to get you.

FLO: Why, I've never been so insulted in my life.

HACKENBUSH: Well, it's early yet.

FLO: Well, I'm leaving. I'm certainly not going to stay here with these men.

TONY *runs to the door.*

Medium Close Shot—Tony

He opens the door to show her the way out.

HACKENBUSH *(offscreen)*: You're not leaving—they're leaving.

Medium Shot—Hackenbush, Stuffy, and Flo

STUFFY *wraps the fur around* FLO *and starts to drag her to the door.*

HACKENBUSH: Now come on, I want you fellows to get out of here. *(He grabs the other side of the fur and pulls in the other direction. The fur rips)*

FLO: Oh, my cape.

HACKENBUSH: Come back here with my woman.

TONY *helps* STUFFY *pull* FLO. HACKENBUSH *continues to tug on her other arm trying to keep her in the room.*

FLO: Oh!

HACKENBUSH: You fellows are busting up a beautiful romance. What's the matter with you?

TONY: Doc, get her out—she's gonna make trouble.

Medium Shot—Another Angle—the Four of Them

HACKENBUSH: You've got her all wrong. This is my aunt and she's come to talk over some old family matters.

TONY: I wish I had an aunt look like that.

HACKENBUSH: Well, take it up with your uncle.

TONY: Hey, Doc!

Three Shot—Tony, Hackenbush, and Flo

FLO *sits down at the table and begins to powder her nose.*

TONY: Doc, you're playing with fire.

HACKENBUSH: I notice you didn't mind getting scorched.

TONY: Well, I got fire insurance.

HACKENBUSH: Well, you better get accident.

Two Shot—Stuffy and Flo

He gestures toward the door with his thumb, telling her to leave.

FLO *(returns the gesture)*: Scram! Blow! *(*STUFFY *leans over and blows the powder in her compact into her face. A great cloud of powder obscures both of them)* Oh! Oh! Oh! Oh!

STUFFY *runs to the door and follows* TONY *out of the room.*

HACKENBUSH *slams the door shut and* FLO *jumps up and dusts herself off.*

HACKENBUSH: How do you like those cheap chiselers horning in on us? *(He walks back to the table and holds the chair for* FLO*)*

FLO: Thank-kew.

HACKENBUSH: Thank-yo.

Medium Close Shot—Hackenbush

He starts to sit at the table across from her; he misses the chair and crashes to the floor. She LAUGHS *offscreen.*

Two Shot—Flo and Hackenbush

He picks himself and the chair up off the floor and sits. They look around the flowers at each other again.

FLO: Oh, ah—how about a little Scotch?

HACKENBUSH: Why, I'd love it. *(He starts to hand her his glass)* Oh—ah—I'll ring for some. *(He walks to the phone)*
FLO: Thank-kew.
HACKENBUSH *(runs back to her)*: Thank-yo. *(He goes back to the phone)*

Medium Close-up—Hackenbush
HACKENBUSH *(on the phone)*: Will you have the bellhop hop up with some hopscotch?

Medium Shot—Hackenbush and Flo
He crosses back to FLO.
HACKENBUSH: I'll flip you to see who pays for it.
FLO: Oh, Doctor.
There is a KNOCK *at the door.*

Medium Close Shot—Door, Opening
TONY, *in a bowler hat, a huge dime-store handlebar mustache, holding a hotel passkey on a large ring, and smoking a cigar, enters.*

Two Shot—Flo and Hackenbush
They look at him perplexed.

Medium Close Shot—Tony
He stands there.

Two Shot—Tony and Hackenbush
TONY *(trying to add a brogue to his Italian accent)*: I'm O'Reilly, the house detective.
HACKENBUSH: Don't talk so loud—your mustache will drop off.

Medium Shot—Flo, Hackenbush, and Tony
TONY *(looking at* FLO*)*: Have you got a woman in here?
HACKENBUSH: If I haven't, I've wasted thirty minutes of valuable time!

198

TONY: Well, you better get her out of here! This is the last time I'm going to tell you.

HACKENBUSH: The last time? Can I depend on that?

Long Shot—the Room
TONY: Yes. *(He walks to the couch)* Because this time I'm going to stay all night.

Medium Close Shot—Tony
He sprawls on the couch.

Two Shot—Flo and Hackenbush
FLO *is furious.*

Medium Close Shot—Tony
TONY: This looks like a tough case.

Two Shot—Flo and Hackenbush
HACKENBUSH *(looking at* FLO*)*: So does this!

Medium Close Shot—Tony
TONY: I think I'll call me assistant. *(He* TOOTS *a whistle)*

Two Shot—Flo and Hackenbush
They look toward the door.

Medium Long Shot—the Room
The door opens and STUFFY, *dressed like he thinks Sherlock Holmes looks, and leading* TWO BULLDOGS, *enters. He crosses to* FLO *and looks through his magnifying glass at her bare shoulder. (See film still 22.)*
FLO: Oh!

Medium Close Shot—Hackenbush
HACKENBUSH: If you're looking for my fingerprints, you're a little early.

199

Two Shot—Flo and Stuffy

STUFFY *continues to study her shoulder. He takes his Sherlock Holmes pipe out of his mouth; his mustache is attached to the pipe.*

Medium Close Shot—Hackenbush

He looks down toward the steak on the table.

Close Shot—Steak

HACKENBUSH *picks it up with his hand and dangles it in front of the* BULLDOGS.

Medium Shot—Stuffy and Flo

HACKENBUSH *runs by with the steak; the* DOGS *follow him, dragging* STUFFY *behind.*

Medium Shot—Tony

He's on the couch, asleep. HACKENBUSH *runs up to him.*

Close Shot—Steak

HACKENBUSH *puts the steak in* TONY's *pocket.*

Medium Shot—Hackenbush and Tony

HACKENBUSH *jumps back out of the way as the* BULLDOGS *jump on* TONY, *growling for the steak.*

Medium Close Shot—Tony

He falls off the couch. The BULLDOGS *go after him.*

Medium Close Shot—Hackenbush

HACKENBUSH: When you get through with that steak, chew him!

Medium Long Shot—Stuffy, Hackenbush, and Tony

The DOGS *chase* TONY *and in the process wind the leash around* STUFFY's *feet.*

Close Shot—Dogs Running
Medium Shot—Stuffy
He falls to the floor tangled in the leash. The Dogs *pull him behind them, knocking over furniture as they go.*

Medium Shot—Tony
He dives under the table. The Dogs *follow.*

Medium Close Shot—Hackenbush
Hackenbush *(to the* Dogs *as they go under the table)*: Pull in your ears . . .

Medium Shot—Stuffy
He is dragged under the table after them, feet first.
Hackenbush *(offscreen)*: . . . you're coming to a tunnel.

Close Shot—Tony
He comes out from the other side of the table. One of the Bulldogs *jumps out after him.*

Medium Long Shot—Tony, the Dogs, Stuffy, and Flo
Tony *gets up, the* Dogs *nip at his coat and drag* Stuffy *behind him.* Flo *stands in the background baffled. As* Stuffy *slides by, he pulls the rug out from under her. She starts to fall.*

Medium Shot—Tony, the Dogs, Stuffy, and Hackenbush
Tony *runs out the door followed by* Stuffy *who slides behind the* Dogs *as if he were on a sled. As they slide out,* Hackenbush *slams the door behind them.*

Medium Close Shot—Hackenbush
He looks at the door.
Flo *(offscreen)*: It's been a nice, quiet dinner.

201

Medium Shot—Flo and Hackenbush

HACKENBUSH: How do you know? You haven't had any yet. Shall we? *(They cross to the table; he pulls out her chair)*
FLO: Thank-kew. *(She sits)*
HACKENBUSH: Thank-yo!

Two Shot—Flo and Hackenbush

He sits and they try to look at each other around the flowers again. He stands.
HACKENBUSH: Tomato soup? *(He takes the top off a soup tureen and pulls out a can)* Have you got a can opener? *(He looks around, finds it on the table)* Oh, here it is. *(He starts to open the can)*
FLO: Oh, I'm really not hungry. Couldn't we just sit over here? *(She leads him away from the table)*

Two Shot—Flo and Hackenbush

She takes him in her arms. He embraces her.
FLO: I want to be near you. I want you to hold me. Oh, hold me closer! *(She squeezes him)* Closer! *(She squeezes some more)* Closer! *(And some more)* *(See film still 23.)*
HACKENBUSH: If I hold you any closer, I'll be in back of you.
FLO: You're so comforting. *(She runs her fingers through his hair)*
HACKENBUSH: The Hackenbushes were all like that. Shall we sit down and bat it around? *(He leads her to the couch. He sits down and gestures for her to sit next to him. He looks down at the couch waiting for her to sit, and begins to search through the rest of the couch for her. He looks under the cushion, then looks up and sees she's in his lap)* You're a little near-seated—a little nearsighted, aren't you? *(She LAUGHS)*

Medium Long Shot—Hackenbush and Flo

There is a KNOCK at the door.
HACKENBUSH: Oh, no—there's nobody else going to get in. I bolted the door.

There is a louder KNOCK at the door and the door falls forward into the room off its hinges. TONY *and* STUFFY, *dressed as paper hangers, carrying ladders and a great deal of equipment, enter.*

HACKENBUSH: Say, fun is fun!

STUFFY *carries one pail of paste in his hand and another balances on his head. He slops the paste wherever he goes.*

TONY: We come to hang the paper.

HACKENBUSH: How about hanging yourself instead?

TONY *and* STUFFY *set up their ladders on either side of the couch, climb up, and get ready to go to work. (See film still 24.)*

FLO *(gets up)* Well, I'm going to stay right here! *(She sits down again)*

HACKENBUSH: Thank-yo!

FLO: Ahhh!

Medium Close Shot—Tony
He's on the ladder.

TONY: That's right, Stuffy. You work on that side . . .

Medium Close Shot—Stuffy
He's on his ladder. He takes a brush out of his pocket and dips it into the pail on his head.

TONY *(offscreen)*: I work on this side, and we meet on the ceiling.

Two Shot—Flo and Hackenbush
HACKENBUSH *(to* TONY *and* STUFFY*)*: You'll wind up on the gallows, is my prediction.

Two Shot—Stuffy and Tony
They are papering the wall above HACKENBUSH *and* FLO.

Medium Shot—Flo and Hackenbush
The wallpaper drops down in front of them; each sheet of wall-paper is different.

HACKENBUSH *(sticking his head out around the paper)*: I must be a citizen. I just got my second papers!

Medium Shot—Stuffy and Tony
They are on the ladders over HACKENBUSH *and* FLO, *who are still on the couch.*
TONY: Looks like a wet track tomorrow, Stuffy.

Two Shot—Stuffy and Tony
They slop paper and paint on everything.

Medium Shot—Stuffy and Tony
They have completely covered HACKENBUSH *and* FLO.
TONY: I think, Stuffy, we put up a border.
MRS. UPJOHN *(offscreen)*: If he's got a woman in his room I'll see that he's dismissed . . .

Medium Shot—Hallway—Mrs. Upjohn and Whitmore
MRS. UPJOHN: . . . immediately!

Long Shot—the Room
MRS. UPJOHN *and* WHITMORE *enter.*
MRS. UPJOHN: What's going on? Good gracious!

Two Shot—Mrs. Upjohn and Whitmore
FLO *and* HACKENBUSH *are completely hidden from her.*
MRS. UPJOHN *(to* WHITMORE*)*: You're mistaken! There's no woman here!
WHITMORE: No?

Close Shot—the Couch
It's completely covered with wallpaper. WHITMORE *crosses to it and rips away the paper exposing* HACKENBUSH *all alone, reading a book.*
MRS. UPJOHN *(offscreen)*: Hugo!

Medium Shot—the Room
MRS. UPJOHN: What are you doing?

HACKENBUSH: I'm having the place done over. It'll make a lovely honeymoon suite.

Two Shot—Whitmore and Mrs. Upjohn
MRS. UPJOHN: Oh-h-h-h!

Medium Shot—the Room
TONY *unravels a roll of wallpaper in front of* MRS. UPJOHN.

Medium Close Shot—Hackenbush
HACKENBUSH *(on the couch)*: You better go, dear. We're tearing up the floor next.

Two Shot—Whitmore and Mrs. Upjohn
MRS. UPJOHN: Oh, my! Come, Mr. Whitmore, I've a few words to say to you!

Long Shot—the Room
WHITMORE *follows* MRS. UPJOHN *out.*

Medium Shot—the Couch
HACKENBUSH: Boys, you were wonderful!
He jumps up; the cushion falls off the couch and an infuriated
FLO *crawls out of the couch.*
HACKENBUSH: You saved my life!

Medium Shot—Hackenbush, Stuffy, Tony, and Flo
FLO *(to* HACKENBUSH*)*: I'll get even! You—you dirty, low-down, cheap, double-crossing snake!
HACKENBUSH: Thank-yo!
FLO: Oh! Oh!
She turns to leave and as she goes STUFFY *slaps a piece of wallpaper on her rear. She goes out and* HACKENBUSH, STUFFY *and* TONY *shake hands.*

Fade out

Fade in:
Exterior, Garden
Medium Shot—Hackenbush and Mrs. Upjohn
They are seated on a bench; his back is to her.
MRS. UPJOHN: Hugo . . . *(She moves closer)* . . . speak to me.
(He shakes his head "no") I said I was sorry about last night. I
never should have mistrusted you. Isn't there anything I can do
to make you forgive me?
HACKENBUSH: You could take over the notes from Miss Standish.
MRS. UPJOHN: Then would you forgive me?

Two Shot—Hackenbush and Mrs. Upjohn
HACKENBUSH: Well, it would help. *(He turns to her, takes her
hand)*
MRS. UPJOHN: Ohhh!
HACKENBUSH: Emily, I can't hide it any longer. I love you.
MRS. UPJOHN: Oh, Hugo!
HACKENBUSH: It's the old, old story. "Boy Meets Girl"—"Romeo
and Juliet"—Minneapolis and St. Paul.

Medium Shot—Hackenbush and Mrs. Upjohn
GIL *(enters from behind them)*: Mrs. Upjohn! Judy has . . .

Three Shot—Hackenbush and Mrs. Upjohn; Gil in Background
GIL: . . . the papers ready for you to sign.
MRS. UPJOHN: Later, later! Can't you see we're busy?
HACKENBUSH: It's all right, Emily. I'll remember where I left off.

Medium Long Shot—Hackenbush, Mrs. Upjohn, and Gil
HACKENBUSH *leads her back into the sanitarium.* GIL *follows.*
MRS. UPJOHN: Must they do that now? What in the world?

Medium Shot—Whitmore
He walks quickly across the patio.
WHITMORE: Mrs. Upjohn, just a moment, please. (HACKENBUSH,
MRS. UPJOHN, *and* GIL *cross and stop in front of him; a pompous*

206

man with a cane and a bowler hat enters behind WHITMORE) Mrs. Upjohn . . .

Medium Shot—All of Them
WHITMORE: May I present Dr. Leopold X. Steinberg of Vienna. DR. STEINBERG *bows to* MRS. UPJOHN *and* HACKENBUSH *tries to duck out behind her.* WHITMORE *stops him.*
MRS. UPJOHN: Doctor.
WHITMORE: And this is Dr. Hackenbush.
STEINBERG *(bows to* HACKENBUSH): Ah, Doctor!

Two Shot—Hackenbush and Steinberg
STEINBERG: I have a few questions I would like to ask you.
HACKENBUSH *(looking closer at his beard)*: I've got a question I'd like to ask you. Steinberg, what do you do with your old razor blades?
STEINBERG: Huh?!
WHITMORE *(offscreen)*: I've been telling . . .

Medium Shot—Steinberg, Mrs. Upjohn, and Whitmore
WHITMORE: . . . Dr. Steinberg about your unusual case.
STEINBERG: Yes. And I would like to know—what is this ailment—double blood pressure?

Close-up—Hackenbush
He raises his eyebrows.

Medium Shot—Steinberg, Mrs. Upjohn, and Whitmore
MRS. UPJOHN: Dr. Hackenbush tells me I am the only case in history. I have high blood pressure on . . .

Close-up—Hackenbush
He rolls his eyes.
MRS. UPJOHN *(offscreen)*: . . . my right side, and low blood pressure on my left . . .

207

Medium Shot—All Five of Them

MRS. UPJOHN: . . . side!

STEINBERG: Ha! There is no such thing!

MRS. UPJOHN: Oh!

STEINBERG: She looks as healthy as any woman I've ever met.

Two Shot—Hackenbush and Steinberg

HACKENBUSH: You don't look as though you ever met a healthy woman!

STEINBERG *(snarling)*: What?

WHITMORE *(offscreen)*: Gentlemen, gentlemen!

Medium Shot—All Five of Them

WHITMORE: There's a very simple way to settle this. Why not examine Mrs. Upjohn?

MRS. UPJOHN: Splendid! Splendid!

WHITMORE: Right this way, Mrs. Upjohn.

MRS. UPJOHN: Dr. Hackenbush will show you. Then I insist that you apologize to him. Come, Hugo. The idea!

> MRS. UPJOHN, DR. STEINBERG, *and* WHITMORE *go into the sanitarium.* HACKENBUSH *turns and runs out the other way.* GIL *follows him.*

Interior, Sanitarium
Medium Shot—Staircase

> HACKENBUSH *runs up the stairs followed by* GIL.

GIL: Hey, Doc! Where are you going?

Two Shot—Hackenbush and Gil

> GIL *grabs* HACKENBUSH *by the arm.*

GIL: Don't you realize if Steinberg examines that woman, we're through?

HACKENBUSH: I'm through right now!

GIL: Oh, no you're not! Now you got to get in there! Do anything! But stop Steinberg! Come on, you've got to hurry!

208

HACKENBUSH: I'll say I have to hurry. I'm hopping the next banana boat for Central America! *(He pulls away from* GIL *and runs upstairs)*

GIL: Hey, Doc! Where you going?

Dissolve to:
Interior, Hackenbush's Room
Medium Shot—Hackenbush and Gil

HACKENBUSH *runs into his room followed by* GIL.

GIL: Wait, Doc—wait!

The CAMERA PANS *over to* STUFFY *who is attacking the mattress with a knife and taking out the straw.*

Three Shot—Hackenbush, Gil, and Tony

TONY *has joined them. He's wearing a smoking jacket and his hat.*

HACKENBUSH: It's all right with me—go right ahead. I'm not sleeping here tonight.

Medium Shot—Stuffy

STUFFY *opens the closet door.* HI-HAT *is in the closet.* STUFFY *feeds him the straw.*

GIL *(offscreen)*: It's Hi-Hat!

Medium Shot—Gil, Tony, Hackenbush, and Stuffy

GIL *goes into the closet to talk to his* HORSE.

HACKENBUSH: Nonsense—that's a horse!

TONY: No, it's Hi-Hat. We hide him in the closet so the sheriff can't find him.

HACKENBUSH: Is that so? Well, he's not going to find me either, because I'm leaving here right away, boys. *(He takes his suitcase from under the bed)*

GIL: Doc! Doc—wait a minute now—

HACKENBUSH: No—I'll see you again sometime.

GIL: Please, Doc—

209

HACKENBUSH: Just as soon as I get my effects—*(He takes the smoking jacket off* TONY *and stuffs it into the suitcase)* Old Hackenbush isn't going to be with you very long! *(He runs to* STUFFY, *takes his tie off, stuffs the tie in the suitcase)*
GIL: Doc, you can't walk out on us like this!
HACKENBUSH *(takes his suitcase and moves quickly across the room)*: I'll say I can't, I'm going to run out!

Medium Close Shot—the Dresser
  HACKENBUSH *puts his suitcase on the dresser and begins filling it.*
GIL *(comes over to him)*: You can't go, Doc! If you walk out, where will Judy be?
HACKENBUSH: Well, she won't be in jail, and that's where I'll be if I stay here. Besides, what can I do?
GIL: You've got to stop the examination—somehow!
HACKENBUSH: Not today, I don't.
GIL: Are you a man or a mouse?
HACKENBUSH: You put a piece of cheese down there and you'll find out. Well, it's been nice seeing you! *(He puts his suitcase under his arm and moves toward the door)*
TONY: Oh, no you don't! *(*TONY *and* STUFFY *stop him)* If you leave, it's over my dead body!
HACKENBUSH: Well, that's a pleasant way to travel. Look out!
TONY: All right, now look, Doc! Look, Doc! You can't leave Miss Judy in a fix like this.
HACKENBUSH: I know, but the sheriff—
GIL: Doc—Doc! If you leave now, Judy loses the sanitarium.
HACKENBUSH: All right, I'll stay.
TONY: You gonna stay? *(*STUFFY *takes* HACKENBUSH'S *suitcase and* GIL *helps him off with his jacket)* I knew you'd do it, Doc.
GIL: Thanks, Doc!

Dissolve to:
Interior, Examination Room

Medium Shot—Hackenbush
He enters.

DR. STEINBERG *(offscreen)*: So next we will see—

Medium Long Shot—Mrs. Upjohn, Whitmore,
Steinberg, and Hackenbush
She is in an examination chair. WHITMORE *and* DR. STEINBERG
are next to her.

HACKENBUSH: Just a moment. Take your hands off her! A fine
doctor you are. Don't you know you're not supposed to touch a
patient without being sterilized? You don't see me running an
examination like that!

MRS. UPJOHN: No!

WHITMORE: That's true. And I think it would be very interesting
to see just how Dr. Hackenbush does conduct . . .

Medium Close Shot—Hackenbush
WHITMORE *(offscreen)*: . . . an examination.

MRS. UPJOHN *(offscreen)*: Splendid . . .

Medium Shot—Whitmore, Mrs. Upjohn, and Steinberg
MRS. UPJOHN: . . . splendid! Show them, Doctor.

Medium Close Shot—Hackenbush
HACKENBUSH: If you insist, I'll proceed.

Medium Shot—Hackenbush
He stands in front of three washbasins, dips his hands and lets
the water run to his elbows. He washes again. DR. STEINBERG
comes over to look, and he washes a third time, then a fourth.

HACKENBUSH *(to* STEINBERG*)*: In case you've never done it, this
is known as washing your hands.

Two Shot—Whitmore and Mrs. Upjohn
She looks embarrassed.

211

Two Shot—Steinberg and Hackenbush

STEINBERG *watches* HACKENBUSH *as he continues to wash his hands in the same manner.* HACKENBUSH *takes off his watch, put it on a worktable.* STEINBERG *stares at the watch.* HACKENBUSH *picks up the watch and puts it in the washbasin.*

HACKENBUSH: Rather have it rusty than missing. *(He washes his hands three more times, raises his arms in the air, and lets the water run down to his elbows)* You'll go a long ways to see prettier drippings than those.

STEINBERG: Why sterilization? After all, this is not an operation, you know.

HACKENBUSH: Not yet, but I may get hot and operate on everybody in the joint, including you!

Two Shot—Whitmore and Mrs. Upjohn

MRS. UPJOHN: Come, come, Doctor. Aren't you ready?

Medium Close Shot—Hackenbush

HACKENBUSH *(drying his hands on a towel)*: Now, Mrs. Upjohn, I guess I know my business. Of course, that's just a guess on my part, but at any rate, I know a thing or two about cleanliness, and that's more than I can say for that mountain goat standing there!

Medium Close-up—Steinberg

He's shocked and infuriated at the insult.

Two Shot—Mrs. Upjohn and Whitmore

MRS. UPJOHN: Come, Doctor, we're waiting.

**Long Shot—Whitmore, Steinberg, Mrs. Upjohn,
and Hackenbush**

HACKENBUSH: All right, if you insist, we'll proceed at once. Now, Mrs. Upjohn . . . *(He crosses to her)*

Closer—Angle—the Four of Them

HACKENBUSH: . . . I want you to take your arms and let them

wave through the air with the greatest of ease. *(He waves his own arms through the air with the greatest of ease; she imitates him)* Not too swiftly.

MRS. UPJOHN: Like that, Doctor?

HACKENBUSH: Yes, that's splendid.

MRS. UPJOHN: How long do you want me to do this, Doctor. *(She continues to flap her arms)*

HACKENBUSH: Just until you fly away.

MRS. UPJOHN *stops.*

Medium Shot—the Door

TONY *and* STUFFY, *dressed in surgical gowns and masks, enter.*

Two Shot—Hackenbush and Tony

HACKENBUSH *(privately)*: I told you guys to stay down in that room with those pigeons.

Three Shot—Tony and Stuffy, Steinberg Between Them

DR. STEINBERG *scowls at* STUFFY, *who cringes and walks to the washbasins. When* STUFFY *turns to wash his hands we see the back of his surgical gown which says:*

JOE'S

SERVICE

STATION

He dips his fingers in each of the three basins.

WHITMORE *(offscreen)*: Dr. Hackenbush!

Medium Shot—Whitmore, Mrs. Upjohn, and Hackenbush

She is still in the examining chair.

WHITMORE: Tell me, who sent for these men? *(He means* STUFFY *and* TONY*)*

HACKENBUSH: You don't have to send for them. You just rub a lamp and they appear.

Medium Shot—Hackenbush, Tony, Steinberg, and Stuffy

TONY *(shakes hands with* DR. STEINBERG*)*: My name is Steinberg.

STEINBERG: Steinberg?

HACKENBUSH (*privately to* TONY): Nix, nix, that's Steinberg. (*To the real* STEINBERG) Dr. Steinberg, by a strange coincidence, this is another Dr. Steinberg. (*TONY and* STEINBERG *bow to each other*) May I take my great friend and introduce my colleague and good friend, another Dr. Steinberg. (STEINBERG *turns to* STUFFY *and bows.* STUFFY *bows backward, hands on his hips. (See film still 25.) Behind him,* TONY *continues to bow to* DR. STEINBERG—*the real one*) This is a Dr. Steinberg—Dr. Steinberg. Dr. Steinberg, and—ah (*gesturing to* MRS. UPJOHN) Mrs. Steinberg.

Medium Close Shot—Hackenbush and Tony

HACKENBUSH *walks over to an anatomy chart.* TONY *turns to follow him. When he does we see that the back of his surgical gown reads:* "Brakes Relined."
HACKENBUSH: And Doctor, I'd like you to meet another Dr. Steinberg. (*He slaps the picture of the skeleton on the anatomy chart and it rolls up and reveals another anatomy chart*)

Long Shot—All Five of Them

WHITMORE: If Dr. Hackenbush is not going to continue the examination, Professor, may we have your diagnosis please?
STEINBERG (*takes a paper from his pocket and begins to read*): With pleasure. In all my years of medicine, I have never . . .
HACKENBUSH (*takes the paper from* STEINBERG *and tears it up*): In all your years of medicine, why you don't know the first thing about medicine.

In the background STUFFY *is fitting himself out with a head reflector.*

Two Shot—Hackenbush and Steinberg

STEINBERG *juts his chin out at* HACKENBUSH. (*See film still 26.*)
HACKENBUSH: And don't point that beard at me. It might go off!

Three Shot—Whitmore, Tony, and Mrs. Upjohn

WHITMORE: Dr. Steinberg. Do you remember your diagnosis?

Long Shot—All Five of Them
STEINBERG: Certainly. To begin with, her pulse is absolutely normal.

Medium Shot—Hackenbush, Stuffy, and Steinberg
HACKENBUSH: I challenge that.
STEINBERG: Challenge that? You take her pulse!
HACKENBUSH: Pulse?
STEINBERG: Take her pulse!
HACKENBUSH: I—I don't do any pulse work. I'm an acute diagnostician. *(to* STUFFY*)* Take her pulse! Take her pulse!

Medium Long Shot—All Five of Them
STUFFY *reaches for* MRS. UPJOHN's *pulse, takes her purse instead, puts in his pocket, and starts to walk away.*
MRS. UPJOHN: Oh, no, no, no. My purse, my purse, my purse, give me my purse. Oh!
HACKENBUSH *(stops him, takes the purse back, returns it to* MRS. UPJOHN*)*: You must forgive him—he doesn't spell very well, Mrs. Upjohn.
MRS. UPJOHN: Oh, dear, come gentlemen, let us begin. *(She takes* TONY *and* HACKENBUSH *by the hand)*
HACKENBUSH: Oh, you shouldn't have done that. *(Looking at his hands)* Now we're all unsterilized. What's the matter with you?
HACKENBUSH, TONY, *and* STUFFY *run to the washbasins.*

Medium Shot—Hackenbush, Tony, and Stuffy at the Washbasins
HACKENBUSH AND TONY *(sing)*: Down by the old mill stream, where I first met you. *(They wash their hands slowly and carefully)*
As they continue to sing, they walk in a small circle and dry their hands on the backs of each other's surgical gowns.
MRS. UPJOHN *(offscreen)*: Well, I must say I've seen quicker examinations.
HACKENBUSH: Maybe, but you'll never see a slippier one.

STEINBERG: Gentlemen, are you ready to proceed?

The THREE BOYS *cross to* MRS. UPJOHN *and* WHITMORE.

HACKENBUSH: We'll proceed immediately.

WHITMORE: Doctor, and what do you expect to do next?

TONY: The next thing I think we shall do isa wash our hands.

They run back to the washbasin.

MRS. UPJOHN: Oh!

HACKENBUSH: You're absolutely right.

MRS. UPJOHN *(offscreen)*: I have never seen . . .

HACKENBUSH AND TONY *(sing and wash their hands again)*: Down by the old . . .

Long Shot—All of Them

DR. STEINBERG *walks to the washbasins.*

HACKENBUSH AND TONY *(singing)*: . . . mill . . .

Medium Shot—Hackenbush, Tony, Stuffy, and Steinberg

STEINBERG *watches* HACKENBUSH, TONY, *and* STUFFY *as they wash.*

HACKENBUSH AND TONY *(singing)*: . . . stream . . .

MRS. UPJOHN *(offscreen)*: What is the matter with them?

They finish washing and STEINBERG *turns away from them.* TONY *dries his hands on* HACKENBUSH's *gown*; HACKENBUSH *on* STUFFY's *gown and* STUFFY *dries his hands on* DR. STEINBERG's *tails. (See film still 27.)*

STEINBERG: I don't know—what is this—get away from me. *(He pushes* STUFFY *away)*

HACKENBUSH: Everything is going to be all right. Nurse! *(Yelling)* Sterilization—sterilization!

Medium Shot—Door

THREE NURSES *enter with clean surgical gowns and hold them up.* HACKENBUSH, TONY, *and* STUFFY *each step into a gown, arms first.* TONY *and* STUFFY, *however, embrace the* NURSES. TONY *lets go but* STUFFY *hangs onto his* NURSE.

MRS. UPJOHN (offscreen): Oh, are they mad, or what is it?

HACKENBUSH: No, we're not mad, we're just terribly hurt, that's all.

MRS. UPJOHN (offscreen): Ohhh—ohhh!

HACKENBUSH (he separates STUFFY and the NURSE and as STUFFY pulls away he takes the NURSE's uniform with him): Hey, just a— just a moment. Just put the gown on, not the nurse, eh? Come here.

The nurse in her slip runs out screaming.

Medium Close Shot—Hackenbush

He is using the water carafe for a telescope.

HACKENBUSH: How is it a dame like that never gets sick.

Medium Shot—Mrs. Upjohn, Steinberg, and Stuffy

MRS. UPJOHN: But I am sick. Doctor, will you pay attention to me?

Two Shot—Hackenbush and Tony

HACKENBUSH *is still looking through his water-carafe telescope.*

TONY *stares through an ultraviolet light, using it as a telescope.*

HACKENBUSH: You'll have to get in line, Mrs. Upjohn. There's three orders ahead of you. *(He and TONY put their telescopes down on the desk and cross to the door)* Say, that nurse, poor girl, may be out there catching her death of cold. *(He looks into the doorway and* YELLS *down the hall)* Say, nurse—sterilization!

Medium Shot—Mrs. Upjohn and Steinberg

In the background, STUFFY *is playing with a large heat lamp.*

TONY *(offscreen)*: Hey, Doc, get away from there.

STEINBERG: This is absolutely insane.

Medium Close-up—Hackenbush

HACKENBUSH: Yes, that's what they said about Pasteur.

217

Medium Shot—Stuffy, Steinberg, and Tony

STEINBERG: Ach, this is ridiculous. Put the patient in a horizontal position.

**Medium Long Shot—Stuffy, Steinberg, Tony,
Whitmore, and Mrs. Upjohn**

STUFFY *and* TONY *flip* MRS. UPJOHN's *examination chair backward and turn it into an examination table but they push it too high and her feet are above her head.*
STEINBERG: Be careful, gentlemen.
MRS. UPJOHN: Oh, oh, oh!
They push the table even further until her legs are straight up in the air. STUFFY *dangles a sign from her feet:* "Men at Work."
HACKENBUSH *runs over, takes the sign off and throws it under* WHITMORE's *feet.* STUFFY *begins to drag* MRS. UPJOHN, *still turned upside down on the examination table, around the room.*

Medium Shot—Mrs. Upjohn, Stuffy, Tony, and Whitmore

The table and MRS. UPJOHN *have been forced into a right angle. She clings to the sides.* STUFFY *drapes a towel over her and begins to lather her face.* WHITMORE *tries to pull him away.* TONY *adds more towels and begins to shave her, using a blunt medical instrument for a razor. (See film still 28.)* STUFFY *takes a basin of water and begins to wash* MRS. UPJOHN's *hands.*
WHITMORE: Here, give me that. What are you doing? *(He takes the basin from* STUFFY*)*

Medium Long Shot—All of Them

The examination table is now back in its sitting position. HACKENBUSH *is shining* MRS. UPJOHN's *shoes.* STUFFY *is drying her hands and* TONY *is massaging her scalp.* DR. STEINBERG *passes in the background and* WHITMORE *is tearing his hair.* HACKENBUSH *stops shining* MRS. UPJOHN's *shoes and begins drying his own back and legs with the towel he was using to dry her shoes.* STUFFY *is cranking the examination table up and down.* MRS. UPJOHN's *legs fly in the air.*

Medium Close Shot—Steinberg, Whitmore, Hackenbush, Tony, and Stuffy
STEINBERG: But there is one indisputable test.
WHITMORE: What?
STEINBERG: The X-ray!
WHITMORE: The X-ray!

Medium Long Shot—All of Them
TONY, STUFFY, *and* HACKENBUSH *run around the room.*
TONY AND HACKENBUSH *(shouting)*: X-ray . . . X-ray . . .

Medium Close Shot—Stuffy
He pretends to shout and hands out newspapers.
TONY *(offscreen)*: X-tray! Extray! Extray!

Medium Long Shot—All of Them
STUFFY *slams a newspaper into* DR. STEINBERG'S *gut;* HACKEN-BUSH *slides a chair behind* DR. STEINBERG *and he collapses in it.* STUFFY *immediately begins cranking* MRS. UPJOHN *up and down again.*

Close Shot—Stuffy
He goes to the lever on the wall marked:
Overhead sprinklers
FIRE ONLY
He looks up at the ceiling and pulls the lever.

Medium Close Shot—the Overhead Sprinklers
The water begins to flow.

Medium Shot—Hackenbush, Tony, and Stuffy
They run across the room.

Medium Close Shot—Stuffy
He hides under the instrument stand. The water pours on it and knocks him down.

219

Medium Shot—Whitmore, Mrs. Upjohn, and Steinberg

They run to the door and start to leave.

Medium Shot—Corridor—Hi-Hat

He comes trotting down the corridor with PIGEONS *riding on his back.*

Medium Long Shot—Examination Room

HACKENBUSH *is standing on a desk.* DR. STEINBERG *turns and runs away from the door as* HI-HAT *trots into the room.* HACKENBUSH *jumps off the desk and onto* HI-HAT. *The* PIGEONS *flutter away.*

Medium Shot—Tony

He climbs upon the examination table and then jumps onto HI-HAT's *back. By now everything in the room is soaked and water begins to collect on the floor.*

Medium Long Shot—Examination Room

STUFFY *runs behind* HI-HAT *and jumps aboard joining* HACKENBUSH *and* TONY, *and* HI-HAT *trots out of the room.*

Fade out

Fade in:
Interior, Barn
Medium Close Shot—Stuffy

He is sprawled in the hay. He is holding his sock between his toes, drying it over a small bonfire. As the CAMERA PULLS BACK, *we see that he is surrounded by* HACKENBUSH, GIL, *and* TONY. *They all look miserable.*

GIL: Well, I certainly messed things up for Judy.

HACKENBUSH: You messed things up? I suppose Old Doc Hackenbush didn't throw a nasty monkey wrench.

TONY: You no throw the monkey wrench. I'm the guy that did it.

HACKENBUSH: Now listen, it was nobody's fault but mine. *(*STUFFY

220

sits up, WHISTLES *for attention, and points to himself)* Now I don't want any more arguments. It was all my fault.
TONY: I think he's right. It was his fault.
HACKENBUSH: Oh, it was my fault, eh? That's the thanks I get. I get you the first shower you had in years and you turn on me like a snake in the grass.
STUFFY WHISTLES; GIL *looks up.*
GIL: Someone's coming.
TONY: The sheriff!

Long Shot—Stuffy, Hackenbush, Gil, and Tony
They all get up, run, and hide.

Medium Shot—the Barn Door
It opens. JUDY *comes in carrying blankets.*

Medium Shot—Gil
He's hiding in a wagon. He peeks over the side, sees JUDY, *and smiles.*
GIL: Judy!

Medium Long Shot—Judy, Gil, Tony, Stuffy, and Hackenbush
GIL *jumps out of the wagon. They all run forward to greet* JUDY.
HACKENBUSH: You're the prettiest sheriff . . .

Medium Close Shot—All of Them
HACKENBUSH: . . . I've ever seen.
JUDY: Oh, you thought I was the sheriff?
HACKENBUSH: We're taking no chances.
JUDY: No, I just brought you these blankets. I thought it might make it a little more comfortable living out here.
STUFFY *takes all the blankets and jumps on them.*
TONY: Hey, get up—get up.
GIL: You should worry about our comfort after the way we bungled your affairs.

221

JUDY: You did your best, Gil.

GIL: Yes, but our best was none too good.

HACKENBUSH: Ah—tell me, Miss Standish, is the water still running in the examination room?

JUDY: Well, after tomorrow, I'm afraid that's Mr. Morgan's worry.

TONY: Morgan . . .

Three Shot—Tony, Gil, and Judy

TONY: . . . he no gotta the sanitarium yet.

GIL: Oh, a lot of things will happen before tomorrow.

JUDY: The sanitarium doesn't matter any more. Gil, you were right. I've been taking things far too seriously. It's much better this way. Now I can be free, I—I won't be tied down, I—I can enjoy myself and—and really laugh. *(She starts to cry)*

GIL: Oh, Judy, please.

Two Shot—Stuffy and Tony

TONY: Don't cry, Miss Judy. I feel sad, but I laugh—I laugh—Stuffy hesa laughing too. Look. Go on and laugh, Stuffy. *(TONY laughs; STUFFY opens his mouth to laugh and collapses in silent hysterics on TONY's shoulder)*

Medium Shot—All of Them

HACKENBUSH *looks very sad.*

TONY: Hey, look. Look—looka Hackenapussa—laugh—go ahead —laugh—

HACKENBUSH *(a feeble attempt)*: Hee-haw. Where did that come from? *(He looks around.* JUDY *runs to the window)*

Medium Shot—Judy at the Window

In the background several BLACK CHILDREN *are jumping rope in the yard.* GIL *joins* JUDY *and tries to comfort her.*

GIL: It can't be that bad, Judy.

Three Shot—Hackenbush, Tony, and Stuffy

HACKENBUSH *leads* TONY *and* STUFFY *out.*

Medium Shot—Gil and Judy at the Window

CHILDREN *are in the background.*

GIL: Look at those kids. Laughing—happy. Come on, you're just a kid. Laugh, be happy. *(He sings)*

The day is through . . .

Two Shot—Judy and Gil

He holds her and SINGS.

GIL:

The sun descending has brought to you
No happy ending—but you can face the setting sun and say
Tomorrow is another day.

Medium Shot—Another Part of the Barn—
Hackenbush, Tony, and Stuffy

HACKENBUSH *is reading the racing sheet.* TONY *is attending to* HI-HAT *and* STUFFY *is sitting by himself, looking glum.* HI-HAT *begins to nibble the straw on* STUFFY's *hat.* STUFFY *doesn't notice.*

GIL *(sings offscreen)*:

You've had your share of tears . . .

Medium Close-up—Judy

Shooting over GIL's *shoulder.*

GIL *(sings)*:

. . . and trouble.
But every care will be a bubble.

Two Shot—Gil Singing to Judy

GIL *(sings)*:

If you can face the setting sun and say.
Tomorrow is another day.

Medium Close-up—Stuffy

He looks around the barn door.

Two Shot—Gil singing to Judy

GIL *(sings)*:

> Some days a little rain must fall
> The skies can't all be blue.

Medium Close-up—Judy

Shooting over GIL*'s shoulder.*

GIL *(sings)*:

> Sometimes a little tear must fall
> To make a smile break through
> Today is gone, it's all behind you

Closer Two Shot—Gil and Judy

GIL *(sings)*:

> A brighter dawn will surely find you
> If you can face the setting sun and say
> Tomorrow is another day.

They embrace.

Exterior, Barnyard
Medium Close-up—Stuffy

He smiles, watching GIL *and* JUDY. *He* PLAYS *a few notes on a flute.*

Medium Shot—Stuffy, Gil, and Judy

He PLAYS *the flute to* GIL *and* JUDY. *They smile at him and he dances away from them to where the* CHILDREN *are playing. The* CHILDREN *follow him, tugging at his coat as he* PLAYS *the flute and dances for them.*

Medium Shot—Group of Young Boys

They are shooting craps on the ground. With the line of CHIL-
DREN *behind him,* STUFFY *dances over to the* BOYS.

BOY: O dice, don' come twosies—

CHORUS:

Di-a-di-a-di-a-di-a-da—twosies.
BOY: Baby needs new shoesies.

CHORUS:

Di-ah-di-a-di-a-di—shoesies.
BOY: Come on.
CHORUS: Yeah.
BOY: Seven.
CHORUS: Man.

Medium Close Shot—Stuffy

He TOOTS *his flute.*

Medium Close Shot—Three of the Boys

BOY *(points to* STUFFY*)*: Who dat man?

Medium Shot—Stuffy and Children

All the CHILDREN *follow* STUFFY *as he* PLAYS *the flute.*
CHORUS *(singing)*:

> Who dat man? Who dat man?
> It's Gabriel.
> Oh, Gabriel's blowin' 'cause he needs us.
> We gotta follow where he leads us.
> Blow that horn, Gabe, we is comin'.
> Followin' everywhere you go.

Medium Shot—Stuffy and the Children

They stop in front of a window. STUFFY *hears the* VOICES
SINGING *and looks in.*
WOMAN'S VOICE *(offscreen)*: Hal-le-lu-Hal-le-lu—

Medium Shot—Group of Black People
They are doing various domestic chores.
CHORUS: *(hums)*

Medium Close Shot—Stuffy and the Children
He approaches the window; they follow.
CHORUS: *(hums)*

Close Shot—Two Women Playing Checkers
CHORUS: *(hums)*

Medium Close-up—Man
He adjusts his collar and puts a derby on.
MAN AND CHORUS: Hal-le-lu—

Medium Long Shot—Group
CHORUS: *(hums)*

Medium Close Shot—Stuffy
He looks in the window, TOOTS *his flute.*

Medium Close-up—Man in Derby
He sees STUFFY.
MAN AND CHORUS: Who dat man?

Medium Shot—Stuffy and the Children
He comes to the door, followed by the CHILDREN, *and* TOOTS *his flute.*
CHORUS: Who dat man?

Medium Close-up—Stuffy
He PLAYS *his flute.*

Medium Shot—Group in Doorway
They all look at STUFFY.
GROUP: It's Gabriel, it's . . .

226

Close-up—Man with Derby
He looks at STUFFY.
MAN AND CHORUS: . . . Gabriel! Oh-h-h!

Medium Shot—Group and Stuffy
He dances away from the house. The CHILDREN *follow him.*
CHORUS:

      Gabriel's blowin' cause he needs us.
      We gotta follow where he leads us.

Medium Long Shot—High Angle—Stuffy and the Children
He dances through the barnyard, the CHILDREN *following him.*
CHORUS:

      Blow that horn, Gabe, we is comin'
      Followin' every . . .

Medium Shot—Stuffy and the Children
He leads them. He sees something offscreen and stops.
CHORUS: . . . where you go.

Medium Shot—Another Cabin
The cabin is crowded. The PEOPLE *are* SINGING *and dancing and having a party. The building shakes.*

Medium Close Shot—Inside the Cabin
A group of PEOPLE *are dancing; a* BAND *is in the background.*

Medium Close Shot—Stuffy and the Children
They are looking at the party. They walk toward it.

Medium Close Shot—Interior, House
STUFFY *is at the doorway looking in at the party.*

Medium Close Shot—the Party
The BAND *is* PLAYING *away.*

Medium Shot—Couples, Dancing
Medium Shot—Ivie Anderson
CAMERA *shoots past the* MUSICIANS *to* IVIE.
IVIE *(sings)*:

> Come on and jam-bo
> A jam what am-bo

Medium Close Shot—Stuffy Dancing in Doorway
He's enjoying himself immensely.
IVIE *(offscreen, singing)*: Jam, Mister Bambo.
STUFFY TOOTS *on his flute.*

Medium Shot—Piano Player; Other Musicians in Background
GROUP: Who dat man?

Medium Close Shot—Stuffy
He TOOTS *the flute.*

Close Shot—Man
He has a piece of straw in his mouth, PLAYING *the banjo. He looks at* STUFFY.
MAN AND GROUP: Who dat man?

Medium Shot—Stuffy in Doorway
The MAN *opens the door as* STUFFY TOOTS *the flute.*

Medium Close-up—Man with Straw in His Mouth
Others are in the background.
GROUP: Who dat man?
MAN: Why it's Gabriel!

Medium Close Shot—Stuffy and Another Man in Doorway
STUFFY PLAYS *the flute.*

228

Medium Shot—Stuffy and Group

STUFFY, *followed by the* GROUP, *dances away, having a great time.*

GROUP *(singing)*: Oh, Gabriel's blowin' cause he needs us . . .

Medium Long Shot—Stuffy; Everyone Following Him *(See film still 29.)*

They dance out of the yard, into the barn to where GIL *and* JUDY *are waiting for them.* TONY *and* HACKENBUSH *join them.*

CHORUS *(sings)*:

> We gotta follow where he leads us
> Blow that horn, Gabe, we is comin'
> Follow everywhere you go
> Oh, Gabriel's blowin' cause he needs us
> We gotta follow where he leads us
> Blow that horn, Gabe, we is comin'
> Follow everywhere you go.

Medium Long Shot—Stuffy and Group

He PLAYS *the flute in the middle of the barn and the* CHORUS *dances around him.*

CHORUS *(sings)*:

> Blow that horn—Gabriel
> Blow that horn—Gabriel
> Blow that horn—Gabriel

Medium Shot—Stuffy and Children

He is surrounded by them.

CHORUS *(sings)*:

> Blow—that—horn—

Medium Close Shot—Group

A GROUP OF ADULTS *blow their* TRUMPETS.

CHORUS: Blow that horn.

Medium Shot—Gil, Judy, Tony, and Hackenbush

GIL and JUDY *are on a haystack;* TONY *is at their feet, guzzling booze from a corn jug.* HACKENBUSH *is in the background. They're all watching the* SINGING *and dancing.*

GIL *(singing):*

> Tomorrow is another day.

STUFFY *joins them.*

Medium Close Shot—Gil, Judy, and Stuffy

STUFFY *reaches up to a calendar which is conveniently placed on a beam in the barn and begins tearing off the pages, making the days disappear.*

Medium Shot—Children

As they SING, STUFFY *joins them, dances in the center and conducts.*

CHORUS *(singing):*

> Tomorrow—za-zu-za-zu-za
> Tomorrow—za-zu-za-zu-za
> Tomorrow—za-zu-za-zu-za

STUFFY *conducts* IVIE's *solo. She comes to the center.* STUFFY *follows her.*

IVIE *(singing):*

> I gotta frown, you gotta frown—
> All God's chillun gotta . . .

Two Shot—Judy and Gil

They are listening.

IVIE *(offscreen, singing):* . . .

> frown on their face.

Medium Close Shot—Ivie; Others in the Background

She cuts loose.

IVIE *(sings)*:

> Take no chance with that frown
> A song and a dance turn it upside down
> Ho—ho—ho. Za-zu-za-zu.

Medium Close Shot—Ivie
IVIE *(singing)*:

> All God's chillun got rhythm
> All God's chillun got swing

Medium Close Shot—Ivie; Others in the Background
IVIE *(sings)*:

> Maybe haven't got money
> Maybe haven't got shoes
> All God's chillun got rhythm
> For to push away their blues—Yeah!

Medium Close-up—Ivie
IVIE *(sings)*:

> All God's chillun got trouble
> Trouble don't mean a thing

Medium Shot—Ivie; Others in the Background
IVIE *(sings)*:

> When they start to go ho-ho-ho de-ho
> All your troubles go 'way—say—
> All God's chillun got swing

Medium Shot—Musicians
They are PLAYING.

Medium Shot—the Children
They come running in.

231

Medium Long Shot—Ivie and Group

She is surrounded by the MUSICIANS *and* CHILDREN.

CHORUS:

> All God's chillun got rhythm.

Medium Close-up—Ivie

IVIE *(sings)*:

> Ba-da-la-da-da-da-da-da

Medium Shot—Ivie and Group

CHORUS *(sings)*:

> All God's chillun got rhythm.

IVIE *(sings)*:

> Da-da-la-da-da-do-yeah!
> Ba-da-la-da-oh yeah!

Close Shot—Ivie; Others in the Background

IVIE *(sings)*:

> Maybe haven't got money—ho
> Maybe haven't much swing

Medium Close Shot—Ivie; Others in the Background

IVIE *(sings)*:

> All God's chillun got rhythm for to push

CHORUS:

> For to push

IVIE:

> For to push

CHORUS:

> Push

IVIE:

> For to push

CHORUS:
          Push

IVIE:
          A . . .

CHORUS:
          A . . .

IVIE:
          . . . way

CHORUS:
          . . . way

IVIE:
          Their . . .

CHORUS:
          Their . . .

IVIE AND CHORUS:
          Blues. . . .

Medium Shot—Ivie and a Fat Man
They begin to jitterbug.

Close-up—Fat Man
He spins.

Close Shot—Musicians Playing
Long Shot—Everyone
STUFFY in the center; FOUR COUPLES jitterbug around him.

Medium Shot—a Couple
They are jitterbugging.

Medium Shot—Couples
They are jitterbugging.

Medium Long Shot—a Couple
Jitterbugging.

233

Medium Close-up—Girl
She twirls around.

Medium Close-up—Man
He dances to her.

Medium Shot—a Couple Jitterbugging
Long Shot—Couples Jitterbugging
Medium Shot—Couples Jitterbugging
Medium Long Shot—a Couple Jitterbugging
Medium Long Shot—Another Couple Jitterbugging
Medium Shot—Couple Jitterbugging
Medium Long Shot—Line of Couples Jitterbugging
Medium Shot—Couples Jitterbugging
Close Shot—Man Playing a Trumpet
Medium Long Shot—Couples Jitterbugging
Medium Shot—Couples Jitterbugging
The CAMERA PANS *with them as they dance off.*

Medium Shot—Stuffy
He picks up a pitchfork and dances forward; OTHERS *follow him.*

Medium Long Shot—Hackenbush
He is dancing in the background; CHILDREN *in front of him.* TONY *joins him and dances behind him.*

Medium Shot—Barn—Morgan, Whitmore, and Others
They look suspiciously at the DANCERS.

Medium Long Shot—Hackenbush, Tony, and Stuffy in Crowd
They see WHITMORE *and* MORGAN. *They run off. The* CHIL-DREN *continue to dance.*

Medium Close Shot—Tony, Hackenbush, and Stuffy
They crawl under a wagon and hide.

234

Medium Long Shot—Morgan and His Men

Shooting through the spokes of the wagon. They're still watching the dancing and looking for HACKENBUSH, TONY, *and* STUFFY.

Medium Shot—Hackenbush, Tony, and Stuffy

They are hiding under the wagon. HACKENBUSH *takes some axle grease and smears it on his face.*

CHORUS *(offscreen, singing)*:

> All God's chillun got rhythm.

Medium Close-up—Hackenbush and Tony

HACKENBUSH *smears more black grease on his face.*

Medium Close Shot—Whitmore, Morgan, and Sheriff

They watch.

CHORUS *(offscreen, singing)*:

> All God's chillun got rhythm.

Medium Close Shot—Hackenbush, Tony, and Stuffy

They look out from under the wagon.

Medium Shot—Hackenbush, Tony, and Stuffy

They crawl out from under the wagon, their faces covered with black grease. Only one side of STUFFY's *face is covered with grease. They wave their hands in the air and join the chorus dancing. They move to the front of the line for the finale.*

CHORUS *(singing)*:

> Hey—hey, ho—ho, hey—hey, ho—ho
> Cause all God's chillun got swing
> Swing—swing—swing.

Medium Shot—Morgan, Whitmore, and Sheriff

MORGAN APPLAUDS.

235

Medium Shot—Hackenbush, Tony, and Stuffy
They look up.

Medium Close-up—Chorus Man
MAN: It's de sheriff!

Medium Long Shot—Everyone
HACKENBUSH, TONY, *and* STUFFY *run into the* CROWD *and try to sneak out.*

Medium Shot—Everyone
SHERIFF: Hey, you! *(He reaches for* HACKENBUSH *and the* FAT MAN *gets in the way)*
FAT MAN: I ain't done nothin'!
HACKENBUSH *(running away)*: You've got nothing on me, my skirts are clean!
WHITMORE: Yeah? This letter from Florida says you're a horse doctor!

Medium Shot—the Barn—Hackenbush
WHITMORE, MORGAN, *and the* SHERIFF *run after him. Several bales of hay fall in their way.*
MORGAN: Put 'em all under arrest!

Medium Shot—Hi-Hat
HI-HAT *sees* MORGAN *and gets angry.*

Medium Long Shot—Morgan and His Men
He stops in front of HI-HAT *and calls to the* SHERIFF, *who is chasing* HACKENBUSH, TONY, *and* STUFFY.
MORGAN: They won't run, Sheriff, if you . . .

Medium Close Shot—Morgan
MORGAN: . . . break their legs.

236

HI-HAT *chases* MORGAN *who jumps in a hay wagon to get out of* HI-HAT'*s way.*
VOICE *(offscreen):* Get that horse—get that horse!

Medium Close Shot—Judy and Gil
They are looking into the barn.

Medium Long Shot—Hi-Hat
He has MORGAN *cornered in the hay wagon.*

Medium Close Shot—Judy and Gil
JUDY: What's wrong with that horse?
GIL: Why, he goes wild every time he sees Morgan or hears his voice.
GIL *lifts* JUDY *up over the rail and into the barn.*

Medium Long Shot—Hi-Hat and Morgan
HI-HAT *rears up, getting angrier.* MORGAN *looks scared.*
MORGAN: Get out!

Medium Close Shot—Hi-Hat
He moves back, trying to kick WHITMORE *who is hiding under the wagon.*

Medium Long Shot—Hi-Hat and Morgan
HI-HAT *continues to paw the ground and frighten* MORGAN.

Medium Long Shot—the Barn
The SHERIFF *and his* DEPUTY *chase* HACKENBUSH *and* TONY *around a bale of hay. They pin* TONY *down.*
DEPUTY: Hey, come here, you! Where do you think you're goin'?

Medium Shot—Morgan in Wagon
HI-HAT *kicks the wagon with his hind legs, splinters it, and* MORGAN *cowers into the corner.*

237

Medium Close Shot—Whitmore

Shooting through HI-HAT's *legs we see* WHITMORE *under the wagon.*

Medium Shot—Whitmore

HI-HAT *moves around the wagon and kicks viciously at* WHITMORE.

Medium Close Shot—Whitmore Under Wagon

He tries to get out but HI-HAT *won't let him.*

Medium Shot—Morgan, Whitmore, and Hi-Hat

MORGAN *is in the wagon;* WHITMORE *is underneath.* HI-HAT *keeps them at bay.*

Medium Shot—Sheriff and Tony

The SHERIFF *lunges at* TONY *but gets tangled in hanging ropes.*

Medium Close Shot—Stuffy

He is clinging to a hanging rope up in the rafters. He begins to swing on it.

Close Shot—Tony and Sheriff

The SHERIFF *is caught in the other end of* STUFFY's *rope. As* STUFFY *swings above him, the* SHERIFF *is pulled into the air (offscene)* STUFFY *descends into the scene as the* SHERIFF *is yanked up into the rafters.*

Medium Shot—Sheriff

He hangs by a rope in the rafters.
SHERIFF: You can't get away with this!

Medium Long Shot—Hi-Hat

He kicks the wagon again.

Medium Long Shot—Deputy and Hackenbush
HACKENBUSH *is running away: the* DEPUTY *stumbles over a barrel and falls flat on his face.*

Medium Long Shot—Hi-Hat
He continues to kick the wagon with his hind legs.

Medium Close Shot—Whitmore
He is under the wagon. HI-HAT's *legs crash into the wheel.*

Medium Close Shot—Hi-Hat
MORGAN *jumps out of the wagon and heads for a window.*

Medium Close Shot—Whitmore Under Wagon
MORGAN *(offscreen)*: Get the horse!

Medium Shot—Judy and Deputy
JUDY *is in the wagon. She picks up a horse collar.*

Two Shot—Judy and Deputy
She drops the horse collar over him.

Medium Shot—Hi-Hat and Whitmore
HI-HAT *kicks at* WHITMORE *under the wagon.*

Medium Close Shot—Hi-Hat's Legs
He kicks WHITMORE *and* MORGAN *who has now joined* WHITMORE *under the wagon.*

Medium Shot—Stuffy
He jumps up into the wagon.
VOICE *(offscreen)*: Hey, you!

Medium Close Shot—Stuffy
He jumps onto HI-HAT *and turns and starts to ride away.*
VOICE *(offscreen)*: . . . Stuffy!

Close Shot—Morgan and Whitmore Under Wagon
MORGAN: Stop that horse! Don't let him . . .

Medium Long Shot—the Barn
STUFFY, *riding* HI-HAT, *leaps over the low barn door.* GIL *and* JUDY *watch him go.*
MORGAN *(offscreen)*: . . . get out of here.
GIL: Did you see that horse jump?

Medium Long Shot—Hackenbush
He runs into a wire stall, still chased by the DEPUTY *waving a club.*
HACKENBUSH: And I'm doing some pretty fancy jumping, myself!

Medium Shot—Tony in the Rafters
He drops a chandelier.

Medium Shot—Hackenbush and Deputy
As the DEPUTY *runs after* HACKENBUSH, *the chandelier drops on his head knocking him down.*
SHERIFF *(offscreen)*: Let me off this rope!

Medium Close Shot—Morgan and Whitmore
Under the Wagon
MORGAN *starts to come out, bangs his head on the wagon and knocks himself out.*
SHERIFF *(offscreen)*: I'll throw you all in jail! Get me down!

Medium Shot—Sheriff
He is dangling in the ropes and still hanging.
SHERIFF: Take me out of here!

Medium Long Shot—the Barn
HACKENBUSH *and* TONY *run for the gate.* JUDY *and* GIL *join them and they run out.*

SHERIFF: This is no way to treat the law! You'll never get away with this. I'll get you!

Medium Close Shot—Deputy
He is sprawled in a corner, gagged, and with the horse collar binding him.

Medium Long Shot—Gil and Judy,
Followed by Hackenbush and Tony
They stand at the foot of a haystack, looking for HI-HAT.
GIL: There he goes!

Long Shot—Stuffy Riding Hi-Hat
They gallop across a field. HI-HAT *hurdles a fallen tree and then a low stone wall.*

Medium Long Shot—Tony, Gil, Judy, and Hackenbush
HACKENBUSH: If he's headed south I'd like to make a reservation.

Medium Long Shot—Stuffy on Hi-Hat
HI-HAT *hurdles a snappy looking roadster.*

Medium Shot—Gil, Judy, and Tony
GIL: Look at that horse! He cleared the automobile!

Medium Close Shot—Hackenbush
HACKENBUSH: I wish I could clear mine.

Medium Shot—Judy, Gil, and Tony
JUDY: Darling, perhaps that's why he never won a race! He's a jumper!

Two Shot—Gil and Judy
GIL: Am I a sap! I have a steeplechase horse and I don't know it!

241

Long Shot—Billboard
It says:

GRAND STEEPLECHASE
SPARKLING SPRINGS TRACK
Coming Saturday

STUFFY, *on* HI-HAT, *rides up to the billboard.* STUFFY *seems to think that* HI-HAT *can hurdle the billboard which is at least twenty feet high.* HI-HAT *stops suddenly in front.* STUFFY *sails through the billboard.* HI-HAT WHINNIES.

Fade out

Fade in:
Exterior, Race Track
Series of Dissolves:

A) *Horses Walking Around the Paddock*
B) *People Walking Around the Grounds*
C) *Crowd in Grandstand*
D) *Horses Walking on the Track to Starting Line*

Dissolve to:
Medium Shot—Large Blackboard
It reads:

SIXTH RACE
SPARKLING SPRINGS STEEPLECHASE
$50,000. ADDED 2 MILES 3 YRS & UP

CAMERA PANS DOWN *the list of names to:*

ADDED STARTERS
4804 HI-HAT——STUFFY

MORGAN *and* WHITMORE *are standing in front of the board.*
MORGAN: We're going to find that added starter and see that he doesn't start.
MORGAN *and* WHITMORE *exit.*

Dissolve to:
Exterior, Stables

242

Medium Long Shot—Morgan and Whitmore
They walk past the stables. The SHERIFF *enters with* HIS MEN.
MORGAN: They're not pulling any fast ones on me. Hi-Hat's not running in this race.
WHITMORE: Ah, but Hi-Hat isn't a jumper.
MORGAN: He was doing plenty of jumping in the barn last night.
WHITMORE: Hmmm, but he can't beat your horse.
MORGAN: Well, I'm not taking any chances. My money's riding on Ski-Ball and that's not all. If Hi-Hat wins, Stewart'll give that money to the girl and we can kiss the sanitarium good-by.
SHERIFF: Well, Morgan, you've got nothing to worry about. Hi-Hat's not on this track.
MORGAN: Well, you see that he doesn't get on. Put a man at every gate. If that nag slips by you it means your job.

Medium Shot—Awning—Hackenbush
He is sitting on the awning looking through field glasses. TONY *and* STUFFY *jump in and join him.*

Long Shot (Through the Field Glasses): Ambulance
It is driving through the gate entrance.

Three Shot—Hackenbush, Tony, and Stuffy
HACKENBUSH *holds the field glasses as* TONY *and* STUFFY *try to look through them at the same time. (See film still 30.)* HACKENBUSH *breaks the glasses in half and gives* TONY *and* STUFFY *each their own part.*
HACKENBUSH: Here, keep me posted.
TONY *and* STUFFY *look through their glasses.*

Medium Shot (Through One Lens of the Field Glass):
Gil and Judy
They are riding in the ambulance. As they pass, we see a sign on the ambulance:
SPARKLING SPRINGS RACE TRACK
AMBULANCE

Medium Shot—Tony, Stuffy, and Hackenbush

TONY: He made it! *(He means* GIL *and* JUDY*)* He made it! (STUFFY APPLAUDS *wildly)* Go ahead, Stuffy, go to it. Good luck!

STUFFY *runs up the awning and out.*

HACKENBUSH: Ride'em, cowboy! You know we're heading for the last lockup.

TONY: Come on, Doc, we get a reserved seat. *(They go up the awning and leave)*

Long Shot—Ambulance

It stops near a CROWD OF PEOPLE.

Medium Close Shot—Gil and Judy in Ambulance

She's in a nurse's outfit and he's in an ambulance driver's suit.

JUDY *(see sees* WHITMORE, MORGAN, *and the* SHERIFF *offscene and pokes* GIL*)*: Gil.

GIL *pulls his hat over his eyes so they can't see him.*

Medium Shot—Sheriff, Whitmore, Morgan, and Deputy

SHERIFF: I've got a man on every gate. There's no sign of 'em.

MORGAN: Well, see that there's no sign of 'em until after the race.

Medium Shot—Gil and Judy in the Ambulance

They are trying not to be noticed. There is a great rumbling in the rear of the ambulance.

GIL: Whoa! Hi-Hat!

Medium Shot—Sheriff, Morgan, Whitmore, and Deputy

They look over at the ambulance.

Medium Shot—Ambulance—Gil and Judy

HI-HAT *is shaking the ambulance. His activity causes the sign to fall off the ambulance. Underneath it, a sign says:* STANDISH SANITARIUM.

Three Shot—Whitmore, Sheriff, and Morgan

MORGAN: If you believe in signs, Sherlock, take a look at that ambulance.

MORGAN, *the* SHERIFF, *and* WHITMORE *start running toward the ambulance.*

Medium Long Shot—Ambulance and Crowd

MORGAN, *the* SHERIFF, *the* DEPUTY, *and* WHITMORE *run toward the ambulance.*

Medium Shot—Ambulance

The SHERIFF *and* TWO DEPUTIES *run up, see* JUDY *in the front and they move around toward the back.*

Medium Shot—Ambulance

GIL *tries to stop the* SHERIFF *and the* TWO DEPUTIES *from opening the ambulance.*

GIL: Now wait a minute, Sheriff!

SHERIFF: Don't you start anything, Stewart!

Medium Close Shot—Judy

She has come around to the back of the ambulance.

Medium Shot—Ambulance Doors

The SHERIFF *opens them and sees* HI-HAT *in the back. He puts* GIL *in the ambulance with* HI-HAT *and shuts the doors.*

SHERIFF: Ha-ha! We'll put this baby under lock and key. *(To a* DEPUTY*)* You keep searching for those other mugs.

Medium Close Shot—Judy

She takes off her cape and nurse's cap.

Medium Shot—Upper Grandstand—Tony and Hackenbush

They look down at the track.

Medium Long Shot—Stairway—Stuffy

He looks up at TONY *and* WHISTLES.

Medium Shot—Hackenbush and Tony at Railing

TONY: Stuffy! What's the matter?

Medium Long Shot—Stairway—Stuffy

He opens his arms and gestures wildly. He turns, takes a top hat from a PASSERBY *and throws it away. The* MAN *chases* STUFFY.

TONY *(offscreen)*: What's the matter? Stuffy!

Two-Shot—Hackenbush and Tony

TONY: Hi-Hat's gone.

Medium Shot—Upper Grandstand—Tony and Hackenbush

The BUGLE *sounds post time.*

TONY: The race is going to start.

HACKENBUSH: They won't start the race till we find Hi-Hat!

Dissolve to:
Interior, Stable
Close Shot—Can of Harness Soap

TONY *digs out a paddleful of soap.*

Close Shot—Tony

He is standing near a wall with the paddleful of soap.

Medium Shot—Tony

He flips the soap under a saddle onto ONE OF THE HORSES *just as* TWO GROOMS *are saddling him.*

Dissolve to:
Exterior, Track
Medium Shot—Morgan, Whitmore, and a Jockey

MORGAN *(To the* JOCKEY*)*: Now listen, son, you're riding this race to win. I don't care what you do, as long as the judges don't see you doing it.

Long Shot—Morgan and Whitmore
They watch the JOCKEY *mount his* HORSE. CROWDS *of* PEOPLE *are in the background.*
VOICE *(offscreen)*: All right men, go to your horses.

Close Shot—the Jockey; Morgan and Whitmore in Background
The JOCKEY *starts to mount but* TONY'S *harness soap was there first and the* JOCKEY *and the saddle falls to the ground at* WHITMORE *and* MORGAN'S *feet.*

Long Shot—All the Jockeys
They are all falling to the ground as they try to mount their HORSES.

Close Shot—a Jockey on the Ground
The harness soap falls on his face.

Close Shot—Morgan's Jockey
JOCKEY *(holding a handful of harness soap)*: Soap!

Dissolve to:
Medium Shot—Side of Grandstand—
Bugler; Stuffy in Background
The BUGLER *holds his bugle to his mouth.* STUFFY *is behind a tree, watching him.*

Medium Close-up—Stuffy
He watches the BUGLER.

Medium Close Shot—Bugler
He blows on the bugle but no sound comes out. Instead, a large soap bubble forms at the end of the horn. The bubble bursts. The BUGLER *looks puzzled.*

Medium Close-up—Stuffy
   He gets another idea and runs off.

Dissolve to:
Medium Shot—Horses
   They move toward the track.
ANNOUNCER'S VOICE *(offscreen)*: We are sorry for the delay, but the horses are now coming on the track.

Long Shot—Three Judges on Platform
A JUDGE: Twenty-five minutes late.
ANNOUNCER'S VOICE *(offscreen)*: The horses are parading . . .

Long Shot—Horses on Track; Crowd in Foreground
ANNOUNCER'S VOICE *(offscreen)*: . . . past the grandstand. Only eleven are headed postward.

Medium Long Shot—Grandstand
   STUFFY *walks to the background, turns on a conveniently placed wind machine. Hundreds of hats blow in the air and onto the track.*
ANNOUNCER'S VOICE *(offscreen)*: Hi-Hat, the added starter is missing. This is the third running of the fifty-thousand-dollar . . .

Long Shot—Morgan and Whitmore in Their Box
   They hold on to their hats. PEOPLE *are* SCREAMING *as their hats fly off.*
ANNOUNCER'S VOICE *(offscreen)*: . . . added jumping classic.

Long Shot—the Crowd
   Hats fly onto the track.
ANNOUNCER'S VOICE *(offscreen)*: What's this? What's this?

Medium Long Shot—Three Judges on Platform
   They lose their hats.

Long Shot—the Track
More hats fly over. The HORSES *rear up.*

Medium Shot—Stuffy
He sits in the branches of a tree.
TONY *and* HACKENBUSH *run over to him.*
TONY: Hey, Stuffy! Stuffy!

Three Shot—Stuffy, Tony, and Hackenbush
TONY *and* HACKENBUSH *are on the ground;* STUFFY *is still in the tree.*
TONY: Did you find him? Did you find the ambulance? *(*STUFFY *shakes his head "no")* Well, keep on looking. We know it came in.

Exterior, Track
Medium Long Shot—Race Track
ATTENDANTS *are picking up the hats and tossing them back to the* CROWD.
ANNOUNCER'S VOICE *(offscreen)*: Now that the storm of hats has subsided, the stewards have ordered the track cleared for action.

Medium Shot—Morgan's Box
MORGAN: Get all your men. Don't stop searching till you find 'em.
A COP *brings* MORGAN *and* WHITMORE *their hats.*
GUARD: Here you are, boss.
ANNOUNCER'S VOICE *(offscreen)*: And the hats are being returned to the customers. And the horses are back . . .

Medium Shot—Morgan and Whitmore
They put on their hats. WHITMORE*'s is much too small for him and he throws it down in disgust.*
ANNOUNCER'S VOICE *(offscreen)*: . . . on parade toward the starting point.

Medium Shot—the Three Judges on Platform
They put on their hats.

ANNOUNCER'S VOICE *(offscreen)*: They are going back now, up to the starting post.

Close-up—Man in Crowd
He puts on a hat that is much too small for him.
ANNOUNCER'S VOICE *(offscreen)*: And everyone is getting his own hat . . .

Close-up—Another Man in Crowd
He puts on a derby that's much too large for him.
ANNOUNCER'S VOICE *(offscreen)*: . . . we hope!

Long Shot—the Horses
They are lining up at the starting line.
ANNOUNCER'S VOICE *(offscreen)*: The horses are coming back to the starter now. They are very fractious. They are . . .

Medium Shot—No-Parking Sign
TONY *runs up and picks it up and smashes it against a tree and turns it into a "Parking" sign.*
ANNOUNCER'S VOICE *(offscreen)*: . . . giving the boys quite a bit of trouble after the excitement. First Legion is acting very badly. Sun Helmet is . . .

Dissolve to:
Close Shot—Tony
He is holding the parking sign as he rides on an auto bumper.
TONY: Free parking. Here you are. Free parking.

Long Shot—Tony
He jumps off the bumper of the car. A great many other cars are around him.
TONY: Get your free parking. *(He motions to other cars to follow)* Come on—come on . . .

250

Long Shot—Starter on Platform
The HORSES *line up.*
ANNOUNCER'S VOICE *(offscreen)*: They're coming up this time. Almost in an even line.

Long Shot—Grandstand
Shooting down at the entrance tunnel we see dozens of cars driving onto the track. The CROWD *watches, confused.*
ANNOUNCER'S VOICE *(offscreen)*: The starter has his flag up. And it looks . . .

Medium Shot—the Three Judges
They look at the cars pulling onto the track.
A JUDGE: Look! Look! Look!
ANNOUNCER'S VOICE *(offscreen)*: Wait a minute.

Long Shot—the Track
Cars begin driving onto the track.
ANNOUNCER'S VOICE *(offscreen)*: What is this? A horse race or an automobile race?

Medium Shot—the Starter and Horses
He sees the cars and turns to look up at the JUDGES' *stand for directions. The* HORSES *rear up.*

Long Shot—the Track
The cars drive along the track.

Medium Long Shot—Three Judges on Platform
A JUDGE: Hold those horses!

Long Shot—Starter
STARTER: Hold it! Hold it!

Medium Long Shot—the Track
More cars drive up on the track.

251

Medium Close Shot—the Starter

He throws his flag down in disgust. Then he throws his hat away.

Long Shot—the Entrance Tunnel

More cars drive up on the track.

Close Shot—Hackenbush

He sits on a fence, watching the cars drive past.
HACKENBUSH: Plenty of room! Nice fresh parking today! Right ahead, folks!

Long Shot—the Track

The cars are jammed. COPS *and* ATTENDANTS *try futilely to straighten things out.*

Medium Shot—the Horses

They move in a snarl, excited and confused.

Long Shot—the Entrance Tunnel

THREE COPS *try to stop more cars from coming onto the track.*

Medium Shot—Hackenbush

As TWO COPS *run toward him, he jumps off the fence and onto a passing car.*

Close Shot—Hackenbush

He rides on the running board of a limousine.

Medium Long Shot—the Entrance Tunnel

COPS *run to the back of the tunnel.*

Close Shot—Hackenbush

He is riding on the running board.

Medium Shot—Hackenbush

He opens the back door of the car, crawls on the floor past THREE WOMEN PASSENGERS.

HACKENBUSH: You girls got anything on for tonight? *(And he crawls out the other side)*

Medium Long Shot—Hackenbush

He ducks in among the cars.

Medium Shot—Stalled Cars

TONY, *carrying the parking sign, climbs onto the top of a car. The* COPS *chase him.*

COP: Hey, get out of here!

Medium Long Shot—Snarled Cars

HACKENBUSH *jumps from one roof to another roof with the* COPS *chasing him.*

Medium Long Shot—the Track

More cars drive on.

Medium Long Shot—the Entrance Tunnel

HACKENBUSH *continues over the car roofs.* PEOPLE *grab at him and knock him down. He jumps off the roof and runs among the cars. Then he jumps back onto a roof of a car.*

Medium Shot—Hackenbush

He rolls off the roof of one car and down toward the ground.

Medium Shot—Hackenbush

He appears between two cars. He runs out with COPS *chasing him.*

Medium Long Shot—the Entrance Tunnel

TONY *runs in and joins* HACKENBUSH, *who is also running.*

HACKENBUSH: Going my way?

Medium Long Shot—the Track

TONY *and* HACKENBUSH *run out pursued by the* COPS. *There are dozens of jammed cars as the* DRIVERS *try to straighten things out.*

Medium Long Shot—Three Judges on Platform

The JUDGES *are frantic.*

A JUDGE: Get 'em out of there! Get em out of there!

Long Shot—the Track

The cars try to back out of the track.

Medium Shot—Clubhouse

PEOPLE *stand on the porch.* STUFFY *enters and* WHISTLES. HACKENBUSH *and* TONY *join him. All three of them run.*

TONY *(running)*: Hey Stuffy? Did you find Hi-Hat?

STUFFY *shakes his head "no."*

HACKENBUSH *(running)*: Well, keep looking, he must be around somewhere.

Long Shot—Highway

The ambulance drives along the road and stops near a car wreck.

Medium Shot—Ambulance

The SHERIFF, *who was driving, jumps out.*

Medium Shot—Judy

Shooting toward the wreck we see JUDY *lying on the ground.*

Medium Shot—Ambulance

The SHERIFF *runs to the back, opens the door.* GIL *and* HI-HAT *are still in the back.*

SHERIFF: Get that horse out of there! There's been a terrible wreck. Come on, hurry up! Help me!

254

Medium Long Shot—Near the Wreck

The SHERIFF *runs down to where* JUDY *is sprawled in the grass.* GIL *runs to her and kneels next to her.*

Medium Close Shot—Gil and Judy

JUDY *winks at* GIL *and tells him* "Shush." *He smiles and picks her up.*

Medium Shot—Near the Wreck

GIL *picks up* JUDY. *The* SHERIFF *is struggling with a stretcher in the background.*

GIL: Come on, Sheriff, we've got no time to lose. *(*GIL *carries* JUDY *toward the ambulance)*

SHERIFF: Is she alive?

Medium Shot—Ambulance

GIL *gives* JUDY *a quick kiss when the* SHERIFF *isn't looking and carries her into the ambulance. The* SHERIFF *throws the stretcher back in, goes to the front of the ambulance and* GIL *partially closes the ambulance door. When the* SHERIFF *is gone, he opens the doors and he and* JUDY *climb out.*

GIL: Get going, Sheriff! I'll take care of her.

SHERIFF: All right.

Medium Long Shot—Ambulance

It drives away. GIL *runs over to* HI-HAT.

Long Shot—the Track

All the cars are gone now.

STARTER: Come on—come on.

ANNOUNCER'S VOICE *(offscreen)*: Well, here we are again.

Medium Shot—Three Judges on Platform

They look through their field glasses.

ANNOUNCER'S VOICE (offscreen): The horses are coming up. They're not in too even a line.

A JUDGE: Come on, before something else happens.

Medium Long Shot—the Track
The STARTER holds up the flag.

STARTER (to ONE OF THE JOCKEYS): Turn your horse around!

ANNOUNCER'S VOICE (offscreen): They're very nervous and skittish—but it looks like he's . . .

Medium Shot—Three Judges on Platform
They look nervous.

ANNOUNCER'S VOICE (offscreen): . . . going to send them away.

Medium Long Shot—the Track—Starter

STARTER: Now, easy, easy. . . . Go!

ANNOUNCER'S VOICE (offscreen): Yes. Yes . . . and there they go!

Medium Shot—Three Judges on Platform

A JUDGE: At last!

Medium Shot—the Track—Hackenbush and Tony
They hide behind a bush just outside a curve in the track.

ANNOUNCER'S VOICE (offscreen): Demon is third. Sun Helmet is . . .

Medium Shot—the Horses, Racing

ANNOUNCER'S VOICE (offscreen): . . . fourth and Green Goddess—there's Ski-Ball . . .

Medium Shot—Hackenbush and Tony
They move to the rail.

ANNOUNCER'S VOICE (offscreen): . . . showing the way in the center of the track—by two lengths—at least . . .

Medium Long Shot—Section of the Track—
Hackenbush and Tony
They lift up the rail and rearrange the track.
ANNOUNCER'S VOICE *(offscreen)*: Sun Helmet is second—Green
Goddess is third . . .

Long Shot—the Horses Racing
ANNOUNCER'S VOICE *(offscreen)*: . . . and Flying Demon is fourth.

Medium Long Shot—Hackenbush and Tony
They rearrange the rail so that the HORSES *ride into the field.*
ANNOUNCER'S VOICE *(offscreen)*: Now they're going around the
first turn with Ski-Ball in front by two lengths. First Legion is
second by a head—wait . . .

Medium Close Shot—the Starter
He watches the HORSES *leave the track. He's confused.*
ANNOUNCER'S VOICE *(offscreen)*: . . . a minute! What is this?

Medium Shot—the Three Judges
They're stunned.
JUDGES: What is . . . what's happened now?

Medium Shot—Morgan and Whitmore
They're furious.
MORGAN: Get me the riot squad.
WHITMORE *leaves.*
MRS. UPJOHN *(joining* MORGAN *in his box)*: Oh, Mr. Morgan,
don't get excited.
MORGAN: I'm not excited! Shut up!
MRS. UPJOHN: Oh!

Long Shot—the Track
The HORSES *trot back onto the track.*

257

Close Shot—the Starter

He watches it all, still confused.

ANNOUNCER'S VOICE *(offscreen)*: Quiet please. Your attention . . .

Long Shot—the Horses

They move farther onto the track.

ANNOUNCER'S VOICE *(offscreen)*: Quiet please. Your attention.

Exterior, Stables
Long Shot—Gil

He pulls up in a horse-drawn water wagon. STUFFY *runs up to him.*

GIL: Stuffy!

ANNOUNCER'S VOICE *(offscreen)*: The stewards have ruled this . . .

Medium Close Shot—Gil and Stuffy

GIL *is at the reins of the water wagon.* STUFFY *starts to climb up to join him.*

Medium Shot—Gil

He gets down from the wagon.

ANNOUNCER'S VOICE *(offscreen)*: . . . and have ordered the horses back to the starting post. Now, ladies and gentlemen . . .

Close Shot—Gil

He starts to unhitch the HORSES *from the wagon.* TWO COPS *approach.*

GIL: Stuffy! Scram!

Medium Shot—Gil and Stuffy

GIL *helps* STUFFY *jump on* ONE OF THE HORSES *and he gallops away pulling the water wagon. The* COPS *jump onto the back of the water wagon.*

ANNOUNCER'S VOICE *(offscreen)*: . . . if you will all please be patient . . . who knows, we may yet have a horse race this afternoon. The horses . . .

Medium Long Shot—the Track
> *The* HORSES *come back to the starting line to start the race again.*

ANNOUNCER'S VOICE *(offscreen)*: . . . are back at the starting point. And now the boys are turning them about.

Medium Long Shot—the Track—Stuffy
> *He rides the water wagon onto the track. The* COPS *are still on the back.*

ANNOUNCER'S VOICE *(offscreen)*: They are very nervous—very fractious—they're having . . .

Medium Shot—Morgan's Box
> MORGAN *and* MRS. UPJOHN *watch, stunned, as the water wagon pulls up to the track.*

ANNOUNCER'S VOICE *(offscreen)*: . . . quite a bit of trouble.

Medium Close Shot—the Three Judges
JUDGES: Get that wagon off of here.

Medium Long Shot—Stuffy
> *He races the water wagon down the track. The* COPS *still cling to the back of the wagon.*

Medium Close Shot—Stuffy
> *He is riding the* HORSE.

Medium Close Shot—the Cops
> *They are riding on the back of the water wagon.*

Medium Shot—Stuffy
> *He turns to crawl back over the* HORSE *to the wagon.*

Close Shot—Stuffy

He pushes the water-pipe lever.

Close Shot—Cops on Wagon

The water from the pipe hits both Cops in the face and knocks them off. They fall to the ground.

Medium Shot—Stuffy

He laughs and turns to get back on the Horse.

Medium Long Shot—Stuffy

He gets back on his Horse.

Close Shot—Stuffy

He throws away his battered top hat.

Medium Shot—Morgan

He is looking through his field glasses.

Close Shot—Stuffy

He puts on his racing cap.

Medium Close Shot—the Three Judges

A JUDGE: Get off of there!

Medium Long Shot—the Track

As STUFFY passes the JUDGES' platform he breaks his mount loose from the water wagon and flashes ahead. He's riding HI-HAT!

Medium Shot—Morgan Box

The SHERIFF and his DEPUTIES enter.

SHERIFF: Hi-Hat . . . Hi-Hat, he got him away from me. I don't know where he is.

MORGAN: Who do you think that is, stupid? Take a look at the track!

260

Medium Close Shot—Stuffy

He is now in his jockey racing silks, hurrying HI-HAT *to the starting line.*

Medium Close Shot—the Three Judges

A JUDGE: Number seven!
ANOTHER JUDGE: Why, that's Hi-Hat!

Long Shot—the Track

HACKENBUSH *and* TONY *hide behind a hedge to watch the start of the race. The* STARTER *drops his flag. The race begins.*
ANNOUNCER'S VOICE *(offscreen)*: They're coming up to the start this time—and the starter has his flag raised—and there they go! Ski-Ball is going to the front . . .

Long Shot—the Rail

STUFFY *rides in on* HI-HAT, *hurdles the rail and joins the race.*
ANNOUNCER'S VOICE *(offscreen)*: . . . But here comes Hi-Hat! He's over the fence—he's on the track . . .

Medium Close Shot—Stuffy Riding Hi-Hat

He is trying to catch up with the race.
ANNOUNCER'S VOICE *(offscreen)*: . . . and he's in the race!

Medium Shot—Tony and Hackenbush

They are CHEERING *him on.*

Medium Shot—Stuffy on Hi-Hat

He's racing his heart out trying to catch up.
ANNOUNCER'S VOICE *(offscreen)*: Ski-Ball is going to the front. First Legion is second. Flying Demon is third.

Medium Shot—Mrs. Upjohn, Whitmore, and Morgan

They are watching the race intently; MORGAN *through his field glasses.*
ANNOUNCER'S VOICE *(offscreen)*: Sun Helmet is fourth . . .

Medium Long Shot—Stuffy Riding Hi-Hat

He is almost up to the other HORSES.

ANNOUNCER'S VOICE *(offscreen)*: . . . and Green Goddess is fifth. Now there goes Hi-Hat . . .

Medium Shot—Stuffy Riding Hi-Hat

He begins to pass the other HORSES. *(See film still 31.)*

ANNOUNCER'S VOICE *(offscreen)*: . . . he's moving up between horses!

Medium Long Shot—the Horses

STUFFY *moves to the head of the race.*

ANNOUNCER'S VOICE *(offscreen)*: And look at him go! And he's moving up there at the leaders—and it's Ski-Ball still in front—but now here comes Hi-Hat between horses—and now he's challenging the leader!

Medium Close Shot—Morgan's Jockey on Ski-Ball

He sees STUFFY.

Medium Close Shot—Stuffy Riding Hi-Hat

ANNOUNCER'S VOICE *(offscreen)*: There's Ski-Ball in front by a length . . .

Medium Close-up—Morgan's Jockey

ANNOUNCER'S VOICE *(offscreen)*: . . . and one half. Hi-Hat is second by three . . .

Medium Shot—All the Horses Racing

ANNOUNCER'S VOICE *(offscreen)*: . . . quarters of a length. First Legion is third by a length and one half—and Flying Demon is fourth. Now Ski-Ball is . . .

**Medium Close Shot—High in the Grandstand—
Tony and Hackenbush**

JUDY *and* GIL *join them.*

ANNOUNCER'S VOICE *(offscreen)*: . . . going out on the edge and they're coming to the . . .

Long Shot—the Horses

They move toward a low stone wall. They all jump except HI-HAT.

ANNOUNCER'S VOICE *(offscreen)*: . . . first barrier now. And Ski-Ball . . .

Medium Close Shot—Stuffy on Hi-Hat

HI-HAT *refuses to jump.*

ANNOUNCER'S VOICE *(offscreen)*: . . . takes it, but . . .

Medium Close-up—Stuffy on Hi-Hat

STUFFY *shows him a picture of* MORGAN.

ANNOUNCER'S VOICE *(offscreen)*: . . . Hi-Hat refuses. He's turning back—but wait a minute! Wait a minute—he's going to try it . . .

Medium Long Shot—Stuffy on Hi-Hat

HI-HAT *turns, rears up, and goes right over the wall.*

ANNOUNCER'S VOICE *(offscreen)*: . . . once more. There he goes! He's going after it this time—and he's over!

Medium Close Shot—Gil, Judy, Hackenbush, and Tony

GIL: Oh! Your idea worked, Judy!

ANNOUNCER'S VOICE *(offscreen)*: He's over—and Ski-Ball's still . . .

Medium Close Shot—Stuffy

He kisses the picture of MORGAN *and the picture blows out of his hand.*

ANNOUNCER'S VOICE *(offscreen)*: . . . in front by two lengths!

Close-up—Picture of Morgan

It falls to the ground.

Medium Close Shot—Gil, Judy, Hackenbush, and Tony
JUDY: Oh, he's lost Morgan's picture!

Medium Long Shot—Stuffy Riding Hi-Hat
He passes most of the other HORSES.
ANNOUNCER'S VOICE *(offscreen)*: He's picking up his heels—and he's going up on the outside this time—and here he is at the leader!

Medium Close Shot—Gil, Judy, Hackenbush, and Tony
JUDY: Can you shout like Morgan?
HACKENBUSH: No, but Morgan can. *(He leaves and* TONY *follows him)*

Medium Long Shot—the Horses
Medium Close Shot—Stuffy and Morgan's Jockey
They are neck and neck.

Medium Shot—Mrs. Upjohn, Whitmore, and Morgan
They are watching the race.
MRS. UPJOHN: Oh! Something's happened to the loud-speaker!

Close-up—Microphone
It has been dropped into a piece of newspaper.

Medium Shot—Tony
He is holding the microphone. He starts up the steps into the grandstand.

Medium Long Shot—the Horses
Long Shot—the Horses
They approach another barrier.

Medium Close Shot—Stuffy on Hi-Hat
He searches for the picture of MORGAN *that he'll need to get* HI-HAT *over the next wall. (See film still 32.)*

264

Medium Close Shot—Morgan and Tony
MORGAN *is looking through the field glasses.* TONY *grabs them and looks through.*
TONY: Let me take a look.
MORGAN: Give me those glasses! *(Grabbing them back)* You've got your—

Medium Close Shot—Gil, Judy, and Hackenbush
They are standing by the loud-speaker.
MORGAN'S VOICE *(over the loud-speaker)*: It's you!

Close-up—Hi-Hat
He rears when he hears MORGAN'S VOICE.

Close-up—Stuffy
HI-HAT *pulls away.*

Medium Long Shot—the Horses
They go over the barrier.

Close Shot—Stuffy
He nods toward the stands in thanks.

Close Shot—Gil, Judy, and Hackenbush at Loud-speaker
HACKENBUSH *(to* GIL*)*: You take care of Judy and I'll take care of Morgan. *(He leaves)*

Medium Long Shot—Stuffy Riding Hi-Hat
He moves to the front of the pack.

Medium Shot—Morgan's Jockey on Ski-Ball
He's still in the lead. He sees STUFFY *coming.*

Medium Long Shot—Tunnel Beneath the Grandstand
TONY, *chased by the* COPS, *tosses* HACKENBUSH *the micro-*

phone and runs out. HACKENBUSH *takes it and runs. The* COPS *don't notice him, and continue to chase* TONY.

Medium Shot—the Horses
MORGAN'S JOCKEY *and* STUFFY *are neck and neck.*

Medium Close Shot—Morgan's Jockey and Stuffy
MORGAN'S JOCKEY *hits* STUFFY *with his crop.*

Three Shot—Mrs. Upjohn, Whitmore, and Morgan *(See film still 33.)*
MORGAN: I hope the judges didn't see that.

Medium Shot—Stuffy
Close Shot—Stuffy
He looks ahead, sees the next barrier.

Long Shot—All the Horses
They race toward the next wall.

Close Shot—Stuffy
He looks over to the grandstand, clutches his ear.

Medium Close Shot—Hackenbush
He comes over to MORGAN.
HACKENBUSH: Mr. Morgan *(he shoves the microphone in his face)*, would you mind telling the radio audience what a heel you are?
MORGAN: Oh, come back later. Oh, I've had enough of this! *(He gets up and starts to chase* HACKENBUSH*)*

Close-up—Hi-Hat
He hears MORGAN'S VOICE *over the loud-speaker and heads for the wall.*

Close-up—Stuffy
He LAUGHS.

Long Shot—Stuffy Riding Hi-Hat
They go over the barrier.

Medium Long Shot—Morgan, Whitmore, and Mrs. Upjohn
MORGAN *(to* HACKENBUSH *who is running away)*: If the police can't take care of you, I'll take care of you myself! *(to* COP*)* Keep that man away from me, do you understand!

Long Shot—the Horses Racing
Medium Close-up—the Horses Racing
Medium Close Shot—Feet of the Horses Racing
Close Shot—Hi-Hat and Ski-Ball (Morgan's Horse)
Close Shot—Stuffy
Medium Long Shot—Morgan, Whitmore, and Mrs. Upjohn
MORGAN *(to* COP*)*: Get around there—and stay there! And see that I'm not disturbed again today!

Close Shot—a Small Dog
A microphone is tied to his neck.

Medium Close Shot—Hackenbush, Tony, and Dog
The DOG *is in* HACKENBUSH's *lap. The* DOG *runs offscreen.*

Medium Long Shot—Mrs. Upjohn, Morgan, and Whitmore
The DOG *jumps toward their box.*

Close Shot—Morgan and Whitmore
The DOG *falls on* MORGAN.

Medium Close Shot—Morgan, Whitmore, and Mrs. Upjohn
MORGAN *(screaming at the* DOG *and, without knowing it, into the microphone)*: Get out of here! Get out of here!

Close-up—Hi-Hat
He hears MORGAN'S VOICE *and rears.*

Close-up—Stuffy
He smiles when he hears MORGAN'S VOICE.

Medium Long Shot—the Horses
They go over the barrier.

Long Shot—the Horses
One HORSE *and* RIDER *fall.*

Medium Long Shot—the Horses Racing
Close Shot—Stuffy

Medium Close-up—Morgan's Jockey on Ski-Ball
He looks at STUFFY.

Close Shot—Morgan's Jockey's Foot
It reaches over and pulls STUFFY's *foot out of his stirrup.*

Medium Shot—Morgan's Jockey on Ski-Ball and Stuffy
STUFFY *almost falls from* HI-HAT.

Close Shot—Stuffy
He threatens MORGAN'S JOCKEY *with his crop.*

Long Shot—Ski-Ball and Hi-Hat
MORGAN'S JOCKEY *tries to pull* STUFFY *off of* HI-HAT.

Medium Shot—Morgan, Whitmore, and Mrs. Upjohn
HACKENBUSH *tumbles over several* COPS *and into the box.*

Long Shot—the Horses
HI-HAT *and* SKI-BALL *are neck and neck in the lead.*

Long Shot—Hi-Hat and Ski-Ball
They approach another barrier. Both HORSES *stumble and both* MORGAN'S JOCKEY *and* STUFFY *go into the water.*

Close Shot—Gil and Judy

She turns her eyes away.

Medium Shot—Morgan's Box

MORGAN *looks at the race through his glasses. The* COPS *are holding* HACKENBUSH *and* TONY.

Medium Long Shot—the Water

STUFFY *and* MORGAN'S JOCKEY *stagger to their feet and the* HORSES *run away.*

Medium Close Shot—Stuffy

He staggers out of the water. He, MORGAN'S JOCKEY, *and both* HORSES *are covered with mud.*

Medium Close Shot—Morgan's Jockey

He gets on the HORSE *and gets back in the race.*

Long Shot—Stuffy

He gets on the HORSE *and rides after* MORGAN'S JOCKEY.

Close Shot—Morgan's Box

MORGAN *is looking through his glasses. The* COPS *hold* HACKENBUSH.

MORGAN: Ski-Ball has the lead!

Long Shot—the Horses Racing
Long Shot—the Crowd
Long Shot—the Horses

MORGAN'S JOCKEY *is ahead of* STUFFY.

Close Shot—Stuffy and Morgan's Jockey

They are neck and neck.

Close Shot—Gil and Judy

They CHEER STUFFY *on.*

Long Shot—Stuffy and Morgan's Jockey

MORGAN'S JOCKEY *is in the lead.*

Close Shot—Morgan's Box

The COPS *hold* HACKENBUSH *but he manages to shove the microphone, now disguised as a flower, into* MORGAN'S *face.*

HACKENBUSH: Smell this.

MORGAN: Ah, get away . . .

Medium Shot—Stuffy and Morgan's Jockey

MORGAN'S JOCKEY *is still ahead.*

MORGAN (*offscreen*): I don't want to smell anything. Get him out of here! Get him out of this box. Get him out of here! How many men does it take to do this. Come on, Ski-Ball!

Medium Shot—Morgan, Mrs. Upjohn, Whitmore, Hackenbush, and the Cops

The COPS *hold on to* HACKENBUSH.

MORGAN: Come on, Ski-Ball!

Medium Close Shot—Stuffy and Morgan's Jockey

They are neck and neck.

Long Shot—Ski-Ball and Hi-Hat

The TWO HORSES *are neck and neck.*

Long Shot—the Finish Line

The HORSES *streak across.*

Medium Close Shot—Morgan, Whitmore, Hackenbush, and the Cops

MORGAN: Ski-Ball wins!

Close Shot—Gil and Judy

They're crushed.

Medium Close Shot—Hackenbush and Sheriff
The SHERIFF *is holding him.*
HACKENBUSH: Okay, Sheriff, where do you arrange for a cell with a Southern exposure.
SHERIFF: Come on!

Close Shot—Gil and Judy
She comforts him.
JUDY: Gil, Hi-Hat couldn't have tried harder. We were just unlucky.

Long Shot—the Winner's Circle
MORGAN'S JOCKEY, *still on his* HORSE, *preens.*

Medium Close-up—Stuffy
He looks very disappointed.

Medium Close Shot—Morgan and Whitmore
They hurry onto the track.
MORGAN: Great race, Ski-Ball.

Medium Shot—Morgan and Whitmore
They approach MORGAN'S JOCKEY *to congratulate him.*
MORGAN: Great race, Ski-Ball. *(but the* HORSE *rears up in anger at* MORGAN *and throws the* JOCKEY *off)*

Medium Shot—Morgan and Whitmore
The HORSE *chases them to the rail. They jump over.*

Medium Close Shot—Stuffy
He watches MORGAN *and* WHITMORE *being chased and suspects something is wrong.*

271

Medium Close Shot—Morgan and Whitmore
They are on the ground with what they think is their HORSE *rearing up, threatening to kick them.*
MORGAN: Get him out of here! Get him out of here!

Medium Close Shot—Stuffy
He jumps off his HORSE, *runs over to the winner's circle, scrapes some mud off, throws it in* MORGAN'S JOCKEY'S *face.*

Medium Close Shot—Morgan's Jockey
The mud hits him in the face.

Medium Close Shot—the Three Judges
The watch the winner's circle.

Medium Close Shot—Stuffy
He wipes the mud off the saddle exposing the number seven— HI-HAT's *number. He wipes the mud from his sleeve showing his number seven—* HI-HAT's *number.* HI-HAT's *the winner after all! He gets very excited.*

Medium Close Shot—Judges
A JUDGE: That's number seven.

Close Shot—Whitmore and Morgan
They're shocked.
JUDGE *(offscreen)*: Hi-Hat's the winner.

Close Shot—Stuffy
He WHISTLES, *kisses* HI-HAT, *and everybody* CHEERS.

Close Shot—Whitmore and Morgan
They don't cheer.

Medium Shot—Hackenbush and Tony
HACKENBUSH *is still under arrest.*

272

HACKENBUSH: Hi-Hat wins. Sheriff, cancel my reservations.
TONY: It's Hi-Hat. It's Hi-Hat.

Close Shot—Gil and Judy
JUDY *(grabs* GIL*)*: Gil, come on. Come on, I want to put the wreath on the winner. *(See film still 34.)*

Medium Shot—the Railing—Morgan and Whitmore
They leave as HACKENBUSH *and* TONY *go to the winner's circle.*
HACKENBUSH: One more yell out of you and he'd have jumped over the grandstand.
MORGAN: Ah, ah, you!
TONY: Stuffy!

Medium Shot—Stuffy and Tony, Hi-Hat in the Background
STUFFY *and* TONY *hug each other.*
HACKENBUSH: Stuffy, you were wonderful!

Closer Shot—Hackenbush, Tony, and Stuffy
TONY: Some ride! Oh, boy!
HACKENBUSH: I haven't seen so much mudslinging since the last election.

Medium Shot—Hackenbush, Tony, and Stuffy
STUFFY WHISTLES; TONY *and* HACKENBUSH *bend over to make steps next to* HI-HAT. STUFFY *climbs up on their backs onto* HI-HAT.

Medium Long Shot—Winner's Circle
GIL *and* JUDY *place the wreath around* HI-HAT*'s neck.*

Medium Long Shot—the Track
All the BLACK CHILDREN *from the stables run onto the track.*

273

Medium Long Shot—the Track

STUFFY *on* HI-HAT, *led by* JUDY *and* GIL, TONY, HACKEN-BUSH, *and* MRS. UPJOHN *join with the* BLACK PEOPLE *and* SING.

CROWD *(singing)*:

> All Gawd's chillun got money . . .

Close Shot—Stuffy Riding on Hi-Hat

CROWD *(offscreen, sings)*:

> All Gawd's chillun got dough . . .

Medium Close Shot—the Children

They follow behind STUFFY.

CROWD *(sings)*:

> Gabriel's blowin' cause he needs us . . .

Medium Close Shot—Gil, Hackenbush, and Mrs. Upjohn

CROWD *(sings)*:

> We gotta follow where he leads us . . .

Long Shot—Tony, Judy, Gil, and Entire Group

They walk triumphantly forward in front of HI-HAT.

CROWD *(sings)*:

> Gabriel, blow that horn!

Close Shot—Stuffy on Hi-Hat

He PLAYS *his flute and* HONKS *his horn.*

Medium Close-up—Tony and Judy

TONY *(sings)*:

> On blue Venetian waters together, hi-de-hi-de-hi!
> Get your tootsie-frootsie ice cream!

Close Shot—Hackenbush and Mrs. Upjohn

HACKENBUSH *(sings)*:

I got a message from the man in the moon for you—just you!

(spoken to MRS. UPJOHN*)*: Emily, I've a little confession to make. I really am a horse doctor. But marry me, and I'll never look at any other horse!

MRS. UPJOHN *throws her arms around him joyously.*

Long Shot—Judy and Gil in Front of Hi-Hat

Everybody is still marching forward in victory.

GIL *(sings)*:

If you can face the setting sun and say . . .

Medium Close Shot—Hackenbush and Mrs. Upjohn

HACKENBUSH *grins and chews on his cigar.*

GIL *(offscreen, sings)*:

Tomorrow . . .

CROWD *(sings)*:

Za zu—za zu za—za zu!

Close Shot—Tony and Judy

They are happier with every step.

GIL *(offscreen, sings)*:

. . . tomorrow . . .

CROWD *(sings)*:

Za zu—za zu za—za zu!

Close Shot—Judy and Gil

They lead HI-HAT *and sing.*

GIL AND JUDY *(sing)*:

Tomorrow is another day!

275

Long Shot—Judy, Gil, and Everybody

They walk forward in victory. STUFFY, *on* HI-HAT, *is in the center. (See film still 35.)*

Fade out

Fade in:

The End

Fade out